CAN
CHINA
LEAD?

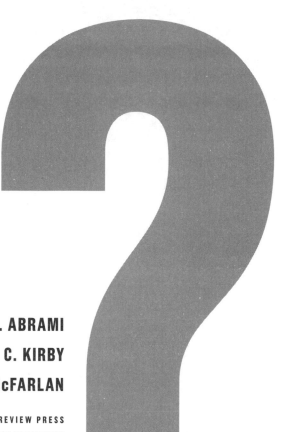

REGINA M. ABRAMI

WILLIAM C. KIRBY

F. WARREN McFARLAN

HARVARD BUSINESS REVIEW PRESS
BOSTON, MASSACHUSETTS

Reaching
the Limits
of Power
and Growth

CAN
CHINA
LEAD?

Library of Congress Cataloging-in-Publication Data

Abrami, Regina M.
    Can China lead? : reaching the limits of power and growth / Regina M. Abrami,
William C. Kirby, and F. Warren McFarlan.
        pages cm
        ISBN 978-1-4221-4415-2 (hardback)
1. Economic development—China. 2. China—Commerce. 3. China—Foreign economic
relations. 4. China—Economic policy–2000– 5. China–Economic conditions–2000–
I. Kirby, William C. II. McFarlan, F. Warren (Franklin Warren) III. Title.
    HC427.95.A27 2014
    330.951—dc23

                                        2013029761

ISBN: 9781422144152
eISBN: 9781422144169

This book is dedicated to
Dean Emeritus Jay O. Light—a great mentor and leader
who brought us together

CONTENTS

RECASTING CHINA'S ECONOMIC MIRACLE

For the past decade, much has been written on how China is going to change, and perhaps lead, the world. We do not agree. True, China has sustained a level of economic growth—nearly 10 percent for over thirty years—that remains unmatched. But China is now at a critical inflection point in realms that go beyond those of economic development.

Lost in the telling of China's dizzying array of infrastructure improvements, its huge foreign reserves, its growing status in international organizations, and the prevalence of its goods around the world has been one constant nonevent: there has been no change in its political system. The Chinese Communist Party (the CCP or "the Party"), founded in 1921 in emulation of the Soviet Union, is still in control, still claiming its role as "vanguard of the People." It stands at the helm of China's economy, state, and society, but no longer can anyone argue easily that it is a source of China's stability.

If anything, the political system created by the CCP stands in the way of the substantive changes needed to transform this country of 1.3 billion people into a place with sustainable foundations for economic growth and social well-being. The question, quite simply, is whether the CCP can constrain itself when its members hold sway over the country's corporations, universities, civic organizations, and, of course, the state. If not, we contend, the China "miracle" as we have known it is coming to an end. The changes necessary to ensure greater accountability at the highest levels of these organizations will require either internal checks on Party authority or more dramatic political change.

We do not make these claims lightly. We acknowledge that substantial positive changes have unfolded in recent decades. Most important, Chinese standards of living have improved markedly. This improvement has been uneven, and much remains to be done. China is still only eighty-ninth in the world in per capita GNP, and its Gini coefficient of economic inequality is higher than those of the two other countries to which it is often compared—the United States and India. Still, overall incomes in China have risen significantly, and the Chinese people now enjoy a far greater degree of freedom than was ever known under the rule of Mao Zedong (1949–1976). The countryside has also been transformed, most notably by three forces: the recommercialization of agriculture, the spread of industry, and the waves of rural to urban migration that have integrated China in new ways. Access to education in China has improved greatly, as has the quality of China's university system. Chinese businesses compete globally, now going head-to-head with North American and European corporations in telecommunications, heavy machinery, and renewable forms of energy. At home, China's new middle and upper classes have developed expanding appetites for international luxury goods, travel, and international real estate.

China is thriving by most comparative measures. But it faces major unmet challenges. The lack of accountability, transparency, and ease of operating in this market, combined with stunning examples of high-level corruption, make both domestic and foreign businesspeople wary. Good roads cannot compensate for poor governance. A robust private sector is limited in scope by sectors of the economy still monopolized by state-owned corporations. Research and development cannot flourish if fears of intellectual property theft persist. Most significant of all is the question of political stability. The turmoil of the most recent political transition reminds us how inadequately institutionalized the Chinese political system still is, more than sixty years after the Communist seizure of power.

By focusing attention on the centrality of politics in China, this book turns the conventional story of the China miracle on its head. Instead of telling the story of how the Chinese government lifted hundreds of millions out of poverty, we emphasize the role of Chinese workers, farmers, and entrepreneurs in lifting themselves out of poverty, once given a decent chance. At the same time, we assess the political reasons that led the CCP to push institutional change in specific directions, resulting in increasingly unsustainable patterns of economic growth and dangerous levels of economic inequality.

Deng Xiaoping, China's principal leader from 1978 until his death in 1997, had likened economic reform to feeling for stones when crossing a river. But China's fault lines today cannot be crossed with such ease. Stepping from stone to stone may be useful in filling gaps in innovation, social equality, access to financial resources, and product quality assurance. There is, however, also the gap between the Party and "the People." It grows wider each time a high-level corruption scandal explodes in the press or is exposed informally by the millions of Chinese blogs now operating as vibrant, if at times suppressed, social spaces for dialogue and criticism on Chinese political and economic matters.

Our attention to the political drivers of China's model of economic reform and its aftermath is critical, we believe, to answering the larger theme of this volume: Can China lead? Will the twenty-first century be the *Chinese* century? We believe that attention to this theme will put our readers on a surer footing as they assess their own strategies for doing business in China, and with—or against—the growing number of Chinese competitors, both private and state-owned, now operating successfully around the globe.

Understanding modern China also requires deep appreciation of the unique forces that led to its emergence in its particular economic form. Historical and political processes continue to shape how business is done. If you don't understand them, your Western-driven decision processes will almost surely bring you to ruin. History suffuses this book because it matters so much in China today and will help define where it is going in the future.

Collectively, we bring to this endeavor many decades of field experience and research in China. In addition to our individual writing on China, we have produced dozens of Harvard Business School cases (see appendix B) that today form the backbone of an HBS course, Doing Business in China in the Early Twenty-First Century, and serve as inspiration for this book. We come to this work with three different perspectives.

One perspective is that of the historian who attempts to understand the roots of today's challenges in China by looking to its past as well as to our contemporary understanding of it. William Kirby shows us that from the ruins of the last dynasty, China's twentieth century was consumed with the task of making China modern and of creating a new Chinese state, at times with tragic consequences. The Chinese people experienced the worst of this during the Maoist period, when neither foreign occupation nor civil war could be blamed for the broken promises of Communist "liberation." The story of twenty-first-century China is part of this larger narrative. The past—of Chinese capitalism, Chinese engineering, and the Chinese Party-State—is very much with us today as we contemplate China's future.

Another standpoint is that of the political economist. Regina Abrami focuses our attention on the economic implications of more than sixty years of CCP rule, the last half of which has been distinguished by greater economic liberalization and global reintegration. Consistent, however, is the fragile relationship between private business and the state. As much of this volume shows, this has been a story of accommodation, conflict, and CCP dependence on the vital economic force provided by the private sector. The CCP's political co-option of private entrepreneurs puts to the test its ability to encourage private wealth while preventing its worst excesses of nepotism, corruption, and illegitimate forms of privatization.

The final perspective is that of a general management expert who views the changes underway in China in terms of the forms of navigation that will be necessary to continue to succeed in this market. Warren McFarlan has seen companies rise and fall on Chinese soil, some of them run by our former students. He has also acted as mentor and witness to dozens of foreign businesses eager to succeed there. Now based both at HBS and at Tsinghua University's School of Economics and Management (Beijing), he has seen private businesses, both local and foreign, grow more pessimistic.

Our distinct viewpoints and area expertise allow us to bring forth a fuller picture of China today and what you, our readers, need to do. The unique historical and political perspective in this book makes it useful for both those who are working in China and those who are totally new to these issues. It is for both the managers in multinational corporations and those who craft their strategies. And it is for a broader, general audience that seeks a deeper understanding of China's path.

We start by making the case that you first need to know how little you know about China. Then, it is important to understand how China got to where it is in 2014, as this long view is surely a basis for forecasting what lies ahead.

As readers will discover, this book provides a sobering reassessment of China's trajectory. While we have great admiration for the country's economic transformation in recent years, we are also compelled to raise words of caution about its future direction if substantive change is not forthcoming. We hope that this volume will be a source of conversation and debate in China and abroad. We want to be clear from the start that this book is not a criticism of the Chinese people or of Chinese culture. It celebrates many of China's extraordinary achievements of the last century, but it also recognizes that institutional change is now necessary, and necessarily difficult. The fault lines that imperil China's future all lead to one place: the current political system's determination to keep a strong (in our view, too strong) hand on the economic life of the country and its citizens.

Each chapter examines the forces that have made China as we know it today, explores what has to change, and concludes with a set of strategic questions for managers interested or invested in China.

Chapter 1:
The Myths and Making of Modern China

What do we really know about China? This chapter examines the persistent myths that have molded our perception of China, its markets, its political system, and its recent economic development. The comparative scope of the Chinese economy, China's global integration, and the centrality of a robust business culture are not new phenomena. The processes through which they have developed have shaped the options open to China today.

Chapter 2:
Party, Inc.: The Rise and Limits of China's Red Capitalism

In this chapter, we examine the Party's levers and levels of control over leading economic forces as well as behaviors that now weaken its legitimacy. Chinese power holders have historically relied on commercial actors to advance their interests (collect taxes, solve social welfare problems, and provide economic growth), while always retaining the ability to constrain them. The era of Communist rule upset this balance profoundly as the Party came first to dominate, then to influence, all businesses of significant scale. The Party has sought to make its base stronger through favoritism to enormous state-owned conglomerates; yet this is at odds with its necessary reliance on private enterprise as the engine of China's future growth.

Chapter 3:
The Engineering State: The End of the Road

Modern China's founding father, Sun Yat-sen, had a vision for what would make China modern. It was all about having a scientific plan— to engineer, as it were, a future that looked fundamentally different from China's past. This chapter shows how the CCP fulfilled this vision in ways that have changed China profoundly but suggests that its obsession with infrastructure may have found its limits. China has been terrific at "hardware." Now can it lead in "software"?

Chapter 4:
Planning Innovation?

China has a long tradition of invention. We consider in this chapter not only why China fell behind, but also if and how it is likely to catch up. We look to new policy efforts in education, from the liberal arts to science and technology, as well as to the innovation strategies of individual firms. We find considerable improvements and exciting developments. However, what the Party-State is ultimately comfortable with in this domain is the great unknown. The future of China lies here, and we see great risk.

Chapter 5:
Achieving Commercial Success in
China: Hazardous Business

Over the past several decades, innumerable enterprises have been launched in China. Many have succeeded, while others have failed. Much of this can be explained using conventional business analysis that all MBA students would understand. Four distinguishing features for achieving success in business in China, however, are not part of a standard curriculum: the all-important role of the Party; the vital role of local Party and state officials as gatekeepers; the extraordinary opportunities offered by the emergence of new physical infrastructure; and the astonishing lags in development of soft infrastructure. These are special challenges in developing a consumer economy where none existed three decades before.

Chapter 6:
Global China: The Limits of Power

China has been, is, and will be a central actor in the global economy. Three forces propel its further international engagement: its dependency on foreign sources of energy and other natural resources; the acquisition by Chinese firms of international technology at the highest level; and the need to balance its trade flows as part of a broader agenda to move from an export-oriented economy toward a domestic, consumer-led economy. These forces are driving Chinese firms to pursue foreign acquisitions at an ever-sharper rate. No longer is the story just about China in Africa, but of China in Europe, the United States, and Canada. At the same time, foreign firms in China increasingly feel squeezed out.

The rise of China as an economic power has not brought forth the levels of "soft power" that were achieved by the United States in the twentieth century and the United Kingdom in the nineteenth century. The ideals of Chinese culture and civilization may be proudly promoted abroad ("Confucius Institutes"), but these are not the values of the regime at home.

Chapter 7:
China 2034: The Future in the Light of the Past

Can China be again—as it was two hundred years ago—a dominant force in the world? Predicting the future of China even twenty years from now is a deeply uncertain exercise. China faces significant internal pressures for which there no longer is the sure safety valve of export-driven growth. The Chinese people and those doing business in China want more, and what they want more of—the certainty of clear air, safe products, and equal economic, educational, and social opportunity—means that the Party-State needs to allow, minimally, for the emergence of a true regulatory state with alternative centers of authority. We doubt it can do this and expect that more profound political change may be the consequence. In the absence of change in the political arena, we believe that China will remain a formidable competitor in global markets for both goods and ideas, but not the dominant one.

Acknowledgments

These chapters reflect our equal efforts and collaboration over several years of teaching and case writing—a joint effort in every sense. For this reason, we are indebted to our students, who with each round of teaching Doing Business in China gave us the benefit of road-testing many of the ideas found here. We also want to express our gratitude to the many firms, government organizations, and friends within China and elsewhere that provided us with their time and insight, and especially to those who allowed us to prepare cases on their China operations.

This work was collaborative in other ways as well. We especially owe our gratitude to Tracy Yuen Manty, who worked alongside us tirelessly for four years. She has been a source of our success in so many ways. In addition, we would like to acknowledge our appreciation to Paula Alexander, Maureen Donovan, Molly Forte, Iacob Koch-Weser, Kate Pilbeam, Alison Ring, Jan Simmons, Luz Velazquez, and Weiqi Zhang, each of whom helped with portions of our work; and most recently, to Erica Zendell, who assisted us greatly in bringing the final drafts to conclusion. We have also benefited from the valuable suggestions and insights provided by our colleagues, Professor Elisabeth Köll and Professor Li Jin.

Professor Xia Donglin and Professor Jia Ning at Tsinghua University's School of Economics and Management have been especially helpful in introducing us to a variety of Chinese companies and facilitating the opportunity for us to study them. We are deeply grateful for the support of Harvard Business School's Division of Research and the strong encouragement of HBS deans Jay Light and Nitin Nohria.

Finally, we are especially indebted to our editor, Melinda Merino, for her patience with often dilatory authors and her numerous suggestions in helping to structure the book and forcing us to think more deeply about our managerial conclusions. Our three anonymous reviewers also helped us to improve our work. For this, we thank them. We take full responsibility for all the material in this book.

1

THE MYTHS AND MAKING OF MODERN CHINA

Irrationally held truths may be more harmful
than reasoned errors.

—Thomas Henry Huxley, 1880

On September 28, 2012, Bo Xilai, the charismatic Party chief of a major Chinese municipality, a former provincial governor, former Minister of Commerce, and son of a well-respected revolutionary elder, was expelled from the Chinese Communist Party (CCP). A Party princeling—that is, a person with direct family links to the highest level of the Party's political elite—Bo had crafted a reputation as one of China's most suave and charismatic politicians. He had won praise for aiding the transformation of cities weighed down by dying industries and for protecting the interests of Chinese businesses in the face of foreign competition.

He was now accused of abusing his power in a variety of ways: of being corrupt; of having covered up his now-convicted wife's murder of a British citizen; and (for good measure) of having "improper sexual relations with a number of women." Even as he faced trial on slightly reduced charges in August 2013, Bo's conviction the following month was a foregone conclusion.

The fall of Bo Xilai, a man who seemed destined for senior leadership in China, was the country's biggest political scandal in decades. What does it mean? Was his demotion from Communist hero to greedy villain a demonstration of the CCP's recognition that even its leading members must stand for judgment before the Chinese state and its laws? Or was the dramatic show trial that Bo received in 2013 proof that, in this time of China's growing power, stunning prosperity, and claims to global leadership, its ruling Party and its political culture remain rooted in an earlier age? Is the rule of law, in other words, still subservient to the ever-shifting political needs of the Chinese Communist Party?

More than thirty years ago, at the beginning of China's three-plus decades of economic reform, there was another show trial. In November 1980, Jiang Qing, Mao Zedong's widow and one-time Shanghai actress, found herself in court. Standing alongside Zhang Chunqiao, Yao Wenyuan, and Wang Hongwen—the other members of the "Gang of Four"—she stood accused of causing great disharmony and other crimes through her role in the Cultural Revolution (1966–1976). She was declared guilty in the official press before the proceedings even began. Her first court-appointed lawyer called her "the criminal." The trial of the Gang of Four was broadcast nightly across China, offering the Chinese people an image of chaos brought to order. Held for four years awaiting trial, the Gang was ultimately convicted of counterrevolutionary activities. All served long prison sentences and died in obscurity, Jiang Qing by her own hand in 1992.

Decades apart, we have two politically sensitive, high-profile cases. Of note is their position at the start and recent point of China's era of "reform and opening," that is, the period of market-oriented policies that began under Deng Xiaoping in late 1978. Each also came at a moment when the CCP's legitimacy had come into question. In both cases, a show of order was made as if the government, not the CCP, were running things. So much has changed over the past thirty-five years, and yet—in this realm at least—seemingly so little. What does this tell us about China's capacity for future growth—indeed, its capacity for leadership? If China emerges as a global leader, what kind of leader might it be? The answer depends on what you believe of modern China's story and the role of the Chinese Communist Party in it.

This is a history that we need to retell and that you need to know. One simply cannot understand the complexities of modern China without understanding their roots. For many books on China, "history" is the story of recent events. Not this one. China was not born yesterday. What made China modern did not begin in 1949, when the CCP came to power, or even in 1978, when a market economy began to reemerge. Rather, China's current rise has been a century and more in the making. The CCP put it on a unique path, to be sure, but that path is in many ways a fuller incarnation of plans previously written, with consequences for the fault lines that we identify in the chapters to follow.

To put it another way, we must look back in order to see what is ahead for this country of 1.3 billion people. After all, China's rise has been predicted for more than a century. At the turn of the twentieth century, as now, there was a robust market for "rise of China" books. They had familiar titles: *The Dragon Awakes*; *China Awakened*; *Sun Yat Sen and the Awakening of China*; *Rising China*; and, an unusual entrant, published in 1904, *New Forces in Old China: An Unwelcome but Inevitable Awakening.*[1] Today, we again have such titles: *The Dragon Awakes*; *China's Rise*; *The Rise of China*; *China's Ascent*; *As China Goes, So Goes the World*; and, perhaps most forcefully, *When China Rules the World.*[2] But what do we really know of this rise of China and of the CCP's role within it?

Let us start with a question that we use to kick off our course: How old is China? When we pose this question, we can rely on Chinese and foreign students alike to give a stock answer: "More than five thousand years." This is the answer you will find in every textbook. We think of it differently: China is home to an ancient and great civilization: indeed, the longest, continuous civilization in world history. But China is also a very young country. As a political entity, "China" did not exist until 1912, when the Republic of China—Asia's first republic—was proclaimed as the successor to the Qing empire. China is, in this respect, a relatively modern phenomenon.

The writing of China's modern history has been built on several myths that are so widespread that they have gained the appearance of truth. Without dispelling them, we are poorly equipped to address the conventional wisdoms that underpin official depictions of the role of the CCP in China's economic development or even of the country's current economic challenges. Such reconsideration is needed to answer the broader question of this volume: Can China lead? We need to know where this new country has been in its first century before assessing the inevitability of its dominance in its second.

Enduring Myths

The "new China" of the twentieth century was founded on the ruins of the Qing, or Manchu, empire, the last imperial dynasty to rule over Chinese and neighboring lands. For those not familiar with portrayals of Chinese history, the Imperial period (221 BCE–1911 CE) can carry with it a variety of simplifying, totalizing generalizations. Below, we look at several of the myths that have clouded our vision of modern China.

Myth: China Has Always Been Unified

From the unification of neighboring states by the self-proclaimed "First Emperor of Qin" in 221 BCE, political unity has been a consistent ideal—one stressed all the more because it was so often lacking in practice. The borders of China-based empires were not fixed. The imperial period was, at its foundation, based on constant cycles of change, of unity and disunity (see table 1-1). When the Qin dynasty first conquered its neighbors and declared the first empire, it standardized the writing system, weights, measures, and currency. These measures lasted much longer than its empire, whose history can be measured in decades. And when its successor dynasty, Han, fell in 220 CE, there followed a three-and-a-half century period of disunion (220–589 CE) between the northern and southern territories that included the Three Kingdoms period, Six Dynasties period in the south, and Sixteen Kingdoms in the north. It was not until the time of the Sui (581–618 CE) and Tang dynasties (618–907 CE) that one could speak of reunification.

What we see upon examination of China's early imperial history is a cyclical process of destruction and revitalization. These cycles were based on the passing of the so-called mandate of heaven (*tianming*), without which a dynasty could not be considered legitimate. The emperor, considered the "son of heaven," was expected to fulfill his filial duties by acting as the ritual intermediary between the cosmic and the mundane. If an emperor (and by extension, his dynasty) failed to satisfy his obligations and the government was in disarray (which was said to be indicated by natural disasters), it

TABLE 1–1

Timeline of Chinese dynasties

Ancient period	Xia	2100–1600 BCE
	Shang	1600–1050 BCE
	Zhou	1050–256 BCE
	Warring States period	473–221 BCE
Early imperial era	Qin	221–210 BCE
	Han	221 BCE–220 CE
	Age of division	220–589 CE
	Sui	581–618 CE
Mid-imperial era	Tang	618–907 CE
	Song	960–1279 CE
	Yuan (Mongol)	1279–1368 CE
Late imperial era	Ming	1368–1644 CE
	Qing*	1644–1912 CE
Modern era	Republican period	1912–1949 CE
	People's Republic of China	1949–present

*Also romanized as Ch'ing.

was considered not only justified but also right for the citizenry to rebel and pass the mandate on to a new dynasty. There were multiple transitions of the mandate, each resulting in a new state with unique geographic boundaries (see figures 1-1, 1-2, 1-3, and 1-4).

Moreover, the expansion of the borders of the empire beyond the Chinese cultural realm during the mid and late imperial periods was led, above all, by foreign dynasties. First, during the Yuan (or Mongol era, from 1279 to 1368), China was briefly part of the Mongol-led Eurasian imperium. Then again, under the Qing

FIGURE 1-1

Sui dynasty

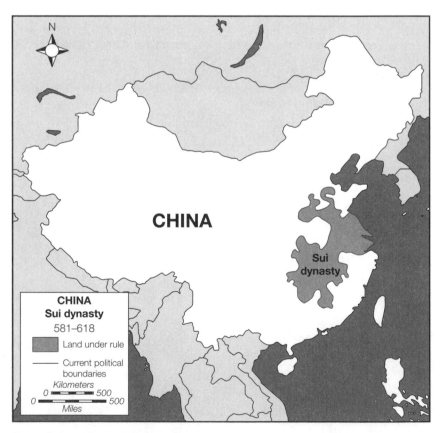

Source: Courtesy Minneapolis Institute of Arts.

dynasty (an era of governance by Manchus lasting from 1644 to 1911) the empire comprised much more than the Chinese lands of the Ming (1368–1644) and came to include the Qing's Manchurian homeland, Mongolia, Xinjiang (Eastern Turkestan), and Tibet, among its far-flung parts. Thus, in geographic terms, China today is the Qing without the Manchus, an empire without an emperor.

This is quite an achievement. After all, the world into which the Chinese Republic was born was still a world of empires. These multinational, multicultural, spatial regimes included the

FIGURE 1-2

Yuan dynasty

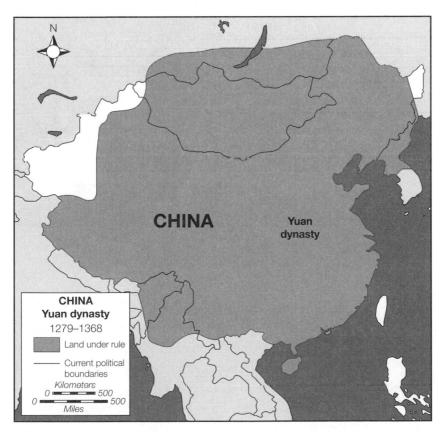

Source: Courtesy Minneapolis Institute of Arts.

FIGURE 1-3

Ming dynasty

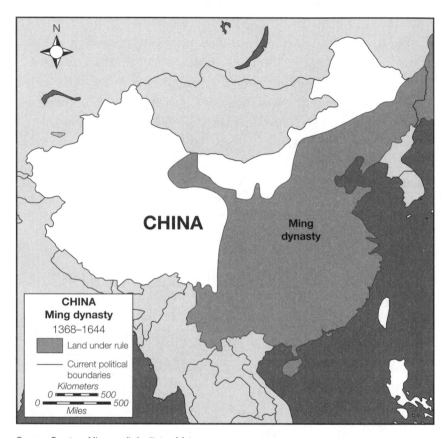

CHINA

Ming dynasty

CHINA
Ming dynasty
1368–1644
Land under rule
Current political
boundaries
Kilometers
0   500
0   500
Miles

Source: Courtesy Minneapolis Institute of Arts.

Ottoman, Romanov, and Habsburg empires, which had their roots
in medieval and early modern times; the "new" imperia of the
British and the French, who together governed most of Africa, all
of the Indian subcontinent, and much of Indochina; and the Great
Qing Empire of the Manchus. Today, of all the world's empires that
existed a century ago, only the Qing (now China) remains.

The concept of Chinese unity must therefore be seen as a rather
modern phenomenon. How long can it last? "Empires wax and
wane; states cleave asunder and coalesce." This famous first line

FIGURE 1-4

Qing dynasty

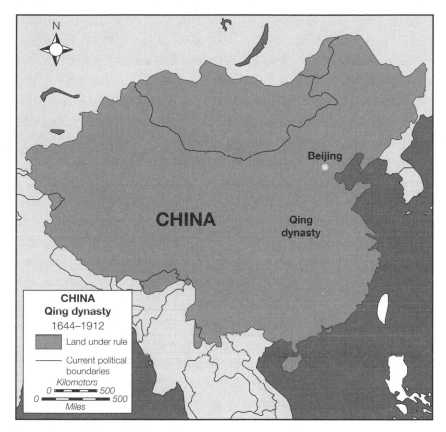

CHINA

Qing
dynasty

Beijing

CHINA
Qing dynasty
1644–1912
Land under rule

Current political
boundaries

Kilometers
0 ▬▬ 500
0 ▬▬ 500
Miles

N

Source: Courtesy Minneapolis Institute of Arts.

of *The Romance of the Three Kingdoms* captures the history and
challenge of Chinese unity today. Perhaps the Chinese Communist
Party works so hard to promote unity in textbooks because it
knows just how hard it is to maintain the harmony of class, creed,
and ethnicity across the realm that is China today.

Even in a politically unified empire, as in periods of political disunity, regions matter. All of China—an area the size of the conti-
nental United States—may be on Beijing time, but its citizens wake
at different times, speak in separate dialects, eat distinctive dishes,

worship diverse deities, and dream quite different dreams. But these regional differences are not only cultural. In modern China, economic life is also centered largely on *regional* economies, what scholars call *macro regions*. For business, there is one important lesson here: despite the recurrent dream of what Shanghai newsman Carl Crow counted as *400 Million Customers* (1937), there has never been just one, national China market.[3] There have been, and still are, very few goods for which there are clear national markets. China is instead a series of interlocking regional economies, with populations the size of European nations, or larger.

The Bo Xilai case demonstrates the endurance of regional power bases in a supposedly unitary state. Like the warlords of the early twentieth century, provincial party secretaries in the People's Republic of China (PRC) often have untrammeled political power, even absolute power, as in Bo's case, where he held all the power and prestige of his position in Chongqing until the moment he was stripped of it. So the Western CEO who believes that she can make use of connections in a Beijing ministry to ensure a business's reach nationwide is almost surely on a fool's errand. Government is indeed powerful in China, but there are many governments—national, provincial, municipal, local—and there are just as many Party committees. The interests of each layer of government do not always intersect. Without local patrons, partners, and customers, Beijing can seem very far away.

Myth: China's Culture Is Confucian Culture

Great empires in history were able to rule large and differentiated landscapes with very small bureaucracies because of enduring systems of shared values. Even as other empires waxed and waned, the place we call China today became home to the world's longest continuous civilization, with the longest continuing (if periodically reinterpreted) set of philosophical and literary traditions.

The common cultural denomination assigned to China has often been called "Confucianism," with the myth being that the Chinese are of singular mind and habit. The idea of Confucianism, however, is too general to capture the multiple traditions of Chinese culture, and instead better reflects what had been a means to impose order through adherence to moral principle and proper conduct according to one's status.

Until the twentieth century, this meant a hierarchy of ruler over ruled, elite over commoner, elder over younger, male over female. It also meant that the study of Confucian traditions defined not only how to be a scholar but also how to be powerful and moral. At the elite level, success was determined through a torturous education and examination system that aimed to bring the most learned men in the realm into the service of the state. Today, what Japanese scholar Ichisada Miyazaki once called "China's Examination Hell" continues through the higher examination (*gaokao*) for college entry.[4] It too tests for political correctness, as well as for math, science, and composition, to determine who will be admitted to China's most prestigious universities—places like Tsinghua and Peking universities.

Under Communist rule, when for a time Mao's "Little Red Book" replaced the Confucian classics, the labels changed, at least in principle (for example, in the 1950s, it was farmer over landlord, worker over manager), but the idea of acting properly according to one's status, as determined by the ruling power, was the same and such that China remains one of the most hierarchical and status-conscious countries on earth. Any businessperson who has attended a formal meeting, in which seating is meticulously arranged according to rank and status, knows this. So too do those once labeled "landlord" and "capitalist."

Today, few Chinese know the Confucian classics. Fewer still, perhaps, believe in Mao Zedong Thought and the revolutionary values of his era. Perhaps that is why, when Bo Xilai promoted a return to Maoist morals and urged people to sing "red songs," he sparked such fear in Beijing. When former president Hu Jintao talked of building a "harmonious society" in the early 2000s, his task was all the harder because of a lack of consensus on just what "Chinese values" are today.

Myth: China Has Been Isolated

Scholarship on China (and indeed *in* China) had once emphasized China's insularity vis-à-vis other cultures before being blown open to the world in the era of Western imperialism, from which time it became "the sick man of Asia." There are, to be sure, both symbols and monuments of Chinese defensiveness, such as the Great Wall, but for most of the imperial era, China-based empires routinely crossed borders that were often loosely defined. They did so for good reason: to engage in trade, to adjudicate diplomatic disputes, and to fight wars against external threats.

The Han dynasty, for example, held trade and political relations with what are now Manchuria, Korea, and Vietnam and sent envoys along what much later was called the Silk Road. Before and during the Tang period, travelers from all over the world, including Japan, India, and West Asia, were welcomed into the realm. With merchants and monks came new cultural and religious influences, the most important of which was Buddhism, the transformative influence of which can be compared only with that of the much later opening to the West in the nineteenth century.

By the Qing period, private Chinese entrepreneurs also moved abroad, maintaining ties with their mainland families. At the end of 2011, the Chinese diaspora population had reached over 40.3 million.[5] Today, some estimate the population at nearly 50 million. It is most concentrated in Asia, in such places as Singapore, Thailand, Malaysia, Vietnam, Burma, and the Philippines, but the Americas (6 million) and Europe (2 million) also have long- and well-established overseas Chinese populations. Beyond this, perhaps 750,000 citizens of the People's Republic are currently working in African countries.

China's current boom is incomprehensible without recognition of its long-standing engagement with the wider world, including the world of overseas Chinese, contact with which was constrained for only the smallest period of time, a by-product of Mao Zedong's reckless quest for Chinese self-sufficiency. Yet the myth persists that China was historically isolated until the Communist "reform and opening" of the late 1970s. The truth is simpler: the Maoist period of self-seclusion was the exception that proves the rule of China's internationalization.

Today even China's scandals and purges have an international dimension. Defense Minister Lin Biao was allegedly fleeing to the Soviet Union when his plane crashed in 1971. The Tiananmen protests of 1989 found a global audience because CNN and other networks were in Beijing to cover the visit of Soviet leader Mikhail Gorbachev. And Bo Xilai was purged in part because he was suspected of covering up his wife's alleged murder of an Englishman who may have helped secure the family's assets abroad and their son's admission to London's exclusive Harrow School.

Myth: China Could Not Develop Capitalism

The conventional view of earlier Chinese and Western scholarship was of a strong cultural bias against commercial activity that kept China from realizing all but the "sprouts" of capitalism. In the ideal social hierarchy, there were four major social categories, with merchants placed on the lowest rung. This ordering reflected a Confucian bias against profit and hence against capitalists, though perhaps no more so than the invocations against profit and usury that marked medieval Europe. Indeed, the Chinese may just have been ahead of the curve. By the fifteenth century, restrictions against merchants taking civil service exams were eliminated, opening an avenue through which they might procure higher status.

By the turn of the twentieth century, China was an autocracy with sizable realms of freedom. It had a highly commercialized economy, and Chinese under Qing rule had the freedom to transact to a degree that was greater than that enjoyed by most Europeans, at least until the nineteenth century. Land was also freely alienable. It was bought and sold, rented and worked, all subject to the forces of the market.

Late imperial China had its landed elites, to be sure, but no class of hereditary estate holders as in France or Prussia. Nor did serfdom exist in any measure like that of Eastern Europe, where it persisted into the second half of the nineteenth century. The population was registered, but it was essentially free to move throughout much of the realm. There were enormous migratory flows even to areas that were officially off limits, such as Manchuria. Goods as well as people flowed largely unimpeded by government regulation. State monopolies all but disappeared. Domestic trade was subject to few administrative barriers and—by any comparative measure—China had remarkably low taxes. Local and long-distance banking systems, and private ones at that, grew.

Central to all of this was the development and protection of property rights and the de facto sanctity of contract. Even without a formal commercial code and in the absence of a system of legal precedents, the rights and obligations negotiated in contracts were normally upheld in magistrates' courts. This in turn facilitated the growth of more-extended forms of private enterprise, such as shareholding partnerships in farming, mining, and commerce. "Corporations" formed around guilds and family lineages were later joined by joint-stock business partnerships, several of which developed into very sizable commercial firms long before the writing of the company laws of the twentieth century.

To sum up, by the late imperial period, China was a lively and dynamic setting for various commercial pursuits from mobile street peddling and small shops to massive domestic trade in bulk commodities, long-distance banking, "chains" of retail stores, and large flows in international commerce. The institutional framework surrounding the vibrant capitalism of late imperial China was well developed, with high levels of commercialization, monetization, and accepted regulatory guidelines.

This great commercial economy—or, more accurately, the large regional economies that comprised it—played a significant role in global flows of goods and specie. These were further internationalized in the late nineteenth and early twentieth centuries. China was, in other words, a place that defied a single characterization. It was dynamic and changing, urban and rural, cosmopolitan and provincial, at peace and at war. It was in the world economy, and it was part of it not just for decades but for centuries prior to the Communist takeover of 1949.

All this was destroyed by Chinese Communism, which threw China backward, economically, in the 1950s, 1960s, and 1970s, while the rest of East Asia roared ahead. The best way to understand the subsequent policies of "reform and opening" is as a return to many of those of prerevolutionary China: allowing family farming, permitting again a form of mixed economy, and encouraging international investment and foreign trade on a large scale.

The basic elements of Chinese economic growth, in other words, were there all along. But as part of the Party's effort to consolidate its power and legitimacy, it constructed a myth of pre-1949 China as a time of singular darkness and gloom—the *hei'an de shiqi*. In effect, to sustain an image of the post-1949 period as a time of liberation and freedom demanded nothing less than that China fall down in order to stand up.

Myth: China "Stands Up"

It is commonly taught in China today that only after the establishment of the People's Republic in 1949 did China, in Mao's famous words, finally "stand up" to the outside world. This is one of the most persistent historical myths. True, the new PRC showed itself to be a power in fighting the United States to a standstill in the Korean War (1950–1953). But did it need to prove that? The Republic of China under the leadership of Chiang Kai-shek had already denied Japan victory in the second Sino-Japanese War (1937–1945).

In defending itself against Japanese aggression, China had shown that it was a major player in world affairs in the 1930s and 1940s, entering into alignments or alliances with three of the world's leading powers—Germany, the Soviet Union, and the United States—in order to fend off the fourth, Japan. Before that, it had been one of the leading citizens of the League of Nations and an active participant in the influential international bodies of the day. By 1943, China was formally one of the great powers and became a founding member of the United Nations. With Japan prostrate, postwar China seemed assured of becoming the leading power in Asia, if in part by default, and necessarily one of the leading actors in the global community.

That did not happen in the early PRC, for Chinese power was largely contained—and, thanks to Mao Zedong, *self*-contained—as China unincorporated itself from the global community: first from the West and then a decade later from its Soviet and Eastern European allies. By the early 1960s, China was diplomatically quarantined, economically isolated, and in a nearly catastrophic military situation where it faced threats from the two superpowers—the Soviet Union and the United States. In effect, China "stood up" only to put itself in the most dangerous strategic position of its modern history.

"Standing up" also meant defining on whose behalf the Chinese Communist Party assumed its vanguard position. Who, in other words, was to be led? The answer entailed a reimagination of "the Chinese" that began even before the Communists seized power.

The Great Qing Empire, as we have noted, was not a *Chinese* state. On the contrary, Sun Yat-sen and other early-twentieth-century Chinese revolutionaries sought to overthrow this "foreign" dynasty and to create a modern Chinese state.

This quest to build a modern nation-state was carried out by extending the boundaries of the Chinese nation (in the sense of Han national-racial identity) to be coterminous with the reach of the sovereign power of the state. In 1912, the first Republic took an inclusive approach, emphasizing in its five-bar national flag that the Republic of China consisted of Han (i.e., Chinese), Manchus, Mongols, Tibetans, and Muslims.

The Nationalist (Guomindang) state, which ruled the mainland from 1927 to 1949, pursued a more racial nationalism and was symbolized by Sun Yat-sen's one-sun flag and his belief that just as the

Chinese "race" had defeated the alien Manchus, it was China's mission to colonize Mongolia, Xinjiang, and Tibet.[6]

Subsequently, although the PRC, established in 1949, promised to restore autonomy to selected "national minorities," its rule, too, has been marked by the overwhelming political dominance of Han Chinese in the governance of the multinational Qing realm. Indeed the great Qing emperors, such as Kangxi (reigned 1661–1722) and Qianlong (1735–1796), have been elevated in recent years, posthumously depicted in film and textbook as *Chinese* patriots. Thus today in the PRC, one can be Tibetan, Uighur, or Mongolian, and still be "Chinese" (*Zhongguoren*) and a citizen of the People's Republic of *China*. By this reasoning as well, the CCP has, and did, claim to have reinforced "unity among the People," thus earning its position as their vanguard.

Perhaps the clearest demonstration of this comes by way of a famous post-1949 political song. Its chorus, repeated again and again, and known by most Chinese of every generation, says: "Without the Communist Party, there could be no new China." It is a vision that permeates official Chinese depictions of the country's social and economic development over six decades and has also influenced foreign observers of China. It is a concept of the Chinese Communist Party as bringer of order, economic development, and social well-being.

Clearly, it matters who gets to write history. Every dynasty writes the history of its predecessor. But it is not easy to gain historical perspective on the present. We need to see the making of modern China in a manner different from the hagiographic depictions of the CCP's role in the country's development. To be sure, in recent decades China has "stood up" in its economic development, with remarkable rates of economic growth, although it is uneven across regions and income inequality is increasing (see appendix A). But the promise given in 1949 of an altogether new China seems elusive. We see instead the return of issues that plagued China on the eve of the Communist victory: a one-party political system in need of reform, stunning stories of high-level corruption, the monopolistic power of state-owned corporations, and a growing sense among the Chinese people that their leadership is not serving them as well as it might.

A quick scan of web pages created by Chinese citizens also gives us an image of rural government thuggery, impressive forgeries, unsafe products, and Party officials who in dress, decorum, and conspicuous consumption have signaled their distance from "the People." Contradictions, more than harmony, characterize this period in China's development. At their root there remains order-making of a particular sort—that of a Leninist Party-State.

The Ruler's Ruler: The Party-State in China

The CCP did not bring the idea of a Leninist Party-State to China. That began with the Nationalist Party, dating from the 1920s. Sun Yat-sen, the father of the Nationalist state, defined its mission as that of tutoring the Chinese people for democracy. "Tutelage," he said, was to last six years. For Chinese under Nationalist rule on the mainland and later on Taiwan, however, it lasted sixty. When the Nationalists were ousted from the mainland in 1949, they were replaced by the Communist Party-State, which survives to the present day.

A Party-State is a one-party state, meaning that the ends of government are directed to protect the power of the ruling party and not the autonomy of law and policy. The Party's self-assigned purpose is not only to direct government but also to remake the polity—a new citizenry for a new nation-state. Chiang Kai-shek's New Life Movement of the mid-1930s, for example, aimed to discipline an undisciplined populace, to give it a sense of obligation to the nation. Mao Zedong took this transformative effort in a more extreme direction, most notably with his "Great Proletarian Cultural Revolution" of the 1960s.

The Chinese Party-State is also a developmental state. It aims to mobilize and industrialize China from the top down. Sun Yat-sen's famous work, *The International Development of China* (1922), was the first attempt to plot the integrated economic development of a reunified China. It remains the most audacious and—still today, many three-, four-, five-, and ten-year plans later—the most memorable of national development programs. Sun's faith that international capital could be mobilized to construct Chinese socialism was shared widely by both Nationalist and Communist leaders. Sun's more concrete plans also left their mark. His two-paragraph proposal to "improve the upper Yangzi" with an enormous dam spawned seventy-five years of effort and debate before work on the Three Gorges Dam finally began in the mid-1990s.[7]

The Chinese Party-State is also a military state. While the Nationalist military took an oath to defend the nation, and did so valiantly during the anti-Japanese war, the People's Liberation Army has sworn its allegiance to upholding the rule of the Chinese Communist Party. It serves the Party first, the country second.

The Bo Xilai scandal also allows us to consider the role of the military anew. When the Communists conquered China, they divided the country into regional military districts that remain to this day. Bo clearly had substantial support within the People's Liberation Army, nationally and regionally. His closeness to military authorities was so alarming to Beijing that after Bo's arrest military leaders nationwide were required to take new loyalty oaths to the Party. It remains as true today as it was the day the People's Republic of China was founded: military power is the heart of the regime. The most important person is not the premier, the president, or the party chief; it is the chairman of the Party Military Commission. Today the roles of chairman of the Party Military Commission, general secretary of the Communist Party, and state president are embodied within one individual—Xi Jinping.

The Chinese Party-State is also in part a dynastic state. Chiang Kai-shek, who ruled the Chinese mainland from 1927 to 1949, and then Taiwan until his death in 1975, was succeeded by his son, Chiang Ching-kuo. In Communist China, there has been no direct succession from father to son, but again the Bo Xilai case presents an important lesson: Bo was a "princeling" and thus a descendent of one of Communist China's founding families. His career, his aspirations, and his demise remind us that the Chinese still live in a dynastic system dominated by conquering families, in which princes vie for the throne when it becomes vacant. Nationalist China under Chiang Kai-shek was said to have four great families. Communist China has at least forty, which hold much more power, influence, and wealth than their Nationalist predecessors.

The Chinese Party-State also allows great authority to be vested within a single leader, with few checks on this individual's preferences. Indeed, the formal titles given first to Sun Yat-sen, Chiang Kai-shek, and Mao Zedong hardly capture the spirit and scope of their domination over subordinates. The results of their time in power, however, do. So, too, do the informal titles, as Mao the "Great Helmsman" suggests. One of the criticisms of Bo Xilai was that he, in emulation of Mao, sought to construct a cult of personality.

To put this context a different way, there are no titular leaders in the Chinese Party-State. Rank and position matter greatly. For the ambitious, it means hitching one's wagon to a superior as a way to get ahead. Meritocracy does not suffice. Whom you know matters, and for this reason as well, the risks of alliances can be great. As recent political events attest, political careers in China rise and fall based on what the highest-ranking individual within a given alliance has done right or wrong. As a result, subordinates are inclined to cultivate as wide a patron network as possible to dodge the worst of consequences.

Against this backdrop, it really is not possible to speak of the autonomy of civil government in China. The individual interests of state bureaucrats lie elsewhere. Moreover, the overwhelming presence of Party members at the highest level of government office ensures that the political ends of government are aligned with Party interests above all else. The oath that Party members are expected to follow also makes this clear. For this reason, China remains a place where there is rule *by* law, but not truly a rule *of* law.

Once again, the case of Bo Xilai is instructive. The Bo case and its sideshows—the trials of his wife, Gu Kailai, and his onetime police chief, Wang Lijun—demonstrate more clearly than ever that the judicial and police systems of the PRC remain politically malleable. As party secretary in Chongqing, Bo used the law as a blunt instrument to imprison and execute his enemies. Then Gu and Wang were subjected to politicized trials in which there was no opportunity for self-defense. Although Bo himself was permitted to contest the charges against him, his trial, too, was carefully managed by the state. Bo's son went on to study law abroad, but the legal skills of even the best attorney would not have been sufficient to help Bo Xilai.

In the absence of legally constituted authority with legal constraints, the symbolic gestures of China's top political leaders carry with them striking, almost imperial influence even to this day. Mao Zedong swam in the Yangzi River to show that it was possible for all China to swim metaphorically upstream in building a Communist society. Deng Xiaoping traveled south in 1992—modeling his trip on the famous "southern tour" taken by the Qianlong emperor in the eighteenth century—to signal support for reviving market-oriented reforms. China's new party secretary, Xi Jinping, has replicated this move, making his own journey southward in December 2012, signaling that continued economic reform was the correct path for China.

It is only after these bold political gestures that the government apparatus begins the policy-making process in earnest, more or less attempting to execute the current line of whatever the Party leadership is thinking. This is not to say that debate is absent, but rather that an attempt to make an assessment of where the Chinese economy is headed, or of what is needed, without keen recognition of trends in high politics is simply foolish.

No less important is reading the politics correctly. Much of what is known of the "China model," for example, is often understood as a state-led program of both economic liberalization and massive infrastructure investment, thus presenting us with a story of political will rather than Party politics and family intrigue.

History Matters

The downfall of Bo Xilai, with which we opened this chapter, captures much that is unhealthy in China's political system. No one can possibly believe that in the distinguishing features of this scandal—the importance of family ties, regionalism, the influence of the military, the politicization of justice, and simple corruption—the Bo case is unique. What is unusual is that all these factors, which have strong roots in history, have risen to the surface at one time for all the world to see. None of this signals the CCP's strength as a political organization; instead, it demonstrates the historic weaknesses of the CCP's political system and its internal tensions.

In the chapters that follow, we will introduce you to individuals, now leading entrepreneurs in China, who have had to navigate this system in order to succeed. As we will show, China's political system is at the heart of understanding the kinds of strategies that have led to business success and failure.

History also matters to Chinese businesspeople today. We were reminded of this in January 2010, when in Manchuria, at a place called Yabuli, the Chinese Entrepreneurs' Forum celebrated its tenth anniversary—the "golden decade," it declared, of private Chinese enterprise from 2000 to 2010. The forum was attended by many of the most extraordinary and inventive entrepreneurs in the world—all of them Chinese. Its leader, Chen Dongsheng, chairman of the Taikang Life Insurance Company, devoted his keynote speech to reminding all in attendance that the first "golden decade" for modern Chinese business had occurred under Nationalist rule in Nanjing, from 1927 to 1937.[8]

Chen's words were well received because he was speaking at a time—roughly the present—when the tensions between private and public enterprise were again on the rise, and with a lesson to those high in government that private business will look elsewhere if the current environment grows less viable.

Another entrepreneur offers an even broader perspective. Lu Guanqiu, the charismatic chairman of Wanxiang Group, was born in the Republican era outside Hangzhou, in Zhejiang Province, a place known as an incubator of entrepreneurship. Lu was born to be a businessman, but he came of age in the early Communist period, truly the worst years in Chinese history to start a business. Nonetheless, he persevered. The small enterprise that he was permitted to establish in a People's Commune in 1969 is now China's largest automobile-parts manufacturer, with $14 billion in sales in 2012. Wanxiang is also now a global and diversified company and a significant employer in the United States.

What is the secret of Lu's success? In public, he credits the same Chinese government that in his youth stifled both entrepreneurship and economic growth. In private, he talks of the more enduring and regional forces that are the true strength of modern China: "We joke that as long as there is a human race, there will be Chinese. Well, as long as there is a market, then you will have people from Zhejiang."[9]

It is often said that the CCP "lifted" hundreds of millions out of poverty in the past decades. But who really did the heavy lifting? Lu Guanqiu lifted his family, his village, and tens of thousands of Wanxiang employees out of poverty, once he was given a chance to succeed.

These stories of extraordinary private entrepreneurs, now case studies in our course, and those that follow in the succeeding pages, allow us to illustrate the promise and limits of China today. In particular, they allow us to assess the enduring and problematic role of the Party in Chinese business and its effect on how economic actors assess their costs and benefits.

The answer to the question "Can China lead?" thus squarely points back to those in power and their willingness to cede some control to market forces and other indirect sources of stability and peace—first among them being the rule of law and the rights of citizens. It is, in other words, time to recognize that control from above may have had its day, and now is a source not only of inefficiency but also of unfairness, lessened transparency, and increasing social tension.

Today China is at a crossroads. The conventional wisdom is that the country needs "economic rebalancing," meaning a shift from an investment-driven, export-oriented model of development to one in which consumer spending and home-grown innovation play a greater role. But China's success ultimately hinges on a larger rebalancing, the elements of which we have begun to lay out in this chapter.

In the era of the People's Republic, China's economy and society changed markedly, and the country has started recovering the entrepreneurial spirit of pre-Communist times only in recent decades. But the influence and reach of the Chinese Communist Party has not diminished. So how will state and society interact to make the best use of the great talent of the Chinese people? How can the Chinese people, and particularly entrepreneurs, know that the country is on the right path? The question of whether China can lead in the twenty-first century depends on whether the CCP can address these questions as they connect to the broad range of dilemmas now facing the country, starting, as our next chapter shows, with the immense power of the country's "red capitalists."

What lessons can we draw from all this? First, history matters. Chinese civilization may be more than five thousand years old, but China as a country is about a century old, and it is still building the institutions of a modern state. Second, China is composed of different regions, each with its own history, culture, economic interests, and at times strong regional leadership. Any China strategy must evolve in a nuanced way, dealing with both the local and the central. Third, the Party-State is omnipresent. You cannot avoid it, so you must learn to deal with it. Engagement with the China market, however, can never be a short-term commitment, for the Party-State is itself composed of a complex of personal, regional, and organizational networks. You need to know them, and this takes time. Fourth, although you may not notice at first, the military remains the foundation of the regime. Like the Great Qing

Empire before it, the PRC is a conquest dynasty and it is still divided into the military districts established during the conquest. Bo Xilai may have had allies in several of these, but not, it turns out, in enough of them. Fifth, as a conquest dynasty the rule of great families endures. You will meet them, their lesser relatives, and their friends, sometimes without warning, in all realms of business. Again: you need to know to whom you are talking. This will never be as easy as it sounds.

Doing Business in China

- Does my firm have focused regional strategies in China or only a national one?

- Does my firm understand the conflicts between relevant Party and government entities as they apply to my firm?

- Does my firm have broad, deep, and long-standing personal networks in China? How can I develop them?

- Does my firm understand the hierarchical relationships among the various people it deals with?

- Does my firm understand the potential importance of the military to it, given our services and products?

- Does my firm know who the relevant power families are in relation to its activities?

2

PARTY, INC.

The Rise and Limits of China's Red Capitalism

Awkward marriages are normally fodder for gossip columnists and celebrity magazines. One union that receives insufficient coverage, however, is that between the Chinese Communist Party and private business. In recent decades, the CCP's top leadership has admitted, at times through remarkable ideological twists, that private entrepreneurs and markets are critical to the country's *socialist* development.

Today, China's "red capitalists"—entrepreneurs with strong political connections—lead large private corporations and oversee state-owned conglomerates. They include the sons and daughters, brothers and sisters of China's ruling elite, and they are rich. At the same time, there has been a deep unease in the CCP toward the development of a truly autonomous private economy. And yet growing numbers of Party members have ascended to the helms of China's most successful private firms. The Party has also created official space for non-Party members and private business leaders to offer their opinions through official "consultative conferences" that serve as honorary legislative bodies.

Alongside these well-connected individuals from private firms are red capitalists of a more official sort. These are the executives leading China's large, globe-spanning, state-owned corporations, many of which have subsidiaries trading on global exchanges. Finally, there are the children of China's political elite who have parlayed political pedigrees into dizzying sums of wealth.[1]

These outgrowths of single-party rule make China different from other models of state capitalism, all of which assume the autonomy of the government. China's red capitalism instead aims to maintain the autonomy, power, and position of the *Party* itself. This objective includes controlling and co-opting the country's richest individuals and largest non-state-owned organizations. If you want to understand the global reach of Chinese companies today, you need to know about China's red capitalists.

As of 2011, the Communist Party of China had 83 million members.[2] The membership comprised 6.3 percent of the country's total population of 1.3 billion. In 2010, more than 21 million Chinese citizens applied to join the Party, with slightly more than 3 million accepted.[3] As members, they became part of China's elite—a group at the vanguard of political status within China and in the past decade increasingly at the helm of business, both state-owned and private—a phenomenon we term "Party, Inc."

This chapter explores the making of "Party, Inc." The Party's role in business is both a bulwark of its support and a challenge to its wider legitimacy. At issue is more than the coexistence of private businesses and powerful state-owned corporations. The vast sums of private wealth accumulated by Party members have done real damage to the moral standing of the CCP as a ruling party and have hampered its capacity for internal control of its members.

In 2012, several unflattering accounts of Party, Inc. appeared in the international press, including one about the family members of the CCP's current general secretary, Xi Jinping. The successes and excesses of businesses tied to the ruling elite contrasted sharply with the challenges faced by small and medium-sized private enterprise owners. Even successful private businesspeople may be insecure in their achievements, since so much of their success still depends on the political dynamics of Party, Inc.

Chinese private enterprise was not set entirely free in the "reform and opening" period that began in 1978. We see instead continuity with earlier periods of the People's Republic. This is not a comfort to today's private enterprises, but it is a reality. Anyone doing business in China today should know the history of relations between the private economy and the CCP. It is a story of accommodation, conflict, and indeed CCP dependency on the success of an old enemy.

Continuity does not, however, mean absolute similarity. Before 1978, there was little illusion of shared interests between the Party and private business. Allowance for private economic activities of any scale did not exist. Today is different. The private economy has reemerged as China's largest employer and the major exporter of manufactured goods. The private economy dominates the service sector and the consumer goods sector. While government oversight of the private economy remains one of the Party's most direct links to the population, rules and controls to regulate market behavior are enforced unevenly from place to place, case to case (in the area of food safety, for example, often only after egregious failure), and often in favor of the politically connected.

Herein lies the paradox of China's economic liberalization. Greater ideological allowance for private economic activity is now necessary, but it also means that the CCP must now defend profit making, even among its members, or risk their exodus. The trend of family members of high-ranking Party officials going into business shows that allegiance to the Party has not superseded a much older set of values: loyalty to one's family and its well-being. Little wonder then that today, when the CCP is most in need of greater internal oversight of the economic activities of Party members, it lacks the will to bring them to account.

This chapter chronicles how China's current forms of business enterprise came to be. This is not history for history's sake.

The evolution of private enterprise is part of the collective memory of China, and the course that it has taken is one reason that distrust between private entrepreneurs and the Party-State remains strong despite the growing list of laws to protect market-based exchanges. Later chapters show through case examples how private entrepreneurs, despite this distrust, have been a critical force behind China's economic transformation. But here the story is of a once-dysfunctional relationship that has become a marriage of convenience between the Party and the private sector.

An Awkward Marriage: The Party and Private Business

When the Communists came to power in China in 1949, they inherited an economy in which leading strategic industries had already been nationalized. China's small heavy industrial sector, all major banks, railways, and critical parts of the energy sector were already under government control. The result was that more than 60 percent of modern industrial output was controlled by the state. (The Guomindang was not called the "Nationalist" party for nothing.[4])

In terms of GDP, however, the Chinese economy was largely private and agrarian. Nonfarming private enterprises were mostly family businesses. These were small and medium-sized businesses or partnerships of a kind that had made China one of the most commercial places on earth. There were also a small number of private companies of great scale or wealth. Most of these were concentrated within China's eastern coastal cities.

In 1949, the question was: what would the CCP do with China's 1.3 million private light industrial manufacturing and commercial businesses? The answer came even before the CCP secured its hold over cities. In 1947, Mao Zedong drew a distinction between two types of capitalists. *Compradores* were those deemed too close either to foreign businesses or to the old regime. *National capitalists* were those judged to serve China primarily and thought potentially loyal to the CCP's "new China" (this was a purely political categorization, as almost every sizable business had some international connection).

The CCP initially praised these national capitalists for their shared struggle against foreign competitors and worked diligently to persuade them to remain in China. Others who had fled were courted to return. Among them was Liu Hongsheng, one of China's leading industrialists who had earlier held positions in the Nationalist government. On his return to Shanghai in 1949, he mobilized other capitalists to join him in support of the CCP.[5] (Liu's sixth son—Harvard Business School class of 1949—opted not to join him.)

But the arrival of hammers and sickles in China's urban landscape was not reassuring to private businesspeople, especially those who knew Soviet history. Recognizing this, the Party told Chinese entrepreneurs repeatedly that they were part of China's multiparty, multiclass "New Democracy." Mao at first cautioned those within the Party who wanted to move ahead too quickly with "socialist transformation."[6] He promised a coalition government and a mixed economy to last fifteen years or more.

The reason for the promise was simple: the Communist Party, then as now, needed private businesses to aid economic development. In June 1952, Chen Yun, the Party vice chairman with economic planning responsibilities, spoke before the All-China Federation of Industry and Commerce, a state-run apparatus founded in 1953 that replaced private chambers of commerce. He announced that "law-abiding" entrepreneurs had little to fear. This was a bit disingenuous, as the CCP had already begun to reshape legal institutions to expand Party control over society.

The promise of coalition government was not kept. Entrepreneurs were moved to pledge allegiance to the Party in an attempt to protect their firms, employees, and families. Some made preemptive declarations of guilt, others "volunteered" to turn over everything, eager to be known as workers. Still others did everything they could to make themselves look insignificant. The commercial sectors—Shanghai, Tianjin, Chongqing, Guangzhou, and other large cities—came under a political microscope. By 1953, harsh punishments against the private sector had been meted out in these places.

There was at first some geographic variance: private firms in smaller cities such as Chengdu, defined mostly by small family workshops and petty commercial trade, initially fared well. Of the 450,000 businesses investigated in China's nine major cities, three-quarters were found to have engaged in "illegal activities." In Chengdu, however, only one-third of investigated firms were found to be in *any* violation of the law.[7] Soon enough everyone was swept into the new system. The regime steadily increased its control over once-private assets, judging firms by their levels of support for socialist development and values.[8]

By 1956, China's economy was fundamentally changed. Private industrial and manufacturing businesses ceased to exist, and dividends that had been promised to owners ended. Even small retail shops were "transformed," changing the urban landscape of cities both big and small. In the countryside, a millennium of private land ownership came to an end. Farming households were forced into cooperatives where they were encouraged to produce according to plans and quotas.

There was only one way to be legitimate in China, and that was to build socialism. Even so, while People's Squares, revolutionary songs, blaring speakers, and the *People's Daily* aimed to celebrate a "new China," the golden age of socialism never came. Instead, the rapid elimination of traditional trading networks created shortages across the economy, and some second thoughts.

Months after the CCP had declared socialist transformation of the economy complete, Chen Yun announced at the National People's Congress in mid-1956 that peddlers had a legitimate place in socialism. He declared them, along with marketplace vendors, to be "productive people," a high socialist compliment to this day. This label distinguished them from those who had been labeled "capitalists."

The change allowed small traders to operate with a high degree of protection, even though they were explicitly engaged in the business of buying, selling, and profit making. The effects were immediate. In Sichuan, for example, rural handicraft workers and traders, newly embedded within supply and marketing cooperatives, began to venture back to urban areas to sell goods to factories and office workers.[9] Newly created state-owned enterprises (SOEs) began to give loans directly to producer cooperatives in urban areas and elsewhere to help them meet their production quotas.

Tensions emerged. Factory workers accused the CCP of having double standards, claiming that it seemed better to be in commerce than production. Still, the CCP had named small traders as laborers, slotting them into what was then the right side of history, a tactic that would be repeated with private entrepreneurs starting in the 1980s.

The position of traders as a good class did not last long. Mao Zedong launched the Great Leap Forward in 1958, taking away residual property rights. China's farmers were forced to live in People's Communes and share with neighbors almost all personal possessions. It was a fundamental attack against both traditional and existing systems of commerce and production. Mao promised something better, a "leap" into communism. Mobilizing China into a frenzy of agricultural and industrial work, the campaign led instead to a spectacular collapse of the Chinese economy (GDP declined 25 percent from 1960 to 1962) and a famine that cost the lives of between 40 million and 60 million Chinese.[10]

The catastrophe of the Leap led to another brief embrace of private production and trade as the state tried to reduce its own burden and deal with the absolute desperation of so many. Many who had been recruited into the state-owned sector during the Great Leap Forward were cast out. Some were relocated to rural areas, while others headed back to small-scale commercial cooperatives of the kind operating in the early 1950s. There was a resurgence of informal traders and beggars in urban areas.

In the countryside, the enormously inefficient People's Communes were dismantled, in fact if not in name, allowing for economic management decisions to occur at lower levels. With this, smaller innovations began to emerge. Among them were the return of household garden plots to families and the introduction of household contracting, identical to what would emerge again in the late 1970s. During this period, something similar to township- and village-owned enterprises (TVEs) also began to appear, with local Party and government officials supporting much of this quietly. Anything beyond this only increased the possibility that they would be accused of taking the "capitalist road."

The subsequent decade (1966–1976) of Mao's Cultural Revolution stopped all of this and pushed back Chinese economic development just when East Asia was taking off with remarkable success. This time, there was no room for adaptations even on the smallest scale in China. Earlier depictions of petty traders as laborers were again overturned. They were now *capitalists*, a term that came to be applied indiscriminately with unfortunate consequences for those so labeled. Words matter greatly in China, but the ideas behind them change over time.

There is a 1957 Chinese film, clips of which we use in our class, which makes this point. The film, *Bu Ye Cheng (The City without Night)*, was initially shown in China as a celebratory tale of the socialist transformation of private business. It showed the human drama of a business family being "socialized" in every dimension—including children turning against parents. Just a few years later, the film was harshly rebuked as a show of "bourgeois humanism," meaning it revealed too much of human feelings and not enough of class natures.[11] By the time of the Cultural Revolution, the film was banned outright. None of our Chinese MBA students had ever heard of it, let alone viewed it. The film's content, of course, remained the same, but its meaning had changed. The lesson of this—still true today—is that China's political climate, not its laws, defines what constitutes legitimate economic activity.

The story of Wu Ying, founder of the Bense Group, is illustrative. Wu Ying's story is emblematic of the rise and fall, and the opportunities and constraints, of private entrepreneurs in post-1978 China. A farmer's daughter who started out with a small nail salon, Wu Ying quickly expanded into other service industries, and ultimately into China's shadow banking and investment sector, a part of the economy estimated at $2.4 trillion in 2012.[12] Her success depended on raising money from others in exchange for significant returns and then lending at a good spread. Wu Ying became one of China's richest women before her thirtieth birthday.

Informal flow of funds at this scale was no secret to anyone in China, including government officials. Indeed, the economic revival of Wenzhou City, in Zhejiang Province, as China's heartland of private business had depended upon it, with local government officials often defending the practice of informal lending.[13] By 2011, the city had nearly two hundred guarantee firms, over one thousand investment firms, over four hundred consignment shops, and nearly fifty pawnshops.[14] Wu Ying was an integral part of this system. She operated without incident despite laws existing against informal private fund-raising and collecting deposits like a bank.

In 2007, her luck ran out. Initially charged with illegal fund-raising, and later financial fraud, she was sentenced to death in 2009 for failing to pay back $55 million raised from private investors. She appealed the Zhejiang Provincial Court's verdict. In 2012, China's Supreme People's Court ruled in her favor, resulting in a two-year suspended death sentence, which will likely be commuted to a jail sentence.[15]

In the run-up to the court's decision, the role of politics (and political sentiments) in Chinese economic life had come into full display. In Wu Ying, all entrepreneurs, large and small, saw themselves and paths earlier taken. In open letters and online social media, they pointed out the government's double standards, highlighting self-made men and women sitting in jail, while naming those better connected who remained free despite identical offenses. Others faulted China's state banking system and its permanent favoritism toward state-owned industries in its lending. Private entrepreneurs, many noted, had little recourse outside of informal finance as a means to start and expand their businesses.

The Party's continued disinclination toward a truly autonomous private sector had put it at odds with the country's economic engine. In March 2012, then-premier Wen Jiabao acknowledged the sensitivity of the Wu Ying case and urged the court to "rely on facts." He also noted that private financial institutions ought to have a greater role in China.[16] One month later, under a new pilot program, Wenzhou City's informal moneylenders were given permission to register as private lenders—something that they had already been doing underground since the start of economic reforms, if not longer.[17]

Today, a boom in private sector peer-to-peer microlending has taken off, with more than four thousand firms now in operation.[18] These companies, among them China Risk Finance (CRF), CreditEase, and PPDai, are underwriting funds for everything from small businesses to weddings and school tuition. Their management teams also keep their political ears close to the ground. As Drew Mason, a major CRF investor, expressed, "regulatory clarity" is not always available in China.[19]

Stories of this kind are not limited to the high-risk world of finance. Cathay Industrial Biotech, a private firm, had been a market leader in the production of a form of nylon. Suddenly, its advantages shriveled as a state-backed company emerged to compete with it. Nylon had been reclassified as a "national security" good. Where the private sector succeeds, the state may follow. Recently, the Chinese government has sought to devise its own internet, its own mobile telecommunication standard, and its own version of Google maps. Known as Map World, the product also defines China's territory to include a well-known set of disputed islands. As the state establishes standards and controls to favor homegrown businesses, especially state-owned enterprises, foreign companies have been driven out of this space.

What's in a Name? How Private Entrepreneurs Became Good Socialists

As noted in chapter 1, private entrepreneurship has a long history in China. While tolerated at points before 1978, its scale and form has undergone tremendous changes over the past three decades.

The unleashing of entrepreneurial talent has been accompanied by extraordinary economic growth (shown in appendix A), creating a middle class of over 300 million people.[20] As appendix A also shows, this growth has occurred unevenly across the country. The conventional story is of market conditions and legal rights as the driving force of this development. We find the ideological shifts that allowed these factors to come into existence to be far more significant.

In 1978, China was a place of Mao jackets, ration coupons, and individuals with heads full of caution forged over decades of political turmoil. As a result, China's economic reformists had the task of convincing "the masses" that what once had been cause for arrest and public humiliation—market-oriented activities and thought—was now the way ahead for China's success.

Patterns of private entrepreneurship have mirrored critical changes in Party ideology. The case of Rong Yiren is a good example. Rong was the nephew of Rong Zongjing, the richest entrepreneur of Republican China. He was the only one of his seven brothers to stay in China. His business—like all businesses—was nationalized in 1956, with Rong himself directing the expropriation of his own firm. Rong then became a strong symbol of a reformed national capitalist—honored in times of ideological relaxation and humiliated in eras of radicalism such as the Cultural Revolution. Rong lived long enough, however, to be rehabilitated politically by Deng Xiaoping and ultimately to serve as a symbol of the return of entrepreneurship as well.

In 1978, Rong was given the resources to set up the China International Trust and Investment Corporation (CITIC), the country's first state-owned investment company and the vehicle by which

Western investors made their way back to China. His son, one of China's first princelings to go into private business, Rong Zhijian (or Larry Yung), restored the family's wealth initially through business partnerships with relatives in Hong Kong, where he moved at the start of economic reforms. He ultimately joined his father at CITIC where he became chairman of its Hong Kong operation (CITIC Pacific) and where his daughter was employed until she was involved in a trading scandal. Rong Zhijian subsequently resigned as well because of the scandal. Now, at seventy years of age, Rong Zhijian has an estimated worth of slightly over $1 billion.[21]

On a wider scale, the transformation of the Chinese economy started more humbly. In 1978, the Party acknowledged that market-based agricultural activities had a rightful place in a socialist economy. On February 29, 1980, an editorial in the *People's Daily* asserted that former industrialists and businesspeople could now be worthy of the term *comrade*.[22] One year later, the government encouraged self-employment in cities, allowing unemployed young people and the unemployable, including ex-convicts and former capitalists, to sustain themselves.

With this, China's boom in registered individual businesses took off. There were fewer than 1 million "self-employed workers" in 1980; that figure reached nearly 13 million by 1989.[23] Among them were not only shopkeepers and farmers, but small workshop owners and artisans who needed to employ others. They were permitted to hire no more than two workers and five apprentices, a limitation that proved almost immediately unsustainable.

In 1987, CCP general secretary Zhao Ziyang acknowledged as much at the Thirteenth Party Congress, giving recognition to private business as a "necessary and useful complement to the public economy."[24] One year later, in 1988, the Chinese constitution was amended, using the term *private economy* for the first time, describing it as "a complement to the socialist economy" and thus entitled to state protection and rights.

That same year, the State Council issued "Tentative Stipulations on Private Enterprises." Although not law, the stipulations elaborated a set of rules and regulations by which enterprises employing more than eight people could rightfully exist. For the first time since 1949, entrepreneurs could register private firms as sole proprietorships, limited liability companies, joint-stock enterprises, or partnerships. At home and abroad, there was growing optimism for what lay ahead for China and the Chinese people.

At the same time, the state continued to discriminate against private enterprises of any significant size or ambition. To survive, private entrepreneurs had to cultivate social and economic ties with government officials, suppliers in the state-owned sector, and customers beyond their immediate environment. For local government officials, the relationship was beneficial in many ways. It aided local prosperity, created employment, and in some cases, led to personal riches.

Forms of cooperation between local government and private entrepreneurs varied across geographic areas and in relation to economic sectors and scale. The case of Wenzhou City in Zhejiang Province is again noteworthy. Wenzhou's commerce has historically been comprised overwhelmingly of private businesses. It was an incubator of entrepreneurs in Qing and Republican times. It was less persecuted than ignored during the Maoist era and emerged, alongside Guangdong Province, as a key area of private-sector development.

In 1979, Zhang Huame started her button business in Wenzhou, unofficially at first, and then as recipient of post–Mao China's very first "self-employed worker" business license.[25] She is still in business. So too is Chen Wenda, whose Wenzhou lighter factory, opened in 1988, along with support from his other enterprises, has allowed him to fill a cellar with Chateau Lafite.[26]

Nearby, Lu Guanqiu forged a different kind of partnership, having obtained permission to create a Commune and Brigade Enterprise in 1969 in a People's Commune in the village of Ningwei outside of Hangzhou. The endeavor eventually became Wanxiang, China's largest auto-components company. Lu's big breaks came at moments of political moderation—in 1973 and then especially in 1979, when he benefited from more-liberal government policies. Wanxiang became the first non-state-owned enterprise to enter the state plan for the production of auto parts.

Entrepreneur-run, nominally collectively owned enterprises such as Wanxiang, while rare at the height of the Cultural Revolution, were common in the early years of market-oriented economic reform. Alongside genuine township- and village-owned enterprises (TVEs), these "red hat"—or nominally publicly owned— firms were the industrial engine that brought "Made in China" to the world. By 1990, collective enterprises, rural and urban, were emerging as the largest employers in China.[27] They were also the country's light manufacturing export engine.

Private entrepreneurship, in turn, became a source of political legitimacy for the CCP. Although private enterprise and entrepreneurialism initially took off in the countryside, it did not take long for growing numbers of educated people to begin to participate.

Ren Zhengfei was among them. Ren was born in 1944 and released from military service in 1982. In 1988, he established a small private company in the experimental Special Economic Zone of Shenzhen, north of Hong Kong. Huawei, as he named his firm, is today the largest telecommunications equipment manufacturer in the world. He is celebrated as a Chinese hero and a valued Communist Party member.

The same cannot be said for Wan Runnan, another such entrepreneur. Born in 1946, Wan was a Tsinghua graduate, well-respected software engineer, and college friend of Hu Jintao, the recent general secretary of the Chinese Communist Party (2002–2012).[28] In 1984, Wan established the Stone Corporation, which by 1989 was the largest private company in China, with over seven hundred employees. He also supported an independent think tank that channeled its opinions to China's more reform-minded leaders, including then–general secretary Zhao Ziyang. Today, Wan is in exile, still subject to arrest in China for his support and funding of protesters, many of them employees who had mobilized in

Tiananmen Square calling for democracy.[29] Wan was expelled from the Party in 1989. His story remains a sobering lesson to this day.

Two men, both Party members, each well connected in his own right, came to different fates. For us, the broader lesson is that neither connections nor wealth can fully counterbalance political missteps in China. With the suppression of mass demonstrations in Tiananmen Square in Beijing in June 1989, this dynamic played out on a larger scale. The Party's resulting leftward turn put private entrepreneurship again out in the cold.

It took another political signal to restart private entrepreneurship in a large way. This was Deng Xiaoping's 1992 journey to Shenzhen. In his Southern Tour talks, he argued that capitalism and a market economy were different things. Thus it was possible, he said, for China to have markets and still be socialist. Similarly, no infusion of private capital, foreign or domestic, could make China capitalist if that was not the CCP's goal. Deng's contorted language at once unleashed new economic growth and yet made clear that China was to remain socialist and under the control of the CCP.

By late 1993, China's economic system became officially known as a "socialist market economy." Subsequent changes in Party discourse granted private entrepreneurs increasing legitimacy. Once again, entrepreneurs, big and small, were portrayed as having a positive role to play in socialist development. Early in the year 2000, then-CCP general secretary Jiang Zemin took matters a step further. Who, he asked in his theory of "The Three Represents," did the Party actually represent? The answer was "advanced social productive forces." With this, the Chinese Communist Party was able to recast private entrepreneurs, now standing alongside workers, farmers, soldiers, and the "intelligentsia," as good for socialism.

Celebrating the eightieth anniversary of the Chinese Communist Party on July 1, 2001, Jiang then expressed support for admitting private entrepreneurs into the Communist Party. Shortly thereafter, the Party's constitution was changed to allow this. The impact was swift, starting at the very pinnacle of political socialization in China—the Central Party School, an organization tasked with providing midcareer training to Party members with positions at varying levels within the CCP and state organizations.

Within a year of Jiang Zemin's recommendation, private entrepreneurs began to take classes at the Party School. They did so at their own expense or through sponsorship of their local governments or business associations. The phenomenon itself was a strong indication of things to come in the new millennium. Who could have predicted that Harvard Business School and other educational institutions in China would be in competition with the Party's own brand of executive education? The cachet and connections generated from studying at the Party School, however, continue to draw private entrepreneurs each year.

From Ideology to Law

Each of the ideological interventions described above was followed by legislative changes that institutionalized the Party's intentions in law and policy. The 1988 change to China's constitution put the phrase *private economy* in a positive light for the first time, describing the segment as a "complement" to socialism. In 1993, the government did away with the idea of "commodity planning" when it introduced the concept of a socialist market economy. At the decade's end, the private sector was again recast within the constitution, and finally as an "essential element" of the economic system. Laws were passed to strengthen market-based exchange and the rights of private entrepreneurs.

As China entered the twenty-first century, it seemed that the state economy was in retreat. In 2002, the National People's Congress proposed a new property law that subjected all forms of property—state, collective, and private—to equal rights and protections before the law. In 2004, the Chinese constitution was amended to assert that "lawful private property" was inviolable. By 2007, over twenty-three thousand private entrepreneurs held seats in the national and local legislatures.[30] Even more came into roles within quasi-governmental advisory bodies—most importantly, the Chinese People's Political Consultative Conference, which meets annually at the same time as the plenary sessions of the national legislature and is meant to represent a broad spectrum of social groups and divergent interests in Chinese society.

The business community responded positively to these shifts. Formerly unregistered entrepreneurs and enterprises came aboveground. The number of registered private entrepreneurs jumped from 1.7 million in 2000 to 4.3 million in 2005. The number of registered private enterprises also skyrocketed, going from 3.9 million firms in 2000 to 11 million in 2005.[31] By the end of the first decade of the twenty-first century, the structural composition of the economy seemed fundamentally different.

At the same time, reforms of state-owned enterprises begun in the 1990s had changed fundamental features of the economy. The percentage of urban employment provided by state-owned enterprises between 2001 and 2010 dropped from 52 percent to 28 percent. Gross industrial output of wholly state-owned firms dropped from 25 percent to 9 percent of the total economy between 1999 and 2010 as the nonstate sector surged.[32]

Putting these changes in political context, it is also apparent that the Party-State had helped itself by shedding once-sacrosanct obligations to workers while simultaneously making the remaining state-owned sector more successful through processes of privatization and mergers and acquisitions. This occurred concurrently with a growing body of law to protect and encourage the private economy and market-based activities.

Perhaps for this reason, no one correctly predicted the political implication of China's changing economic structure, a context wherein the Party inserted itself into a new place—the private sector. At the same time, the Party made it clear that state-owned corporations would maintain control over the country's "strategic industries."

On the Road to 2014

In November 1993, a decision to end the state's responsibility to small state-owned enterprises was made.[33] Many of these largely rural-based firms were heavily in debt and in some cases had been subcontracted to private operators. Others, failing to achieve sustainable economies of scale, were increasingly a burden to local governments. By 2000, it is estimated that 80 percent of collectively owned firms at the county level and below had been privatized.[34]

In many places, governments had begun years earlier to lease collective firms to private entrepreneurs, forging a relationship of mutual dependency and the phenomenon of red hat enterprises, as was the case for Wanxiang. These enterprises and their successors were a source of job creation, tax revenues, and other receipts to local governments all across China. In the best case, private entrepreneurs helped local government officials look good and enjoyed their protection in return. Worse were growing instances of cronyism and unfair competition that made markets unequal in new ways.

A second element of privatization was the elimination of "redundant" state-owned enterprise workers. Even Daqing, the Communist showcase refinery, invoked decades earlier as the Maoist industrial model for China, experienced heavy layoffs.[35] In a further sign of changed times, local Chinese governments were told to show tolerance toward protesting SOE workers. Thousands staged sit-ins outside local government offices across China, especially in its northern rust belt.

The protests made no difference. Between 1995 and 2003, the number of state-owned enterprise workers was cut nearly in half; 43.4 million Chinese workers lost their jobs, the equivalent of putting around two-thirds of the United Kingdom's population—approximately 63 million as of July 2011—out of work. The reduction of state-owned enterprises was no less remarkable, declining from 118,000 to 34,000 firms.[36]

Positive political signaling toward the private sector also encouraged individuals within the state-owned and related sectors, such as government and education, to exit on a large scale in the 1990s. This was a move made not without trepidation if the Chinese phrase for going into private business ("jumping into the sea") is any indication. Some of China's best-known information technology entrepreneurs found their way into the private sector during this period, including Alibaba's Jack Ma, who left a government position, and Liang Wengen, founder of Hunan's Sany Heavy Industry, a heavy equipment company.

Joining these start-up entrepreneurs were individuals who were able to restructure their links with local governments. The Wahaha Group, China's beverage giant, is representative of this kind of shift. Its founder, Zong Qinghou, started out with a license to sell snacks in his home district's school system. Today, he holds 29.4 percent of the Group's shares. Slightly less than that belongs to employees of Wahaha's affiliated joint-stock company, and the remainder is held by a district government within Hangzhou City, located in Zhejiang Province, where the company had its start.[37]

Alongside these new entrants were the old stalwarts of private entrepreneurship—the farmers, shopkeepers, and small manufacturers who, much in the tradition of Walmart's trajectory, bootstrapped their way to tremendous economic success. The story of the Liu brothers is a good example. Descendants of wealthy landlords, Liu Yongyan, Liu Yongxin, Chen Yuxin, and Liu Yonghao survived their family's political persecution to establish China's most successful animal feed and poultry business, New Hope Liuhe Company. While smaller and less experienced at the start, the Liu brothers ultimately were able to compete successfully with the overseas Chinese-Thai entrepreneur Dhanin Chearvanont's Charoen Pokphand Group ("CP Group") in China.

A quick survey of *Forbes*'s 2012 "China's 400 Richest" illustrates this diversity, showing that no single feature, even among the top ten (see table 2-1), links them beyond their extraordinary wealth. Some are not highly educated; others hold doctorates. Their companies range from agribusiness to heavy manufacturing, information technology to real estate development. In terms of generation, some are led by rather young CEOs, such as Robin Li, who founded the search engine Baidu after years of studying and working in the United States. Others are led by individuals who survived economic hardship during the planning period and, in some cases, persecution owing to family background. All benefited from the shifts in Party ideology and subsequent policy changes that began in the 1980s, but the 1990s ended with two events that foreshadowed changes ahead.

The first was the release of China's first "rich list" in 1999, the brainchild of Rupert Hoogewerf, a British chartered accountant based in Shanghai. It illustrated that considerable amounts of wealth had accumulated initially in areas where the CCP's presence had been weak, most notably, the consumer sector. The second was the official release, in 2000, of China's Gini coefficient figures, a measure of overall income inequality. It proved what everyone was already seeing—inequality was increasing. That was also the last official release of China's Gini coefficient.[38]

While there are differing opinions on exact levels, the trend line of this measure is undisputed. Income inequality has worsened

TABLE 2-1

Forbes's China rich list, top 10 (October 2012)

Rank	Name	Company	City	Worth
1	Zong Qinghou	Hangzhou Wahaha Group	Hangzhou	$10 billion
2	Li Yonhong (Robin Li)	Baidu	Beijing	$8.1 billion
3	Wang Jianlin	Dalian Wanda Group	Beijing	$8 billion
4	Ma Huateng	Tencent	Shenzhen	$6.4 billion
5	Wu Yajun	Longfor Properties	Beijing	$6.2 billion
6	Liang Wengen	Sany Group	Changsha	$5.9 billion
7	Liu Yongxing	East Hope Group	Shanghai	$5.8 billion
8	Hui Ka Yan	Evergrande Real Estate Group	Guangzhou	$4.9 billion
9	Yang Huiyan	Country Garden	Foshan	$4.4 billion
10	Hui Wing Mau	Shimao Property	Hong Kong	$4 billion

Source: "China Rich List," *Forbes*, October 2012, http://www.forbes.com/china-billionaires/list/.

dramatically in China. To draw from one study, between 1991 and 1997, China's Gini coefficient increased from 0.37 to 0.40. By year 2000, it had reached 0.44. A subsequent Chinese Academy of Social Sciences study claimed that the number had jumped to 0.47 in 2005, and in December 2012, a report released by a Chinese university reported 0.61 for year 2010, putting China between Bolivia and the Central African Republic.[39]

With this, observers inside and outside China began to raise more pointed political issues linked to income equality, describing the phenomenon as China's "Latin-Americanization," meaning intractable inequality caused by powerful economic interest groups and their government allies.[40] In response, China's political incumbents began to speak of the need to create a "harmonious society." The concept, initially aimed to shift government attention toward improvements in social development and the environment, was linked with the aspiration that all of China might belong to a "well-off society" (*xiaokang shehui*). The slogan today carries a far less positive meaning. It connotes stability at all costs, including suppression of dissenting citizens.

China as Party, Inc.

Over the past two decades, China has not only become more unequal, but wealth has become concentrated in ways that now make efforts to rebalance the economy politically challenging and structurally difficult to execute. Much of this began with the Party's need to support private sector development to meet three macroeconomic goals: lessened debt burdens on the state budget, continued economic growth, and sustained low unemployment.

The Party benefited enormously from its recognition of the legitimacy of the private sector. Support of the private sector allowed the government to shed loss-making industries while ensuring that employment levels did not dip severely. In turn, the structure of the private sector changed dramatically. Between 1991 and 1997, the share of limited liability companies grew from 6 percent to nearly 50 percent of all private firms. Sole proprietorships declined nearly 16 percent in relative terms, while partnerships were on the rise.[41] There were also geographic implications, with China's once-vanguard category of "self-employed workers" now largely concentrated in rural areas.

At the same time, the massive transfer of wealth that got under way had political consequences. Knowledge of backdoor economic dealings and influence peddling by family members of China's political elite is now common, as is contempt for the double standards by which these activities are treated. The description in chapter 1 of the sentencing of Gu Kailai, wife of once-hopeful Politburo member Bo Xilai, is one example. Less notable figures might have been put to death. Tales with less tragic endings also exist, having to do with the influence peddling of relatives and family business dealings such as the recent exposé of former premier Wen Jiabao's family finances.

Private entrepreneurs without connections still need to develop them. Indeed, thirty-five years after China's economic reforms began, we hear private entrepreneurs, domestic and foreign, tell us that it is nearly impossible to conduct business without accommodating the political demands of the Party-State. (We will see more examples of this in chapter 5.)

Other successful entrepreneurs have obtained positions within government and quasi-government bodies, seeking protection of their economic interests through legislative channels. Zhang Yin, the daughter of a People's Liberation Army lieutenant and founder of Nine Dragons Paper Holdings, Ltd., is a good example. Several years ago, she used her position as a member of the Chinese People's Political Consultative Conference to advocate for milder labor laws in China—in line with those of the United States, as she noted.

China's legislature has also included at various points some of the country's richest individuals—Zong Qinghou, Wahaha's founder and chairman; Lu Guanqiu, Wanxiang's founder and chairman; and Wu Yajun, Longfor Properties' chairwoman, among others.

They can be vocal advocates of pro-business policies. These legislators have opposed property taxes, arguing that these will discourage investment in China and possibly reduce employment owing to increased business costs. However, advocates for the poor, especially in rural areas, say that a property tax is the only way to attack the ongoing problem of property hoarding in urban areas and land grabs in the countryside. The latter phenomenon has left some farmers barely compensated by local governments that seize their land in order to lease or sell it to property developers.

With the enrollment of private entrepreneurs and the enrichment of the Party elite, the members of China's legislature are now far richer than the leading officials of the United States. The seventy richest delegates of China's National People's Congress have a combined net worth of $89.9 billion as of 2011. Across all three branches of the US government, the net worth of the 660 top officials is approximately $7.5 billion.[42]

Yet even with new privileges, China's business leaders have grown more vocal in their opposition to the "monopoly-state," by which they mean the dominance of state-owned enterprises over certain sectors. In this they are joined by millions of private entrepreneurs who still do not feel that China has a level playing field. They point to a new fault line in the making—their growing frustration with "hitting the red ceiling" in China, meaning the imposition of barriers of entry into economic sectors and political positions that the Party-State protects.

State control over strategic industries is a key example. While the number of state-owned enterprises has declined, their assets have expanded exponentially. A graph of this trend would reveal two lines running in opposite directions, with the implication being a greater concentration of assets in a smaller number of state-owned businesses. Such concentration of wealth is no accident. It is Chinese industrial policy.

The millennium in China had started with the idea that "the state retreats and the private sector moves ahead," something we saw unfolding in the dramatic increases in private enterprise and legal protections for such businesses. Now that trend has come under threat. A survey of the top twenty Chinese companies on the global *Fortune* 500 reveals how economically powerful state-owned firms have become (see table 2-2). Among China's listed companies, there are few truly private Chinese enterprises. And, given this, the phrase that better describes the relationship between state and economy in the last decade is "the state advances and the private sector retreats," as former premier Zhu Rongji once said.[43]

TABLE 2-2

Top twenty Chinese firms on the *Fortune* Global 500[a]

Rank	Company	Global 500 Rank	City	Revenues ($ millions)	Profits ($ millions)
1	Sinopec Group	5	Beijing	375,214	9,453
2	China National Petroleum	6	Beijing	352,338	16,317
3	State Grid	7	Beijing	259,142	5,678
4	Industrial & Commercial Bank of China	54	Beijing	109,040	32,214
5	China Construction Bank	77	Beijing	89,648	26,181
6	China Mobile Communications	81	Beijing	87,544	11,703
7	Agricultural Bank of China	84	Beijing	84,803	18,860
8	Noble Group	91	Hong Kong	80,732	431
9	Bank of China	93	Beijing	80,230	19,208
10	China State Construction Engineering	100	Beijing	76,024	1,108
11	China National Offshore Oil	101	Beijing	75,514	8,836
12	China Railway Construction	111	Beijing	71,443	489
13	China Railway Group	112	Beijing	71,263	1,035
14	Sinochem Group	113	Beijing	70,990	1,178
15	China Life Insurance	129	Beijing	67,274	1,048
16	SAIC Motor	130	Shanghai	67,255	3,128
17	Dongfeng Motor Group	142	Wuhan	62,911	1,321

TABLE 2-2 *(continued)*

Top twenty Chinese firms on the *Fortune* Global 500[a]

Rank	Company	Global 500 Rank	City	Revenues ($ millions)	Profits ($ millions)
18	China Southern Power Grid	152	Guangzhou	60,538	755
19	China FAW Group	165	Changchun	57,003	2,297
20	China Minmetals	169	Beijing	54,509	754

Source: Adapted from "Global 500," *CNN Money*, July 23, 2012, http://money.cnn.com/magazines/fortune/global50_0/2012/full_list/index.html.
[a] All of the companies listed are fully state-owned or possess a significant government stake.

Fault Lines Ahead

The pervasive influence of the Party in China means that private entrepreneurs are at an enduring disadvantage. Strengthening China's regulatory apparatus is unlikely to help, as rules and regulations do not truly apply to all. As a result, China remains a place where nonregulatory signals are important. This often puts foreign players at considerable disadvantage, as they tend to look for policy lines rather than knowledge about how to read between them.

These trends also have implications for the sustainability of China's Party, Inc. model of development. Successful private entrepreneurs are growing weary of the theatrics of doing business in a system that once again is limiting their field of endeavor. While some are using their access to CCP leaders to express these opinions, others are making their views clear in another way: by shifting family members and capital overseas—a repeat of patterns seen in the pre-1949 period.

Recasting an Economic Miracle

The Chinese Communist Party has had a long and uneasy relationship with the private sector. As before, it needs private entrepreneurs to deliver the promises of prosperity it makes. Today, the state alone cannot deliver what President Xi Jinping has called the "China Dream," as that vision depends on what Chinese entrepreneurs can provide. Yet Party, Inc. continues to limit what entrepreneurs can do. That is why telling the story of China's great economic transformation solely from the Party's perspective is so deeply misleading.

The official history dates China's economic success from a state-led "reform and opening" after 1978, a story centered on Deng Xiaoping's pragmatism and his willingness to experiment. Absent from the official stories are the many roadblocks that private entrepreneurs had to endure. When we hear of China opening its doors, we should remember the real story of the China miracle is about how the Chinese people opened their own doors and found other means to economic prosperity by working around the barriers posed by the Party.

The economic miracle, in other words, was hard-won, and now it is again under threat from within. The chapters that follow will show how existing institutions are a large part of the problem. Even an area of seemingly obvious success, such as the infrastructure state we encounter in chapter 3, may have found its limits.

Doing Business in China

- What is the ownership structure of my industry in China? Is there a significant SOE presence?

- Do I have evidence that the Party-State supports my firm's presence in the regions where we want to operate?

- Do I have evidence that the Party-State supports my firm's presence in China? How recent is that evidence?

- How does today's political climate dictate the best entry and operation mode for my business?

- Is there a way to expand my business in a politically correct way? Does this entail taking on local partners, creating opportunities for indigenous research and development, or producing higher value-added products in the China market?

3

THE ENGINEERING STATE

The End of the Road

Two important and interlocking trends have dominated the last century and shaped modern China's development. The first was a wrenching transition from an elite culture of educated general-ists to a society dominated by technocratic values and technocrat leaders—China today is a society led by engineers. The second trend has been an extraordinary focus on building infrastructure where none existed before.

China's technocratic leadership has focused on the development of infrastructure as a platform for the country's economic growth and social well-being. National infrastructure typically takes a long time to construct, but China is midstream in a rapid build-out.

Since 1995, the total expressway length in China has grown from two thousand kilometers to sixty-five thousand kilometers. Since 2006, there has been a 20 percent growth rate per year in trunk highways. The seven horizontal and five vertical trunk-line sys-tems will at least double again by 2020. The Chinese highway net-work is already the second-largest in the world, yet the government maintains enormous ambitions. Even a highway to Taiwan can be found on Chinese planning maps.

Improvements in road network capacity have facilitated China's booming auto sector: the Ford Motor Company, for example, estimates that the current annual national production of automobiles of 16 million vehicles will rise to 32 million by 2020.[1]

China's improved road and other transportation networks have also been a force of social change, assisting several hundred million Chinese to move out of poor rural areas toward greater economic opportunities elsewhere, and thus fundamentally weakening a critical lever of state control—the household registration (hukou) system.

China's transportation networks have also integrated communities and economies in new ways. For example, China's richest town, Kunshan, has a per capita GDP of legal residents of $52,000. Once an out-of-the-way backwater of Shanghai, it is now connected in every direction by road, highway, rail, and now high-speed rail. As a result, it has become home to booming manufacturing and high-tech industries, none of which would have been possible without the 1.2 million "temporary residents" who have also moved there.[2]

In rail transport, China's 233 miles of track in 1900 expanded to nearly 61,000 miles in January 2013. The network is now second only in size to the networks of the United States and Russia, but the Chinese system carries many more passengers and much more freight volume than any other national system.[3] As a result, a quarter of the world's cargo and passenger traffic is carried on only 6 percent of the world's track. Figure 3-1 shows the steady growth in passenger traffic from 1980 through 2011.

High-speed rail (an average speed of 125 miles per hour or higher) was inaugurated only in 2007, but China's system is already the longest high-speed rail network in the world, with nearly six thousand miles in service.[4] On half of this network, trains reach speeds near 200 miles per hour. The network is expected to nearly triple in size by 2015.

All this seems sudden and overwhelming: China on the march to modernity. But it is in many ways the last act of a play that

FIGURE 3-1

Passengers carried in China: Rail transport (1980–2011)

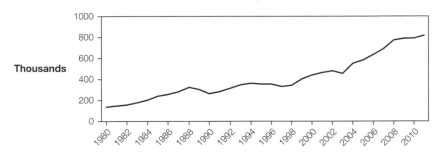

Source: Data from CEIC, taken from the World Bank (WDI), June 3, 2013.

opened a century ago, starting with a shift in educational values toward the hard sciences and all things modern. Over the last century, China has undergone a revolution in values. For nearly a millennium, from the Song dynasty (960–1279) until the twentieth century, the state examination system defined not only what it meant to be a scholar and an official but also what it meant to be rich and powerful. The imperial educational and examination system brought the most learned men in the realm into the service of the state—not because they had been trained in practical matters, but because they had deeply studied what today we would call the humanities. They had studied, memorized, chanted, and metaphorically consumed the classics, and, once in office, they acted according to the enduring principles of human behavior that the *Analects*, *Mencius*, and other great works set out. There has seldom been a higher academic ideal: good people embarking on the living study of great books in order to do good work in society.

There were limits to this system: the absence of the study of mathematics, science, and practical affairs did not mean that the Empire was better governed. In fact, it contributed to the Empire's feeble capacity in the nineteenth century to respond to a militarized, industrialized, and otherwise energized West, resulting in a series of humiliations that would spell the end of a two-thousand-year imperial tradition.

The empire fell in 1911, but for our purposes the more important date is 1905, when the ancient civil service examination system ended. Starting in 1905, Chinese education at all levels began to drift strongly toward the study of those subjects that would lead to *fu qiang* (wealth and power)—primarily mathematics, science, and engineering. Within a decade of that date, the moral foundation of both Chinese government and culture, Confucianism, came under a withering attack, leaving a void in the realm of human and social values. By 1949, when the mainland fell to the Communists, fewer than 10 percent of graduates of Chinese public universities graduated with degrees in humanistic disciplines—and the Communists took that number to the vanishing point.

In the absence of the humanities, two themes dominated in education in the twentieth century. First was the belief that culture and the arts were to serve the purposes of the developmental state. As Mao Zedong put it, literature and art were to be defined as "the artistic crystallization of the political aspirations of the Communist party." (As the twentieth-century writer Lu Xun once observed: all art may be propaganda, but not all propaganda is art.)

A second, more enduring trend was the belief that in an age of science one could quite literally engineer a bright future, a new people. This was the dream of modern Chinese leaders from Sun Yat-sen onward: a government of technocratic expertise, capable of "reconstructing" China with roads, railroads, and dams; a government of huge ambition, as seen in the Three Gorges Dam project, first conceived by Sun Yat-sen in the 1920s, planned by the Nationalists in the 1940s, and later built by the Communist regimes of Jiang Zemin and Hu Jintao. One result of this belief in the power of science is that nearly every member of recent Standing Committees of the Politburo of the People's Republic of China—the seven to nine men who have run the country—have had training in engineering. In 2011 there were 339,700 Chinese students studying overseas.[5] Of these, 194,029 were studying in the United States, with more than half of them majoring in management, science, and engineering.[6]

In 1900, China's infrastructure was wretched by modern standards. Fewer than 250 miles of railroads had been laid. Provincial highways were stone paths at best. Telephones and power lines were rudimentary and fragmented. Although progress was made before World War II, that war, the civil war, and twenty-six years of Maoism left China woefully behind its East Asian neighbors in every technological category. Since the early 1990s, however, the dreams of Sun Yat-sen and other believers in technocracy have been realized. China today is an engineering state. To understand the power and purpose of China's "hardware" now and where it may take us tomorrow, we need to understand its deep roots and its contemporary limits.

Engineering Culture

The Soviet engineer Peter Palchinsky drafted a letter in December 1926 to the prime minister of the Soviet Union contending that science and technology did more to shape society than even communism. The twentieth century, he wrote, "was not one of international communism, but of international technology. We need to recognize not a Komintern [the Communist International], but a 'Tekhintern.'"[7] Ideas like these got Palchinsky shot in Stalin's Russia. For Chinese governments over the past century, however, they have been at the heart of China's nation-building strategy.

The story of the Chinese engineer is different from that of legal, medical, religious, and journalistic professionals—to name but a few of China's modern professions. Lawyers, judges, doctors, priests, and writers all had ambitions for professional autonomy, and all found themselves severely limited by the Nationalist and Communist Party-States. Not so the engineer.

Engineering has been one of the two professions most privileged by the modern Chinese state. The other is the modern military professional, which in China, as in so much of the world, has become perhaps the most uniformly influential profession. But whereas military professionals could choose to support, or endanger, or even overthrow the state, engineers, by contrast, were from the start in the service of state power, national defense, national unity, and national economic development. The relationship between Chinese state power and engineering is, simply put, one of mutual dependency.

China since 1911 has been governed both by militarists and by specialists. China's new specialists were educated increasingly in colleges and universities, abroad or at home, and certified not by their mastery of the Confucian *Analects* but by internationally recognized degrees, particularly in science and engineering. Over the last century, there have been distinguished lineages of Chinese scientific and technical elites. These include the graduates of Shanghai's Jiaotong and Tongji universities, as well as those of MIT and the Technische Hochschule Berlin, and more recently of Tsinghua University and Hong Kong University of Science and Technology. Engineers have fared much better in China's revolutions and upheavals than have their classmates who majored in liberal arts.

China's first official engineer was a railroad man. Zhan Tianyou was the daring chief engineer for the Beijing-Zhangjiakou railroad, completed in 1909, which was the most famous and difficult line planned and built entirely by Chinese in an era when foreigners dominated Chinese railway construction.[8] Zhan founded the Chinese Society of Engineers in 1912 with 148 members. Today China has sixty-four engineering societies, with a combined membership in the millions, and Chinese engineers can now be found the world over, building bridges, roads, dams, power plants, and other high-stake projects throughout Africa, Latin America, Southeast Asia, South Asia, and even the United States, where China Construction America, a subsidiary of the China State Construction Engineering Corporation (CSCEC), has played an important role in recent upgrades to New York's bridge and subway network, among other projects.

Sun Yat-sen's Vision

The dream of engineering and science as the road to a prosperous China was that of Sun Yat-sen. The Nationalist government that came to power in 1927 had aims not unlike those of today's Chinese government. Its fundamental goal was the "development" of China. This meant a strong emphasis on modernizing physical infrastructure, not just political and economic systems. A gleaming capital would rise out of the muddy alleys of Nanjing, a city twice destroyed in the previous century. The cities were industrialized, the countryside electrified, and the provinces joined by networks of railroads, highways, and—most exciting of all—air routes to get what Sun Yat-sen had called the "stagnant race" of Chinese on the move.[9] All this was planned scientifically by a government imbued with a technocratic confidence and cooperating with advanced industrial nations.

One author dates the beginning of "modern China" from the publication of Sun's *Industrial Plan*.[10] In it, Sun proposed a "second Industrial Revolution," in which one hundred thousand miles of rail would be laid, the Yangzi tamed by its Three Gorges Dam, and automobiles manufactured so inexpensively that "everyone who wishes it may have one."[11] Sun's strategies to develop "the vast resources of China ... internationally under a socialistic scheme, for the good of the world in general and the Chinese people in particular" was later taken up by his Communist successors.[12]

Sun's more concrete plans also left their mark.[13] His sketch of a national Chinese rail network, which emphasized political aspirations (linking provincial capitals) over economic relationships, provided the framework for Nationalist and Communist routing plans.[14] Today, at Sun's former home in Shanghai, you can see his original railway and highway plans overlaid (with remarkable congruence) with what has actually been built. His two-paragraph proposal to "improve the upper Yangzi" with an enormous dam spawned seventy-five years of debate and, by the early twenty-first century, the construction of the largest dam ever built.[15]

Sun was the visionary, not the scientist, economist, or engineer. But his visions would prove longer-lived than those of Mao Zedong. Sun believed in a direct relationship between infrastructure and prosperity. He was certain that the wealth of a nation could be measured by the length of its railway lines. Projects of the scale and complexity of those he advocated would bring scientists, economists, and engineers into the center of Chinese government. Known the world over as the "father" (*Guofu*) of modern China, Sun, who died in 1925, was more precisely the founder of the Chinese engineering state.[16]

Reconstructing the National Capital

The Nationalist government aimed to make its mark on China first in its new national capital, the old "southern capital" of Nanjing. Although a former dynastic capital, the city was inherited in a sorry state. It was "notorious for its dim electric light, narrow and uneven roads, and poor telephone service," not to mention its mud and mosquitoes.[17] There was no sewage system except the infested canals, which also served as a source of drinking water for the city's poor.[18] All this was but a challenge. A new Nanjing could be created from nearly nothing.

Within a year of the founding of the regime, the Office of Technical Experts for Planning the National Capital, under the leadership of an American-trained engineer, had developed a detailed and beautifully illustrated design for a reconstructed Nanjing.[19] The city's boundaries were vastly expanded to house both the new government and an anticipated population of 2 million (in retrospect, a conservative estimate). Rail connections were to grow and a huge airport built. Detailed plans were drawn for modern sewage, drinking water, and electric power systems. A new government district of nearly ten square kilometers was to be erected on the site just west of the old Ming palace, and south of the Ming tombs, an imposing Sun Yat-sen Mausoleum. Located at the district's center would be a modern palace complex situated on a north-south axis, dominated at its northern end by a massive Guomindang party headquarters, an international architectural marvel combining features of Beijing's Temple of Heaven and the US Capitol in Washington, DC. A Cultural Center, including an Olympic-sized stadium, would be situated on a nearby mountain.[20] Beyond all this, the city would be beautified. Twelve new parks would be constructed. In Parisian style, trees would line the avenues and electric lights in the shape of Chinese lanterns would line the streets. "Obnoxious and dangerous industries" would be located on the northern bank of the Yangzi, away from the city center. A system of parkways and main roads was conceived, dominated by the grand, six-lane Zhongshan Lu, or Sun Yat-sen Road. A "ring boulevard" was to encircle the new capital, but not, as later in Beijing, at the expense of the city wall. The wall would be retained, perhaps with the thought—times being what they were—that it might be needed. So Nanjing's ring road would run *on top* of the old wall, offering its motorists a panorama of city, river, and suburbs.[21]

Not all of these things were built. A few were, though, and in dramatic fashion: Sun Yat-sen Road was bulldozed forty meters wide through the city center to honor the National Father and was rushed to completion in time for Sun's interment in his stately mausoleum in June 1929. Residents had ten days to leave their homes.[22] The central buildings of the Party-State were indeed located near an old palace, but in the more modest quarters of the old Taiping palace, erected in the 1850s when Nanjing was "Tianjing"—the "heavenly capital"—of the Taiping Heavenly Kingdom. Government ministries, after several years of living in borrowed and occupied buildings, were gradually housed in more properly ministerial quarters. Massive numbers of trees were planted. Seedlings imported from France would later shade a Communist Nanjing.

The most telling point about Nanjing's face-lift was that it was *planned*. Nanjing was the first Chinese city to employ comprehensive zoning and planning regulations on international standards.[23] Its Office of Technical Experts drafted the national legislation for municipal planning and zoning.[24] If Nanjing today can lay claim to be "one of the most beautiful, clean, and well-planned cities in China," this is in part thanks to the determined efforts of Nationalist engineers and public works officials.[25]

Capital cities reflect their governments. When the Communists took over Beijing, they "modernized" it in Soviet fashion. Beijing had been architecturally defined for more than five hundred years by its networks of magnificent city walls, towers, and gates, from those of the Forbidden City, to the Imperial City, to the Inner City and, finally, the Outer City. Of these, all but those of the Forbidden City—today's Palace Museum—have been demolished or diminished. Many were taken down in the 1950s in order to build Soviet-style grand boulevards—upon which there were few cars. Those left after the Great Leap Forward of 1958–1962 were undone during the Cultural Revolution to build a circular subway route that served more as an air-raid shelter than as mass transport. Where walls and moats had once stood was an unused underground. Yet the Communists, too, were heirs of Sun Yat-sen.

Reconstruction

Although Sun Yat-sen had died in 1925, his son Sun Ke drafted in the late 1920s a *fifty-year* plan to construct the railways, harbors, and industries that Sun Yat-sen had envisioned. A National Reconstruction Commission was established, composed of all the ministers of cabinet rank and the heads of every province's Reconstruction Bureau—offices that had been established to institutionalize the developmental mission nationwide. Following Lenin's famous dictum that Communism meant "Soviet Power plus the electrification of the whole country," this Commission focused on electrification, for Sun Yat-sen had written that civilization was now defined by the "age of electricity."[26] In 1924 he had told his Nationalist comrades: "If China wants to learn the strong points from foreign counties, it should, first of all, try to use electricity rather than coal as an energy source."[27] As Yun Chen, a young engineer in the National Reconstruction Commission who would later direct much of China's electrical industries, recalled, electric power, which would promote industry and commerce, permit the exploitation of natural resources, and increase agricultural production, was considered "the people's salvation."[28]

Road building was another Nationalist priority. Sun Yat-sen's vision of "1 million miles of road built in a very short time as if by a magic wand" has still not come to pass, but the fast pace of road building in the 1920s by provincial governments and bus companies started the evolution of China's national road network.[29] Whereas in 1920 perhaps as little as one hundred miles of improved road (theoretically passable by motor vehicle) existed in the entire country outside the foreign concessions, over twenty thousand miles had been built by 1928. That number would reach nearly forty thousand in the first two years of the Nationalist government, with a further thirty-five thousand miles projected.[30]

Chinese and international engineers urged centralization and standardization. Road engineering standards and traffic laws varied enormously from province to province, often from locality to locality. So did road signs and traffic signals, which were famously confusing.[31] Until 1932, cars licensed in one province could not be driven in another. (After extended negotiations, the provinces of Zhejiang, Anhui, and Jiangsu as well as the cities of Nanjing and Shanghai agreed to recognize one another's plates; still, thereafter, cars licensed in one province could travel in another only after paying an additional fee.[32])

It was with great fanfare, therefore, that the Shanghai-Hangzhou Motor Road, connecting two major cities and two provinces, opened on October 10, 1932, as the first section of the Shanghai-Guangxi Trunk Line, itself part of a planned seven-province, eleven trunk-line project of about fourteen thousand miles. This was a typical "modern" road of this region, with alignment and grades of international standard, built on a foundation of broken brick and surfaced with crushed shells and cinders. Some two hundred automobiles drove the seven hours from Shanghai to Hangzhou that day, through dust, accidents, and protests, some completing the return trip the same day—because the road *had* to open on National Day, ready or not.[33]

To knit China together where roads and railroads could not go was the task of civil aviation, which by 1937, through official joint ventures with Pan American Airways and Lufthansa, connected China's major cities on regular schedules.[34] Airplanes for Chinese routes—like automobiles for China's roads—were ultimately to be assembled in China by state-owned enterprises.[35] China aimed to create the capacity to produce its own industries, machines, and tools on a world-class scale.

All this led to China's first integrated system of state-owned enterprises. These new state firms—the China Automobile Manufacturing Company, the China Air Materials Construction Company, the Central Steel Works, the Central Machine Works—were all part of a "new industrial center" of state-owned firms in central China.[36] They were the driving forces of what by the mid-1930s was increasingly called a "controlled" economy. To manage it required a new kind of government official.

A Government of Engineers?

China's rise in international science and technology began seriously in the 1930s. A Nationalist leader argued in 1932 that in order to train talent to meet society's needs, China's universities should stop admitting students of the humanities and law for a decade.[37] That did not happen, but the Nationalist government did require that each university have a school of science, engineering, medicine, or agriculture. Engineering programs at Shanghai Jiaotong, National Central, and Tsinghua universities, to name the most prominent, were among the central places from which the government began to recruit China's first technocracy.

It recruited them into a new superbureaucracy, the National Resources Commission (NRC), to oversee and run China's heavy industry, mining, and defense industries. The NRC became China's largest employer, and it outlasted the Nationalist government. Led by a respected, incorruptible, and crusty scholar, the geologist Weng Wenhao—who also served as president of the Society of Chinese Engineers and in 1948 became premier of the Republic of China—the NRC was the ancestor of today's State-Owned Assets Supervision and Administration Commission (SASAC).

The NRC's mobilization, nationalization, and relocation of industrial plants and talent were essential to China's survival in its eight-year war (1937–1945) against a technologically superior enemy, Japan.[38] When the war ended, the Chinese state and its planners continued in the direction of increased economic control and expanded the state sector and the planned economy at a rapid rate. By August 1947, the NRC's industrial empire employed more than five hundred thousand workers and accounted for 70 percent of China's total industrial capital.[39] All this facilitated the total nationalization of industry in the early People's Republic.

Legacies for Post-1949 China

The new PRC leadership understood that the Nationalist accumulation of state capital had laid the foundation for the PRC's state-owned enterprises.[40] Similarly, pre-1949 trends in the direction of central economic planning anticipated the PRC's early approach to centralized planning. Perhaps the most important legacy of the Nationalist state economy was—or could have been—the human talent developed under it. The large majority of Nationalist economic and industrial planning personnel remained on the mainland when the Communists took power, with NRC men comprising the first staff of Communist planning organs—a fact that rarely makes its way into contemporary history books in the PRC.[41]

The complex legacy of the Nationalist experience may be best demonstrated with one case study. During World War II, a significant number of Chinese engineers were sponsored by the NRC under lend-lease funds for advanced training in major US industries. They were to be industrial leaders of China's postwar development. Some, like An Wang, the creator of the Wang word processor, remained in the United States and had illustrious careers. Most, however, returned to China to pursue careers in the PRC and Taiwan. The first and most selective group of young engineers, composed of thirty-one men from the major NRC divisions, was sent overseas in 1942. Its members were each given several internships over a two-year period in American business and government organizations. Although separated by assignment and professional expertise, the group had a strong sense of cohesion and common mission. The members of this "Society of 31" remained in touch (openly or secretly) for at least four decades after 1949.[42]

After 1949, the group as a whole contributed to the economic activity of three countries: the United States, the PRC, and Taiwan.[43] Three took up permanent residence in the United States; two became project managers for multinational companies, the third a shipping magnate and multimillionaire. Seven made their careers on Taiwan and became leading planners and practitioners of Taiwan's economic miracle from the 1950s to the 1980s. Their ranks included several ministers of Economic Affairs and one premier. Twenty-one remained on the mainland. Seven became chief engineers in sizable state enterprises. Two rose to the rank of "senior" engineer in similar enterprises. Seven others pursued industrial and academic research, of whom four became heads of industrial research bureaus, one ran the Foreign Affairs Office of the First Machine-Building Ministry, and two became professors (one was named vice president of Tsinghua University). Six were named members of the Chinese People's Consultative Conference. Most enjoyed substantial careers in technical work until the Anti-Rightist Movement of the late 1950s, when all of them had their careers destroyed. None escaped political persecution in the Cultural Revolution, and two were "persecuted to death."

From the Purged to the Powerful: Toward a Dictatorship of Engineers

For the large majority of Chinese engineers who stayed on the mainland, the early years of the PRC were still a period for realizing grand industrial plans, and a time for intense cooperation with a new set of international engineering partners from the Soviet Union and Eastern Europe.[44] In 1952, the Ministry of Higher Education began a reorganization designed to take the reforms of 1932 further still, with the aim of "developing specialized colleges, reorganizing and strengthening universities, with the overall focus of facilitating personnel and teachers for industrial development." This led to the establishment of a series of technical and engineering colleges along Soviet models and the reorganization of a number of existing universities, such as Tsinghua and Tianjin, to make them centers of engineering excellence. Taking a page from the Soviet book, more than half of the areas in which degrees were awarded belonged to industrial disciplines.

In the 1950s, a decade of significant expansion in enrollment at Chinese institutions of higher learning, there was a dramatic increase in engineering enrollment. Throughout the 1950s, building on trends from the late Nationalist period, between 30 and 40 percent of university students were engineers, and by 1957–1958, 41 percent of Chinese higher education enrollments were in the field of engineering.[45] Engineers comprised a similarly high percentage of Chinese students abroad during the 1950s, in a web of new cooperative relationships with their Soviet and East European counterparts.

International cooperation among engineers reached its high point during the period of the Sino-Soviet alliance in the 1950s, when China's trade with the Soviet bloc expanded greatly. Over two hundred industrial projects were constructed with Soviet assistance, mostly as turnkey (fully finished) installations. These became the new core of the Communist state industrial sector.

Thousands of industrial designs were transferred from Soviet engineers to their Chinese counterparts. At least ten thousand Soviet and East European engineers and specialists worked in China. Over fifty thousand Chinese engineers and students went to the Soviet Union and its European allies for training.

All of this was undone during the high tide of Maoism. The combination of the Anti-Rightist Campaign, the Great Leap Forward, and finally the Cultural Revolution meant that much of the PRC's inherited generation of engineering talent was placed on ice for twenty years (1958–1978), sacrificed to Mao Zedong's disdain—unique among China's twentieth-century leaders—for the concept of "scientific" planning. As China was led into economic chaos and international isolation, the government rank of engineer disappeared altogether.

It is a measure of the scope of the Maoist catastrophe that the Chinese returned so quickly after 1979 to a developmental ethos with roots in the Nationalist faith in science and engineering. The rank of engineer was restored in 1979 by the State Council. Between the reopening of the universities in 1979 and 2005, the annual percentage of engineering students among all students ranged—as it had in the 1950s—annually between 30 and 40 percent. Among Chinese students studying abroad, the percentage was significantly higher, reaching a peak of 90 percent in 1981, higher even than the 60 percent that was composed of Chinese engineering students abroad in the 1950s and the 54 percent of the mid-1940s.

The Dictatorship of the Engineers

As Maoism and Marxism of any recognizable variant waned on the Chinese mainland, and as the leadership of the People's Republic became an increasingly educated one dedicated to economic development, the role of engineers grew in importance. Deng Xiaoping's Politburo of 1982 had twenty-five full and alternate members, not one of whom had a university education. By 1997, however, the Politburo under Jiang Zemin had twenty-four full and alternate members, seventeen of whom had university educations: fourteen in engineering, two in science, and one in enterprise management. The dominance of the engineering mystique is even clearer when one considers the Standing Committees of recent Politburos of the Chinese Communist Party.

Among the seven members of the Politburo Standing Committee of 1997–2002, under President Jiang Zemin, all but one was certified in engineering; the exception majored in [State] enterprise management at Fudan University. The majority not only had studied engineering but also had practical experience working as engineers. Jiang Zemin himself graduated from the Electrical Machinery Department of Shanghai Jiaotong University—Nationalist China's leading engineering school—in 1947. After the Communist takeover, he served successively as deputy engineer, chief of the works section, and first deputy director of the Shanghai Yimin No. 1 Foodstuff Factory. He was concurrently head of the power workshop and Party branch secretary. He then became first deputy director of the Shanghai Soap Factory and then chief of the electrical machinery section of Shanghai No. 2 Design Division of the First Ministry of Machine-Building Industry. Jiang's energetic premier, Zhu Rongji, graduated in electrical engineering from Tsinghua University and worked both in enterprises and in the State Planning Commission before being purged in the Anti-Rightist Campaign and then resurrected in the 1980s.

Of the nine members of the 2002–2007 Politburo Standing Committee under President Hu Jintao, *all* had engineering education backgrounds and working experience as engineers. Hu was a graduate of the Water Conservancy Engineering Department of Tsinghua University. Similarly, the Politburo Standing Committee of 2007–2012 consisted overwhelmingly of engineers, with eight of its nine members having studied or worked in engineering.

The seven members of China's new Standing Committee who strode onto a Beijing stage in November 2012 carried this tradition further, but with some added diversity. Party chief Xi Jinping had studied chemical engineering at Tsinghua University.

Yu Zhengshen, the former Party secretary of Shanghai, had
graduated from the Military Engineering Institute in Harbin. The
other five included two individuals trained first in statistics and
economics (in one case at the Kim Il Sung University in North
Korea), one in law, and one in history. There is little sign, however,
of tempering China's engineering ambition.

Only this marriage of engineering ambition with Communist political power can explain the physical transformation of
the Chinese mainland over the past twenty years. China may
have moved toward a socialist market economy, but the state's
commitment to building the infrastructure of economic development has never been stronger. Those roads, railroads, airlines,
ports, and telecommunication facilities that Sun Yat-sen thought
necessary to get the Chinese people "on the move" are now doing
so, integrating internal markets and connecting them to international markets while facilitating the movement of goods and
services—not to mention the movement of people through large
internal migrations and significantly increased economic mobility. Whereas the Nationalist highway system was impressive for its
day, it was largely a series of (sometimes connecting) provincial
networks. China's new interprovincial superhighways comprise

FIGURE 3-2

Passengers carried in China: Air transport (1980–2011)

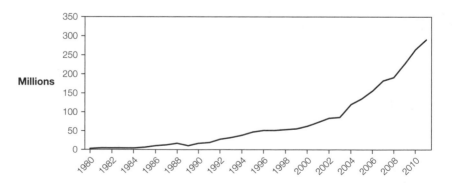

Source: Data from CEIC, taken from the World Bank (WDI), June 3, 2013.

the most ambitious road system since the construction of the American interstate network under President Eisenhower.

A similar story has taken place in air travel. China now has over two hundred modern airports. Figure 3-2 shows the growth in passengers carried inside China from 1980 to 2011. This has been accompanied by an extraordinary growth in Chinese-registered air carrier departures worldwide from 1980 (51,000 departures) to 2009 (2,140,000 departures). No matter where you look, the growth in infrastructure has been extraordinary (similar stories lie in electric power generation and power distribution and pipeline construction, etc.).

The Three Gorges Dam project—which has made the once-isolated wartime capital of Chongqing a great international city and one of the most important inland ports in China—was conceived by Sun Yat-sen and then researched by the NRC in the 1930s and by American engineers—including John Savage, the chief engineer of the Grand Coulee Dam—in the 1940s. It has now been built. Of all the world's governments in the early twenty-first century, only China's had the engineering imagination, political will, and financial resources to complete a project of this scale and to physically relocate the millions of inhabitants in its way.

Similar levels of determination are seen in city settings. Compare the urban planning of contemporary Shanghai with that of Republican Nanjing. Both had ambitious, modernizing plans created by Chinese and international engineers. Communism was at first a lethal preservative for Shanghai. But after five decades of stagnation—in 1987 one could shoot a movie set in 1937 (*Empire of the Sun*) in Shanghai and not worry about the background—the city has been reimagined, replanned, largely rebuilt, and utterly reborn. In only fifteen years' time, construction has involved thirteen subway lines (with at least eight more in planning), four major tunnels under and three bridges over a large river, a massive elevated highway system, and two new world-class airports connected by highway, subway, high-speed rail, and a "magnetic levitation" (the "maglev") train. These are the products of an engineering state unleashed and unchecked.

The State of Infrastructure States

Sun Yat-sen's vision may not yet be complete, but China has become the infrastructure state of which he dreamed. The United States used to be an infrastructure state. Its interstate highway system would become a model for China's. Its Tennessee Valley Authority and Grand Coulee dams inspired those who would plan China's Three Gorges Dam. The American experience also has some sobering lessons for China. The interstate highway system that took a half-century to complete now requires heavy maintenance and is almost impossible to expand. Similarly, what was once the world's largest rail network is now composed of an aging fleet of rails and cars and a limited set of rights-of-way that cannot support high-speed rail, even if there were the political will to build it. In a robust democracy, the ease of mobilizing popular opinion against new infrastructure sometimes ensures that socially valuable infra-structure never gets built. Shanghai—one of eleven Chinese cities to build a subway system—has built one of the world's longest subway networks (439 km) as of February 2013 and plans to add over 350 km in new lines by 2020. By contrast, the city of Boston's big transport project is a *four-mile* extension of its Green Line (the nation's oldest subway/trolley line still in use) that will surely be subject to many legal challenges and much delay.[46]

Today, as for the past century, the planning of infrastructure and the construction of national unity are inseparable. While Sun Yat-sen could set the outline of the national railway system we see today, even he might gasp at the $10 billion cost to build one of the world's most challenging railways from Sichuan to Lhasa, the capital of Tibet. This is above all a political project, moving people (mostly Han Chinese) and goods across the Tibetan plateau to make a physical link with the PRC's most restive and least autonomous "autonomous region."

Much the same can be said about China's enormous investment in mobile telecommunications. The case on China Mobile's rural connection strategy is relevant.[47] Set in rural Yunnan Province, it asks: should China Mobile invest large amounts to connect the last

10 to 15 percent of mountainous Yunnan, where precious few of its inhabitants live? As a pure business case, the answer must be *no*. But this is also a case of "corporate social responsibility" on the part of a major state-owned enterprise, and above all, it is a case of the political extension of state information into every village. At the end of the day, China Mobile had no choice but to connect the most disconnected of villages.

FIGURE 3-3

Mobile cellular subscriptions in China (1980–2011)

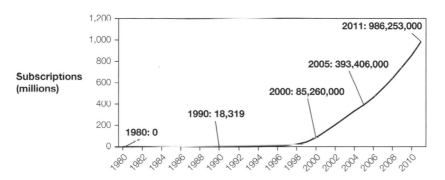

Source: Data from CEIC, taken from the World Bank (WDI), November 27, 2012.

FIGURE 3-4

Fixed broadband internet subscribers in China (2000–2011)

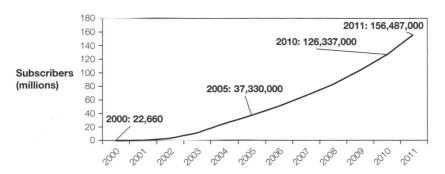

Source: Data from CEIC, taken from the World Bank (WDI), November 27, 2012.

The growth of the telecommunications links and their chang-ing mix is a story of extraordinary growth. The number of fixed telephone lines surged from 1980 (2.14 million) to 2004 (340 million) when it peaked and began to decline.[48] Figure 3-3 shows the growth in the fixed telephone replacement technology, mobile telephones, and their surge in growth from 1990 to 2011. Figure 3-4 shows the concurrent explosive growth in internet users from 2000 to 2011 as fixed broadband internet subscribers jumped from twenty-two thousand in 2000 to 156 million in 2011. In a remarkably short period of time, China has leaped forward to become an electronically net-worked society (with great challenges on information censoring, as will be discussed in chapters 5 and 7).

The Limits of Hardware

Building physical infrastructure, of course, is not an unmitigated blessing—it brings with it a number of complexities. First, just as it brings new sources of supply into the market, it conversely opens markets inside China to international products that had been denied practical access to these markets by an inadequate infrastructure (and in some cases, government policy). Second, the development of infrastructure on a large scale inevitably disrupts the environment and creates adverse by-products.

The case of "Xiamen PX," where civil protest in the port city of Xiamen succeeded in delaying and relocating a major Taiwan-funded petrochemical plant, shows the potential power of civil dis-sent on environmental issues.[49] It also makes clear that China's rising middle and even better-off classes have potential as political forces in their own right. Xiamen citizens rejected the plant on the grounds that it was environmentally damaging and won the day through a peaceful "walkabout"-type campaign that local govern-ment officials could not ignore, even though this multibillion-dollar project had high-level political connections (former Party general secretary Jiang Zemin) and all requisite approvals in Beijing. Today, urban Chinese increasingly expect their homes—most of which are privately owned—to be protected from the scourge of industrial waste. The NIMBY ("not in my backyard") syndrome has come to China.

No example of the growing contrast between government plans and social and environmental impact is bigger or more illustrative than the Three Gorges Dam. The largest hydro project in the world, it today provides electricity to millions, controls floods, and above all has made the Yangzi River navigable to river transport all the way from Shanghai to Chongqing. All of that is good.

On the flip side is the enormous buildup of silt behind the dam, which is both weakening its structure and sharply reducing the amount of electricity that it can produce. The huge lake created by the dam is weakening the hills that tower over it, producing mud slides and—some suspect—leading to broader geologic instability.[50] Furthermore, fields downstream from the dam are being denied important nutrients.

The health risks of the air pollution that have accompanied China's (coal-fueled) energy development and its infatuation with the automobile are very real. Any resident of Beijing knows how very rare a true "blue sky" day has become, and one is reminded of the killer smogs of 1950 London before coal heating was banned.

Looking at the past century of the Chinese infrastructure state, we see its limitations as well as its strengths. The growth of civil aviation in the Republican period, for example, allowed the development of long-distance airmail service for the first time. But it also meant a worsening of postal services on the ground in the Chinese countryside. As one critic maintained, it allowed the Chinese government to "soar above" China's problems on the ground.[51] There were aspirations, too, for international routes as early as the 1930s, when a Nanjing-to-Berlin air route was envisaged. The political limitations of the project emerged during the first flight, which was forced down by Soviet aircraft over Mongolia. The crew members, suffering from broken bones, were sentenced to five years in a Mongolian prison. Only the gracious intervention of the Panchen

Lama of Tibet obtained their release. Technology, in short, is not enough.

As we will see in chapter 4, China's move to mass higher education has been accompanied by a continuing commitment to elite institutions, the "key" universities that meet international standards of excellence, particularly in science and engineering. The percentage of students enrolled in engineering has remained consistently high: between 33 and 40 percent over the last decade. (Among the sons and daughters of high Party officials, the percentage that study engineering in university appears higher still—perhaps more than 60 percent.) The absolute numbers of engineering students have risen even more dramatically. In the higher-echelon, government-funded universities, in 1997 there were 1.26 million engineering students out of total student body of 3.17 million (39.8 percent); in 2005, 5.48 million would-be engineers sat among 15.6 million fellow students (35 percent). Numbers such as these have led to fears in the West of a nation that graduates annually six hundred thousand engineers, compared with seventy thousand in the United States.[52] But perhaps the more important development is that in *qualitative* terms, Chinese universities appear destined to rank among the world's leaders in engineering and applied science in the first quarter of the twenty-first century.

The End of the Engineering Road?

As we stand at a moment of unprecedented influence of engineering talent in modern China, what will the coming decades bring? If the developmental and political trajectory of Taiwan is any guide, the future may belong less to engineers than to lawyers, and to a rather more disputatious political culture. More likely, mainland Chinese political leaders and engineers in coming decades will still be intertwined, but with the rapid growth of the private and "mixed" sectors of the Chinese economies, the state will no longer be the sole or even primary employer of engineering talent. That context should prove conducive to the reassertion of professional associations and a greater degree of professional autonomy on the part of a profession that has not practiced it since 1927 and whose history has been tightly connected with Nationalist agendas and state-led projects of nation building.

For now, China is in the process of realizing the technocratic dream of its twentieth-century founders. Nobody does it better. The mastery of infrastructural hardware has allowed a return to "wealth and power" and permitted China to catch up and, in places, surpass the once–technologically dominant West. But will this be sufficient? What about the software? What about the ideals, the values, the imagination, the education that will define China's future? It is to that more fundamental challenge that we now turn, in chapter 4.

For those doing business in China, the questions raised in this chapter are different from the ones raised in chapters 1 and 2: Does my firm have technologies that will help in the build-out of the new infrastructure or can we use China's infrastructure as a new platform of opportunity? Given the expectations of technology transfer or theft, does my firm have the capacity for sustained reinvention to protect its technological edge? Would a Chinese company like to buy my firm to close its technology gaps? The reality is that in some fields (think railway technology), China is state-of-the-art while in others (as in parts of the pharmaceutical and biotech industries), it is many years behind. Understanding your firm's strength and weaknesses will guide how it wants to address these questions.

Doing Business in China

- What new regional and national opportunities are opened to my firm through new infrastructure development? Alternatively, will infrastructure build-out create problems that my firm has the skills to solve?

- Can my firm get access to infrastructure markets through selective proprietary technology transfer (and not lose control of the technology)?

- Are new service and repair opportunities made available to my firm through this infrastructure build-out?

- Are there new environmental remediation possibilities opening up for my firm as a result of failed infrastructure investments (think water and air pollution)?

- Does my firm have the engineering skills to compete in an engineering culture?

4

PLANNING INNOVATION?

Can China innovate? Does it have the spark to create whole new industries and technologies? For those who would lead, this is an important question. An ambivalent answer is provided by a 2012 joint paper by the China Europe International Business School, the Wenzhou Chamber of Commerce, the Benelux Chamber of Commerce, and Booz & Company. This survey of more than one hundred leading Chinese and international firms over five sectors (industrials, automotive, health and life sciences, consumer goods, and energy) inquired as to China's capacity for innovation at present and in the future. The results showed that foreign firms viewed their Chinese competitors as *almost* as innovative as themselves (with 45 percent finding the Chinese equally innovative or better). Chinese firms were only slightly less optimistic. The idea that China could be a regional and even global hub of innovation was also broadly shared—particularly if issues of talent retention and intellectual property could be better addressed. And more than two-thirds of the leading Chinese firms interviewed expected to extend their R&D presence abroad in the next decade. Yet only a minority of the multinational firms interviewed saw China as a *distinctive* site for innovation. Their strategies for innovation in China have largely been the same as elsewhere.[1]

In short, China is a place where R&D happens, but novel discovery remains rare. It has many patents but few inventions. For this reason, China is a player, a partner, and an acquirer, but not yet a leader. To be sure, China has mastered the hardware of modern development. Over the last century, it has developed military, industrial, and infrastructural capacities that are the envy of other developing countries. It is a global leader in manufacturing both of the most basic and increasingly of the most sophisticated goods. It has the technological capacity to put astronauts in outer space and is likely to send humans to the moon and back within ten years.

Historically, the Chinese have created many breakthrough innovations. Every schoolchild knows that China is the home of great inventions: gunpowder, papermaking (and paper money), printing, the waterwheel, and the compass, among others. Every young Chinese knows of the great Ming admiral Zheng He, whose fifteenth-century fleets, voyages, and accomplishments preceded those of Columbus. To these we can add the extraordinary invention of an enduring civil service, selected on the basis of tested merit. But many Chinese also believe that it is the West, and particularly the Americans, who are the innovative and creative thinkers, while they, despite all of China's ancient inventions and modern revolutions, think of themselves as traditional, or rule-bound, rote learners. When asked why, the answers vary.

Some people blame the engineers. "Most Chinese start-ups are not founded by designers or artists," according to Jason Lim, a blogger on the website VentureBeat, "but by engineers who don't have the creativity to think of new ideas or designs."[2] (One wonders how many successful American companies are really started by designers and artists? The ones started by engineers have become rather more famous.)

Others blame the government for its lack of protection of intellectual property rights. The products of Apple, Inc., have been pirated the world over, but only in China have we seen the emergence of Apple stores so entirely fake that their employees did not know they were not working for Apple.

Still others blame the Chinese education system, with its modernized version of "Examination Hell."[3] How can students so completely focused on test scores in order to enter university possibly be innovators?

In this chapter, we will look at the "software" necessary for China's continued development. What are the frontiers of innovation in contemporary Chinese business? How does the state promote, regulate, or stifle innovation in business? How are international firms mobilized to assist China's innovation, at home and, increasingly, abroad? How is China's educational system adapting to the need for global competitiveness in the education of the next generation of leaders and innovators? Finally, can an innovation culture coexist with a political system that punishes dissent, censors the internet, has little tolerance for failure, and prizes orthodoxy and stability over vision and change?

Innovation from the Bottom Up: The Role of Entrepreneurs

As noted in chapter 1, China has a long history of private entrepreneurialism, with freer markets for most goods than any nation in Europe as late as the early nineteenth century. Chinese commercialism was speeded by market innovations such as experiments with paper currency in the eleventh century and the rise of distinctively Chinese long-distance banking in the nineteenth century. Chinese goods, particularly fine silks and porcelains, gained global markets, and by the late eighteenth century, British and American consumers had become addicted to Chinese tea.

The onset of the Industrial Revolution in the West forced China (like every other part of the world) to play a game of sudden catchup, not just in military technology but also in business enterprise, in a manner that wove Eastern and Western practices together.

A recent case by Elisabeth Köll illustrates the nineteenth-century origin of the modern Chinese textile industry under the great scholar-official Zhang Jian, a man who combined East and West,

imported the first full set of textile manufacturing equipment from
Germany, and in his "company town" of Nantong—which still
erects statues to him—established a hybrid Chinese and American
pattern of corporate social responsibility.[4]

In another case, Köll tells the story of the Rong family of Wuxi,
which became one of the richest families of Republican China.
Rong Zongjing was sent at age fourteen to internationalized
Shanghai for an apprenticeship. Trained in the methods of both
domestic and international banking, he became the most successful industrialist in pre-Communist China, combining international
financing by Japanese capital with his native Wuxi networks of
talent and support.[5] These innovations in forging unexpected alliances and in finance and management helped distinguish the Rong
family from its Chinese and foreign competitors.

In the early Communist era, China would seem less of an inno-
vator than an emulator. In much of its first decade, the People's
Republic was a dutiful simulation of Stalin's Soviet Union. Its
First Five-Year Plan was designed on (and with) Soviet guidelines.
Its first (1954) Constitution was written in imitation of the USSR's
"Stalin Constitution" of 1936. The Soviet Union gave China blue-
prints not only for hundreds of industrial plants but also—and
above all—for the basic structures of Party and state.

China's post-Mao "reform and opening" was marked, especially
in its first two decades, less by innovation than by a loosening of
controls and a tolerance for intellectual piracy and theft. Market
strategy by way of imitation is by no means unique to the evolution of Chinese businesses; the potential scale of economic loss,
owing to the market's size and the seeming indifference of government officials, is. Counterfeiting of luxury goods has been given
the greatest attention in the popular press. It is, however, the lack
of protection given to patented technologies and the theft of trade
secrets—industrial espionage—that led General Keith Alexander,
director of the US National Security Agency, to speak of industrial
upgrading in China as "the greatest transfer of wealth in history."[6]

Entrepreneurial Innovators

Today, we again see an era of imagination, innovation, and challenge in Chinese business, which is deeply integrated with both domestic and international flows of talent and capital. Central to many stories of innovation are Chinese students returning from abroad who aim to bring together their international education with Chinese opportunity.

The story of Edward Tian [Tian Suning] is particularly instructive. A Chinese citizen who came of age in the Cultural Revolution, he spent nearly five years in the United States getting his doctorate from Texas Technology University. In the early 1990s, he returned to China, where he founded AsiaInfo, a telecom start-up. Within three years, it had grown into a company of 320 people with revenues of $45 million. When the authors visited it in 1998, they were struck by its Silicon Valley feel. A hands-on entrepreneurial success with Western culture and Chinese skills, it continues to prosper today.[7]

In 1996, frustrated with the slow pace of technological and service change in the critical telecommunications industry, Premier Zhu Rongji persuaded Tian that it was his duty to leave AsiaInfo to launch a new company, China Netcom. The new company was owned by the Chinese Academy of Sciences; China Railways Telecommunication Control; the Information Network Center of the State Administration of Radio, Film, and Television (SARFT); and Shanghai Alliance Investment Ltd., each of which held a 25 percent share. China Netcom's mission was to build a fiber network linking some three hundred cities. One of the authors wrote a case study in 2001 on the warm, participative culture of this fast-paced, innovative company.[8] He was deeply impressed by the open and creative culture of the firm that brought Western managerial structures to bear on a Chinese state-owned enterprise. The first time the case was taught to a group of Chinese executives (almost none of whom were from the telecommunications industry), it sparked interest and admiration.

But telecommunications is, at the end of the day, under state control in China, sometimes with unforeseen consequences. In 2002, China Telecom, the huge telecommunications giant, was broken apart by the government, and its ten Northern provincial markets were integrated into China Netcom. Overnight, Edward Tian became responsible for an organization of 230,000 people, the vast majority of whom came from the SOE world and were resentful of having a young, Western-trained boss.

The clash between the rigid SOE culture of China Telecom and the more open culture of China Netcom was extraordinary. Edward Tian came to be seen not as a builder but as the outsider from the United States trying to reform an old-time China state-owned enterprise and its embedded culture that most emphatically did not want to reform. Teaching the case six months after the merger to a group of seventy senior Chinese executives, including twenty telecommunication industry executives, was perhaps the most painful teaching moment of one of the author's life. The group aggressively attacked Tian when he appeared in class for his fundamentally "un-Chinese" ways and drove him almost to his knees in abject apology. The group threatened the faculty member with a variety of charges of incompetence for writing about Silicon Valley culture in China in such a positive way. Tian soon stepped down from the executive role and several years later from the China Netcom board. He has gone on to be a successful investor and partner in a Chinese high-technology investment firm.

Meanwhile, China Netcom eventually came to appear to the outside world as a modern telecommunications firm, with all the necessary governance structures to be listed on international stock exchanges. But it remained at heart a state-owned enterprise. When we teach our current case on China Netcom, we ask the MBA students to scour the company's board for the real boss within.[9] Where, we ask, in all the firm's committees, is the Party secretary? This case is a "Where's Waldo?" of Chinese corporate governance. It shows how substance (in this case the strength of state-owned enterprise culture and political control) can triumph over form, despite the most compelling of organization charts.

The difficulties of innovation and transformation even in a high-tech state-owned firm are made clear by this story. Innovation is possible within the constraints of such an enterprise, but innovation is doubly facilitated when the company is backed into a corner by international competitors and is led by a culturally sensitive and politically networked person.

A case in point is illustrated by COSCO (the China Overseas Shipping Company), the state-owned freight shipping organization that is now the second-largest in container volume in the world.[10] Although by 1999 COSCO had been trying to use information technology to modernize its operations for nearly twenty years, very little had happened. In 1999, a scathing report was prepared by the Chinese Academy of Sciences, identifying the IT systems of COSCO as being so inadequate that they represented a point of strategic national vulnerability to China. Unlike most Chinese state-owned enterprises, COSCO competed directly with non-Chinese firms not only on cost but also on service. High-quality service in shipping includes being reliable, having the ability to change destination of cargo, and always having knowledge of the exact current location of a container. With China said to be in a position of national strategic vulnerability in this business, COSCO's CEO made a RMB 1 billion capital investment in SAP, a leading enterprise software package. A multiyear implementation effort touching every aspect of the company—the operation of every cargo shipping office, every customer's office, and every ship—it was ultimately successful in addressing the underlying service problem. Central to this success was Captain Wei Jiafu, CEO of COSCO, an extremely charismatic, long-term employee of the organization and a senior member of the Communist Party. He made this transformation a top corporate priority. The combination of leadership with the right impetus from the government made everything suddenly possible. Within several years, COSCO had reached IT-enabled service capability at a world-class level.

The dividing line between brilliant, iterative improvement and innovation can be hard to draw. It is hard to say, for example, that Microsoft in recent years has been as innovative as Apple. Facebook, Twitter, and others have outgunned Microsoft in creating entirely new services, and in so doing have opened vast new markets. Microsoft has, however, created continual enhancements to its services and has been incrementally innovative. Microsoft continues to invest heavily in R&D. An example is its five-hundred-person Beijing facility, which some executives believe is extremely strong and productive.

A similar dilemma is posed by Baidu, the Chinese search engine leader. With broad sensitivity to the government's concern about unfettered search processes, Baidu has grown massively in the China market, developing a search engine that does not challenge Chinese political orthodoxy (you will find no references to Tiananmen Square in its search results). Its growth and market share are extraordinary. Is this innovation? On the one hand, Baidu did not invent the concept of the online search. On the other, Baidu tailored an organization and production characteristics to deal with broad and regionally differentiated new markets in China. It now has 80 percent market share across a country that has become the world's largest search market. Innovative or adaptive, it is a leading-edge company in a fast-paced, technology-based industry. Its cofounder and CEO, Robin Li (Li Yanhong), who studied information management at Peking University and obtained a master's in computer science at SUNY Buffalo in the United States, was named one of China's "Top Ten Innovative Pioneers" in 2001.

Another pioneering firm is Alibaba, founded by the energetic and imaginative entrepreneur Jack Ma (Ma Yun). His first venture, China Yellowpages, is said to be China's first internet company. When HBS authors first wrote a case on Alibaba in 2000, the company was so small and shaky that they were afraid it would go bankrupt before the case was first taught.[11] The business concept was murky even to the informed reader. Instead of failing, however, the combination of a charismatic CEO and a business-to-business (B2B) portal to enable one company to order products from another company led to great success. Alibaba now serves 80 million members from nearly 250 countries. The success of its auction website, Taobao, eventually forced eBay out of the China market. The timing, creativity, and sheer audacity of Alibaba is another example of China adapting foreign technologies to its needs.

Innovation from the Top Down: The Role of the State

What is the role of the state in the innovation economy? How can it help or hinder originality and innovation? The Chinese Communist Party, after all, is embedded everywhere inside every organization of any significant size. The Party leader in the company reports directly to the Communist Party structure in the municipality or province. Consequently, there is no guarantee of corporate secrecy as to a firm's strategic direction, operational issues, or other matters. This clearly constrains the norms of competitive behavior that are found in other parts of the world and also bleeds off potential advantages of research and innovation.

Innovation requires not just the spark of creativity and willingness to bear market risk, but sustained focus, room to fail, and the government's willingness to bear a lot of disruption in its own processes and controls. In China, the government filter in the background sets a higher hurdle for innovation investments than in the United States. Both AsiaInfo and CreditEase (a Beijing-based microfinance lender) were led by Chinese graduates returning from American educational experiences. Each had broad energy and deep insight as to how information technology could provide value in the Chinese environment. As will be noted in chapter 5, CreditEase has been supported by Chinese regulators because it is helping job-creating organizations gain access to needed capital. But, as described earlier in this chapter, the innovative and successful CEO of AsiaInfo could not operate effectively in the culture of China Netcom as he was seen more as a threat than as a partner, someone who came from a fundamentally different culture than that of a state-owned enterprise. More chilling was the fate of a manager of the Jianlong Group, China's largest privately owned steel company. He was killed by workers in 2009 when he attempted to take his post as general manager of the Tonghua Iron and Steel Company, a failing state-owned firm that Jianlong was acquiring and privatizing. In July 2013, American CEO Charles Starnes was also held captive by employees when he attempted to shut down his Harbin-based factory.[12] This is a world far away from Silicon Valley.

The Infrastructure State as Innovation State

China certainly has the capacity to be a strong regulatory state. The government, however, aims to do much more than to control or regulate. It wants to stimulate innovation from the top. From the late 1970s, a new set of science and technology policies was presented as the engine to make China creative and prosperous.[13]

These efforts sought to revitalize China's science and technology infrastructure. Over time, they became an important conduit to research grants to universities and industries. China created the National Natural Science Foundation of China (NSFC) in 1986 that has aimed, much like its counterpart in the United States, to support precommercial research in universities, by way of a peer-review grant selection process. In the mid-1980s as well, the government began a "Key Laboratory" program aimed to support the work of leading university labs in a range of fields.

In the late 1990s, the old Soviet-style Chinese Academy of Sciences (CAS) sought to ensure the future of the many research institutes under its command.[14] What had been known as CAS's "Knowledge Innovation Program" ultimately led CAS toward a broad range of improvements, demonstrated by the success of its institutes in securing peer-reviewed grants.[15]

Beijing's support of science and technology is not limited to research institutes. In 1988, the state sponsored the development of the Beijing High-Technology Industry Development Experimental Zone (which came to be known as China's Silicon

Valley, or *Zhongguan Cun*), located in Beijing's Haidian District. At the same time, Beijing announced its "Torch" program, which explicitly aimed to further the commercialization of discoveries through the creation of incubators and high-technology zones.

The development of technology parks was also part of China's innovation planning. In 1985, the first high-technology park was developed in Shenzhen, a city already known by that time as a site of private-sector development and policy experimentation.

Over the next decade, high-technology parks became a common feature on any official tour of a major city in China. Funding for these parks came typically through cooperation between local and national governments, as well as from industry itself. Each was, in effect, racing to meet national state planning expectations and the development aspirations of local officials.

Today we can distinguish the variation in science and technology clusters. For example, Shenzhen's high-technology parks have focused on telecom and integrated circuits technology (ICT), while Beijing's "Silicon Valley" was initially dedicated to software development and advanced computing. Shanghai is emerging as the location of the leading biotechnology cluster in China, largely by way of its Zhangjiang High-Tech Park and the Zizhu Science-based Industrial Park. Dalian High-Tech Zone, in contrast, has become known as an area for computer gaming and animation, while Suzhou's "Nanopolis" promises to be a hub for nanotechnologies with application across a range of industries.

Foreign firms have been encouraged to, and many wish to, locate facilities in these parks where talent in their area is concentrated. Microsoft, Motorola, and Siemens, for example, were among the first to do so to align their businesses with Chinese government plans. The Chinese government claimed to support innovation and to protect it even for foreign innovators. Yet there have been limits.

Motorola's long engagement with China is interesting in this respect. Motorola went to China in the heady days of the 1980s and, unlike many Western firms, stayed the course after the Tiananmen crackdown of 1989. For this it was rewarded. Motorola was able to operate without local partners, something unheard of in those days. It subsequently gained a dominant position in the China market. Pressure from the highest levels of the government eventually led Motorola to forge relations with several local partners. By 2001, Motorola had expanded its base of handset, pager, and other equipment suppliers, numbering in the hundreds throughout China. Then the market changed, and Motorola's share of it declined precipitously. Newly forged China-made competitors, notably Huawei and ZTE, took hold in a big way, learning from the company that had once been the best in China. Motorola's loyalty had given it short-term rewards, but its products became obsolete, and as we write, Motorola is being savaged in the Chinese press for the large number of workers it has laid off.

In its 2006 "Medium- and Long-Term Program for Science and Technology Development" (MLP), the government declared it planned to transform China into an "innovative society" by 2020 and a world leader in science and technology by 2050. This was not empty talk. Beijing, after all, had a solid track record of setting out a guideline and watching subnational actors as far down as the village level fall into step through a mix of policies and incentives. In this case, the government aimed to limit China's reliance on imported technology to no more than 30 percent within a few years, to increase R&D funding, and ultimately to leapfrog ahead in what it identified as strategic emerging sectors.

The MLP aimed to ensure that the fruits of Chinese labor remained at home and no longer slipped away in the form of royalty fees, licensing agreements, and second-generation technologies brought in by foreign firms. To further the prospects of local firms, the Chinese government introduced export subsidies that allowed Chinese firms to seek rebates on any export taxes and fees paid, as well as a state procurement policy that required Chinese government ministries and state-owned businesses to procure goods, when feasible, from Chinese-owned companies.

International firms protested strongly. Among them were some of the early advocates of China's accession to the World Trade

Organization. In gaining access to the WTO, China had implemented rather significant reforms to support greater market access to non-Chinese firms, but never to the degree expected. Still, few foreign companies left China. Instead, they have had to recognize the need to show greater support for innovation *in* China. (See more on this in chapter 6.)

This has triggered the recent boom in foreign R&D centers inside China. In 2004, there were more than six hundred foreign R&D centers in China; by 2010, the number had doubled to more than twelve hundred. Pfizer moved its Asia headquarters to Shanghai that year. In 2011, Microsoft opened its Asia Pacific R&D Center in Beijing. General Motors, another longtime player in the China market, opened an Advanced Technical Center comprising several engineering and design labs. Also in 2011, Merck, the giant pharmaceutical company, broke ground in Beijing on what will be its Asia R&D headquarters, scheduled to become operational in 2014 with forty-seven thousand square meters of laboratory and office space.

To push the concept of innovation further still, "incubator parks" have emerged in many large cities, often near universities, with government support to early-stage companies. Innovation Works (China) supports high-tech start-ups in Beijing and Shanghai; Innovation Camp (iCamp) in Shanghai is funded by Chinese and Chinese-American entrepreneurs from Silicon Valley.[16]

Two other areas deserve mention. The US space program over the past five decades has been an enormous source of innovation and product spin-offs for the United States. China, coming from a catch-up position, became—through a combination of building on, "borrowing," and inventing proprietary technologies—only the third country to launch humans into space and is now planning to put humans on the moon. This will require the ability to both invent and adapt numerous technologies that may boost the economy, as the US space program did earlier.

Closer to the ground is China's high-speed rail network. Its senior administrators view it as an earthbound space program, pioneering the integration of a whole new suite of technologies that will allow the safe operation of a train at three hundred kilometers per hour and also enable a variety of spin-off products and services.

The danger in pushing state-led innovation is that the product can get ahead of engineering knowledge and skills. (Think of the British Comet airliners—three of which broke apart in midair in the mid-1950s.) Repeatedly, old operating protocols and new structures run into emerging technologies and not everything works out the first time. The 2011 crash on the high-speed rail system at Wenzhou is an example that cost at least forty lives and led to a decrease in system speeds; this is not unlike the suspension of the US manned space travel program for almost two years after the *Challenger* disaster. Innovation has its risks.

Whenever possible, Chinese firms (state and private) are eager to strike deals to gain access to new technologies that they can shape and build on in innovative ways (as in the scope of the rail project). For example, an agreement with Boeing to buy a large number of Dreamliners for Chinese airlines was directly linked to the decision by Boeing to have the rudders built in China. Had the Chinese not gained access to that technology, the planes would not have been ordered.

The brutal reality is that over time, knowledge about the intricacies of technologies is going to migrate from the originating firm. The only viable long-term way to maintain an edge is to continually invent new technologies and enhance the old ones. Just as Japan caught up with the United States technologically in many industries during the three decades after World War II, China is doing the same.

Acquiring Innovation: Going Abroad

Acquiring and bringing this "hardware" to China is, as we suggested in chapter 3, a long-standing priority. Going abroad to get it by acquisition is something new. Much has been written about the ever-growing wave of Chinese direct investments abroad. In this area, the race for commodity resources has received most of the attention, with front-page stories of China in Africa of special interest. The turn toward the United States and Europe is, however, no less significant, with Chinese firms seeking opportunities for research collaboration and profitable acquisitions that set them ahead of their competitors through technological acquisitions.

As will be explored in chapter 6, there is a supportive policy framework that is helping Chinese businesses go global. But policy alone is not deciding the direction of this trend. The variation of direct investment strategies, ranging from greenfield investments to prized acquisitions, depends also on the firm's leadership and direction.

Take the case of Huawei, the networking and telecommunications equipment and services company. In 1999, Huawei opened its first international R&D center in Bangalore and followed a year later with another center in Stockholm, Sweden. Today, Huawei has twenty-three R&D centers around the world.[17] Huawei's decision to base its US headquarters in Plano, Texas, sparked a short-lived debate in the United States about the international role of Chinese high-tech firms.[18]

William Plummer, Huawei's vice president for external affairs and a former US diplomat, once portrayed the telecommunications powerhouse as "the biggest company you've never heard of," a claim that few would make today.[19] With R&D centers in Boston, Plano, San Diego, Silicon Valley (Santa Clara, California), and Bridgewater, New Jersey, the company intends to operate within leading US innovation clusters. In 2012, it shifted its R&D headquarters from Plano to Silicon Valley, literally taking off from Plano's President George Bush Highway and settling on Silicon Valley's Central Expressway. The new 200,000-square-foot facility earned the company praise from local politicians, who appreciated increased investment and job creation.

In 2010, Huawei recruited John Roese, the former chief technology officer of Nortel, to serve as senior vice president and general manager of Huawei's North American R&D efforts. His appointment came only a year after Huawei recruited Matt Bross, former CTO of the BT Group (formerly British Telecom), to serve as copresident of Huawei USA and CTO of Huawei's R&D, making him responsible for Huawei's entire $2.5 billion R&D budget and scope of activities.[20] Both report directly to Huawei's chairman, Ren Zhengfei, a former Chinese military officer.

Huawei's shift to recruit non-Chinese employees into senior positions is not unique to this Chinese company. Goldwind, one of China's leading wind turbine manufacturers, recruited Tim Rosenzweig, a well-established figure in the clean energy field, to serve as the first CEO of its US headquarters. He in turn brought in executives with records distinguished by cross-cultural experience and industrial expertise.

The patterns of talent recruitment within leading multinational Chinese firms reflect a growing interest in the acquisition of local market knowledge and leading-edge research and development. Today, for example, Huawei has twenty-three thousand non-Chinese employees, many of them playing a role in its R&D efforts around the world.[21] Similar patterns exist in other industries.

Haier, a leading Chinese appliance and consumer electronics manufacturer, has a wide network of global design and R&D centers in the United States (Los Angeles and South Carolina), Japan, Italy, the Netherlands, and South Korea. In 2012, it opened its newest R&D facility in Nuremburg, Germany.[22] For Chinese auto manufacturers, Turin, Italy, is the place to be: JAC, FAW, and Chang'an operate R&D centers there.

In contrast, Sany, a leading heavy industry machine manufacturer, whose main international competitors include Caterpillar and Komatsu, initially attempted to succeed in the European and US markets by relying on its own homegrown talent. A few missteps encouraged the firm to pursue a dual approach in its new market entry strategy, combining a mix of talent and opportunity. Sany now has R&D centers closely tied to its European and US regional headquarters, in Cologne, Germany, and Peachtree, Georgia.[23]

In addition, with its January 2012 acquisition of Putzmeister, Germany's leading cement pump maker, it opened a window into a onetime competitor's technology.[24]

Ren Jianxin, president of ChemChina, the country's largest chemical company, summed up this growing trend: "You can form cooperation agreements with foreign companies; you can also open plants overseas. But for our company, I think the best choice is to make acquisitions. Through acquisitions we can have larger markets, get more advanced technologies, and have more talented people."[25]

ChemChina has certainly followed this conviction, with acquisitions in France, Australia, and Norway, and of Israel's Makhtcshim Agan Industries, the seventh-largest agrochemical company in the world.

In short, we see major innovation gaps that foreign acquisitions and partnerships are helping to fill. For the coming decades, however, how does one train the leaders of the future? This is the job of Chinese universities.

Innovation through the Next Generation: Higher Education

Perhaps the greatest hope for an enduring culture of innovation rests in investments being made in the coming generation of Chinese now attending—or hoping to attend—Chinese universities. The theory is of course that universities are the incubators of innovation.

No country has seen more revolutionary change in higher education than China in recent years. Let us start with the example of Wuhan University, arguably China's oldest modern university. When we think of Chinese universities, we often think only of Peking University, Tsinghua, and a few others. But Wuhan and the surrounding province of Hubei have long been leading centers of commerce, scholarship, and political leadership. It was the great reforming governor-general Zhang Zhidong who in 1893—five years before the founding of Peking University—founded

the "Self-Strengthening Institute" that would become Wuhan
University. It was in Wuhan that the revolution that overthrew the
Qing dynasty in 1912 began. Wuhan hosted one of the two contending
Nationalist governments in 1927 and the retreating government of
Chiang Kai-shek in 1938. It became an industrial center of the early
PRC, and today western Hubei, upriver from Wuhan, is home to the
largest engineering project in world history, the Three Gorges Dam
(and even a "Three Gorges Dam University").

Wuhan University had strong growth before 1949. After having been nearly destroyed during the Cultural Revolution, it is
now a great, comprehensive university, with a faculty of nearly
five thousand, teaching a student body of thirty-three thousand
undergraduates and twelve thousand graduate students. It offers
doctoral degrees in 143 subjects—more than Harvard University.
It is now partnering with Duke University in the development of a
two-hundred-acre residential campus that will house, among other
efforts, a world-class undergraduate program in the liberal arts to
educate the leaders of tomorrow.

Scale and Scope

Wuhan University's recent renewal and expansion is part of a second revolution of higher education in modern China. In the first
half of the twentieth century, China developed strong state-run
institutions (Peking University, Jiaotong University, National
Central University, and, at the apogee of research, the Academia
Sinica) accompanied by a creative set of private colleges and universities (Yenching University, St. John's University, and Peking
Union Medical College, to name but a few). All were Sovietized in
the 1950s and destroyed in the 1960s.

Now Chinese universities are back. Take the case of Tsinghua University. It was founded in 1911 as a two-year, liberal arts
college to send students to the United States. It became a comprehensive university in Nationalist times (John Fairbank, the
pioneer of modern Chinese studies in the United States, learned
his Chinese history there in the 1930s). It became a Soviet-style

polytechnic university in the 1950s. It is now reclaiming its place as a great, comprehensive university—more difficult to get into than Harvard or Yale. In 2016, Tsinghua will open its first truly international college—Schwarzman College, named for the American donor Stephen A. Schwarzman—that will be home annually to two hundred postgraduate students from around the world. The Schwarzman Scholars who reside there will be, Tsinghua believes, the Rhodes Scholars of the twenty-first century.

Simply in terms of the number of students educated, the recent changes are more dramatic than even the great postwar expansion of higher education in the United States or the growth of mass-enrollment universities in Europe in the 1970s and 1980s. In 1978, after a decade of mostly closed universities, Chinese universities enrolled approximately 860,000 students. This number increased very gradually until 1990, when enrollment was about 2 million. In the late 1990s, the government decided to greatly accelerate the pace of expansion, and by the year 2000 there were as many as 6 million students enrolled in Chinese universities.

In the years since then, the overall official numbers—counting all kinds of institutions—have risen dramatically. According to the very ambitious Tenth Five-Year Plan of the Ministry of Education, higher education enrollment was scheduled to reach 16 million by 2005 and 23 million by 2010. But in fact, it has risen even more rapidly, and there are today more than 30 million students in institutions of higher learning (see figure 4-1). By contrast, the United States had about 13 million undergraduate and 2 million graduate and professional students in 2000, with perhaps 15 million undergraduates today. In short, in the year 2000, China had about half as many students as the United States, and today it has nearly double the number enrolled in American institutions. In numbers, at least, the United States has been passed as if it were standing still.

China is thus moving toward mass education. The enrollment of eighteen- to twenty-one-year-olds in universities is set to be 20 percent, having been in the low single-digits for most of the history of the PRC. More than that, China plans to enroll as many

FIGURE 4-1

Higher education enrollment and goals, July 2010

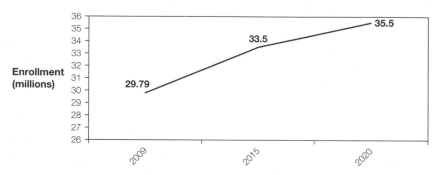

Source: "Outline of China's National Plan for Medium and Long Term Education Reform and Development,"
Ministry of Education, Beijing, July 2010, https://www.aei.gov.au/news/newsarchive/2010/documents/
china_education_reform_pdf.pdf.

as 40 percent of young adults in colleges or universities by the year
2020. By contrast, in 2010, only 28 percent of the US population
reported having a higher education degree.

A once-small teacher's college, Lin Yi Teacher's University had
thirty-five hundred students in the year 2000. It now has thirty-five
thousand. This growth is clear not only in public universities but
in the rapidly growing number of private universities as well. In
Xi'an, the privately owned Xi'an International University did not
exist twenty years ago; today it has thirty-four thousand students.
The case on this university shows that the dynamism of Chinese
universities today is not limited to the public sector: private colleges and universities now account for more than a quarter of
higher educational institutions (HEIs), and they are growing at
an even faster rate than public HEIs.[26] They are remarkably innovative, not least in marketing, recruitment, and placement. The
number of private HEIs grew from 131 in 2002 to 656 in 2009, while
that of public HEIs in the same time span grew from 1,265 to 1,649.

Large companies are also getting into higher education. Alibaba's
Taobao unit has plans for a "Taobao University," first to train
e-business owners, managers, salespeople, and professionals, and in

time to extend business education to more than a million online students seeking the skills to start and sustain small and medium-sized businesses. (Taobao also expects to enroll some twenty thousand students "offline"; that is, in person.)

To put this growth in another light, that of physical space, the "square meterage" of Chinese universities has more than quadrupled in the last ten years. New Chinese universities rise from barren fields in a matter of a few years; more venerable institutions have added second, third, and fourth campuses.

In terms of graduate students, China will soon turn out, annually, more PhDs than any other country in the world. We joke with our Chinese friends that such a number of PhDs hitting the job market at a time of economic uncertainty is a sure prescription for political instability.

Unlike the American expansion of the 1950s and the European growth of the 1970s, this growth of education in China has elements that are consciously elitist. Chinese universities aim to be cradles of high-level, creative researchers; frontiers of scientific research; forces capable of transforming research and innovation into higher productivity; and bridges for international and cultural exchange.

To that end, the Chinese government and many other sources are providing enormous revenues to the leading institutions. Individual winners of recent competitions among universities have received hundreds of millions of dollars each to expend over the next five years. Beyond this, the leading Chinese universities have tapped private, philanthropic, and foundation sources for substantial streams of income. Within ten years, the research budgets of China's leading universities will approach those of leading American and European universities. In the realms of engineering and science, Chinese universities will be among the world's leaders.

International Competitiveness

For American universities, the revolution in Chinese higher education is a challenge both for competition and for cooperation. Although in the latter part of the twentieth century, American universities were, as a group, among the strongest in the world, there is no reason to imagine that this is a permanent condition. After all, about a century ago almost all of the leading universities in the world were German. That is why the leading American and Chinese universities—Harvard and Peking University among them—adopted German systems by the early twentieth century. And yet—at least according to surveys by Shanghai Jiaotong University, whose rankings are taken seriously the world over—in the second decade of the twenty-first century, German universities do not dominate the rankings. Indeed, *not one* of the top fifty in the world was German.

To be sure there is a real silliness to this university rankings game. What is being ranked often has very little to do with education, as distinct from research. Although some in the United States try to measure the quality of undergraduate education by teacher/student ratio, which can be useful, there are few ways of measuring comparatively successful teaching. All of the international rankings focus on research results and prizes, such as the Nobel Prize. Universities glory in having Nobel laureates on their faculty—and they take credit for these noble scholars, even though the work that earned them a Nobel Prize may have been done decades earlier and at another university. (Chinese leaders still crave Nobel Prizes, even as they have shunned three of the four most recent winners born on the soil of what is now the People's Republic.)

Liberal Education

Chinese universities are also now seeking to learn from the Americans how to produce leaders. More exactly, they have come to believe the mantra of American liberal arts colleges that the best leaders are those with the broadest education based in the liberal arts. The idea of a "liberal education" is a concept of German origin that has now established its deepest roots in North America. It means the education of the whole person, not just training the specialist, with the aim of ensuring that graduates are curious, reflective, and skeptical learners—people with the capacity for lifelong learning, as their first job will surely not be their last.

At Harvard, we have just renewed our commitment to this cornerstone of undergraduate education. We have asked the same question that leaders of Chinese universities have asked their institutions: what does it mean to be an educated person in this day and age? We know that all of our curricular drafts and final plans were read at least as carefully in Beijing as they were by our colleagues in Cambridge, Massachusetts.

What we find encouraging about Chinese higher education today is the independent understanding senior faculty and administrators at leading universities have that the general education of their students—in the arts and humanities as well as the sciences and social sciences—will be as important to their, and all of our, futures, as will be their specialized, professional training. Rote learning of facts and theories in a narrow discipline is no longer enough.

Today all Peking University students, even in its Guanghua School of Management, take myriad courses that may include literature, philosophy, and history. There is an elite liberal arts curriculum in the new Yuanpei Program, named for Peking University's famous German-educated chancellor of the early twentieth century, the philosopher Cai Yuanpei. Across the street from Peking University, Tsinghua's School of Economics and Management has implemented perhaps the most imaginative programs in liberal arts and general education to be found in any Chinese university.

Leading American institutions believe that for a truly liberal education, a study of the humanities is essential. Despite a century-long obsession with engineering, we find this view shared increasingly today in China. Perhaps this is because educational leaders in China know better than anyone else what life can be like in the absence of the humanities: Chinese history in the Maoist period shows what dislocation can ensue when a civilization utterly loses its cultural foundations, its moral compass.

The most important revolution in Chinese higher education today may not be its size and scope, but the fact that even under the leadership of engineers, leading institutions have come to understand that an education in the absence of the humanities is incomplete. This is an educational revolution within a revolution, the results of which are not yet clear.

The Importance of Being Innovative

One can surely doubt that creativity can be mandated or that innovation can be planned. Both can, however, be nurtured in different educational and institutional settings. The question, then, is this: does China have a good institutional framework for innovation?

Our answer at present is *no*: the governance structures of Chinese state-owned enterprises and universities still leave too many decisions to too few, too self-important, people. Chinese universities, like state-owned organizations, are still plagued with party committees, and the university party secretary normally outranks the president. (It should be noted that a few extraordinary party secretaries are key to their university's success, but as a rule this system of parallel governance limits rather than enhances the flow of ideas.) Few party secretaries—like few presidents of American universities—look favorably on the prospect of unbridled faculty governance of universities. But the freedom of faculty to pursue ideas wherever they may lead is a precondition for sustained innovation in universities. By any comparative measure of leading international universities, faculty in Chinese institutions have little role in governance. It was not a good sign when China's vice president (and president-designate) Xi Jinping visited China's leading universities in June 2012 to call for *increased* party supervision of higher education.

Deans and presidents everywhere must make decisions and set priorities. In reality, however, many of the best ideas—those that deans and presidents will be compelled to support on their intellectual merits—will come from the mistakenly named "bottom" up, from faculty at the top of their fields. Having an institutional structure to support this is rare anywhere, and in Chinese universities today it is rarer still.

Can world-class universities exist in a politically illiberal system? Perhaps. But perhaps only if they are largely self-governed. German universities in the nineteenth century were subject to much political pressure, but they were the envy of the world in part because they also had traditions of institutional autonomy that fostered and (at times) protected creative thinkers. China's universities today boast superb scholars and among the world's best students. But these students are also forced to sit through courses in Party ideology. They learn a simplified book version of the history of their own country and almost nothing about the historic tragedies of the ruling party. In the realm of politics and history, the disconnect between what students have to learn in order to graduate, and what they know to be true, grows greater every day. This is why, in 2012, when students in Hong Kong were faced with the prospect of enduring "patriotic education" as taught in mainland China, they took to the streets.

Can Chinese universities come to set global standards in the twenty-first century? It is surely possible, simply because of the resources they are likely to have. But here much depends on what happens elsewhere—particularly in the United States, where the great public systems of higher education are in the process of slow-motion self-destruction. The University of California system, once the greatest system of public higher education in the world, has been weakened and made increasingly dysfunctional due to state budget problems. As that great system declines, the leading private universities—the Harvards and Stanfords, for example, which compete with the University of California for faculty and graduate students—may be less challenged and may likely decline as well.

For the moment, American universities still enjoy their hour in the sun as the innovative places to educate leaders. After all, actual Chinese leaders send their kids to American universities, and in increasing numbers. But it is worth recalling that in the 1920s and 1930s, China's paramount leader, Chiang Kai-shek, sent his sons to study in the leading (if quite different) institutions of his day in the Soviet Union (Chiang Ching-kuo) and Germany (Chiang Wei-kuo and Tai An-kuo). Times change. Today there is no shortage of American families who send their children to China. As Chinese universities increase their international offerings, this is a trend to watch.

Perhaps absolute innovation, like absolute leadership and power, is overvalued. In industry as in education, China—like the United States before it—can enjoy for some time what Joseph Shumpeter, the great twentieth-century economist, called the latecomer's advantage: learning from and improving on one's immediate predecessors in a given field. Certainly in business as in education, China has shown innovation through creative adaptation in recent decades, and it now has the capacity to do much more.

So it is clear that China can follow and do creative adaptation. But can China *lead*? Will the Chinese state also have the wisdom to lighten up and the patience to allow the full emergence of what Shumpeter called *Unternehmergeist*, the true spirit of entrepreneurship, be it found in the business world, in the arts, or indeed in politics? On this, we have our doubts.

For the businessperson, all of this creates a complex environment of challenge, risk, and opportunity. China already has world-class engineers, and it seeks to educate its next generations to be creative problem solvers. But can it (and can you) succeed in a realm where academic and intellectual freedom is systematically constrained? Where those governing research, teaching, and learning are politically constrained? Where intellectual property rights remain in their infancy? The problem, we think, is not the innovative or intellectual capacity of the Chinese people, which is boundless, but the political world in which their schools, universities, and businesses need to operate, which is very much bounded.

Doing Business in China

- Who are my Chinese technology competitors?

- What are their strengths? Are they credible competitors? Are their skills close to mine? What is their global strategy? Are they acquiring in my sector? Do they command party and government support?

- Is my firm protecting its core technology skills, or are they so dynamically evolving that I don't have to worry about protection?

- What is my firm contributing to the growth and skills of China, nationally, regionally, and locally? Is it adding enough value to China that it continues to be a welcomed company?

- Is my firm attracting and training good Chinese staff for my firm and ultimately for my competitors and other firms in the region? Have I structured recruitment in a way to manage high turnover among skilled employees?

- Does my firm's foreign headquarters have good, sensitive, cross-border skills as they relate to China? Are my ears really close to the ground?

5

ACHIEVING COMMERCIAL SUCCESS IN CHINA

Hazardous Business

We have focused on the context of the China business environment and how it has emerged. We have recognized the overwhelming presence of the Party-State and the vast economic differences between regions. We have noted the dramatic build-out of hard infrastructure and the challenge of sustaining a culture of innovation in China. All this has been accompanied by 300 million people lifting themselves into the middle class and beyond. In this environment, state-owned enterprises have thrived, and so too have numerous foreign companies and countless local entrepreneurs. Many non-state-owned firms with ambitions for significant growth, however, have failed for reasons that have to do with their inability to design a strategy that suits China's unique environment.

For all enterprises doing business in China, many aspects of a traditional MBA education as they relate to strategy, development, and execution are relevant. Indeed, the curricula at 198 notable

MBA programs in China look much like their equivalents in the West. Strategy, marketing, leadership, entrepreneurship, and supply-chain management are present and useful. There are other topics, however, that are partially ignored or completely forgotten, and that we find to be leading determinants of success or failure in China. Four in particular dramatically differentiate the business environment in China from that of the West. A firm that masters them may meet with success; ignoring them can lead to disaster:

1. Sensitivity and adaptation to the requirements of the Party-State at the national level.

2. Sensitivity and adaptation to the requirements of provincial and municipal Party administrators and government.

3. Identifying the opportunities posed by emergent technical infrastructure and navigating the shoals of weak or nonexistent soft infrastructure.

4. Visualizing and acting on the opportunities of a rapidly emerging consumer economy at both the high-end and mid-market level.

In this chapter, we have chosen a series of companies, some successful and others not, whose stories we think are particularly instructive. We have analyzed their success and failure through those four lenses and highlighted important nuances in execution. Table 5-1 summarizes our analysis of how these four factors affect each firm.

Nation, State, and Party Alignment

The Party-State is critical to the success of all firms, especially if they seek to expand or diversify their activities. Sustained Party-State linkages over long periods of time and across all geographic areas where a firm is active are essential components of any business plan in China; creating and maintaining these relationships

TABLE 5-1

Sources of success and failure of selected companies

This table summarizes the key aspects of each of these commercial enterprises.

Company	National government and Party support	Local government and Party support	National infrastructure	Targets new Chinese consumer	Focuses on national priorities	Succeeded?
Baidu	Important		Enabled its growth	Yes	Yes	Yes
China Merchants Bank	Important		Enabled its growth	Yes	No	Yes
CreditEase	Neutral			Yes	Yes	Yes
Dorm99	Negative			Yes	No	No
Esquel	Important	Important			Yes	Yes
Google	Negative			Yes	No	No
Grace Vineyard	Neutral			Yes	No	Yes
Haidilao	Neutral			Yes	No	Yes
Longtop	Neutral		Absence was a source of failure		No	No
ReSource Pro	Neutral	Highly important			No	Yes
Sealed Air	Important		Company contributes to its improvement		Yes	Yes
UFIDA	Important				Yes	Yes
Wanxiang	Important	Important			Yes	Yes

demands a highly qualified team of public affairs specialists working on your firm's behalf. Some business opportunities that make sense in other countries might be ruled out in China for reasons of government sensitivity. Conversely, strong political favor may be shown to foreign companies that bring special assets to China in terms of technology transfer, new industries, and employment.

Sustained Government Support

While there are many means by which the central government and Party shape China's business environment, the most fundamental is a firm's need for continuous engagement with both of them. No case is more dramatic in this regard than the emergence of Wanxiang, today's global automotive parts giant.

Wanxiang began in 1969 as a Commune and Brigade Enterprise (CBE) in Hangzhou, Zhejiang, in Eastern China.[1] As a CBE, it was a legal entity whose primary purpose was to fulfill government planning objectives, including the self-sustainability of the rural community in which it was based. CBEs were given minimal support from the central government. They depended heavily on the energy, know-how, and relationship-building abilities of their leaders.

Lu Guanqiu, Wanxiang's founder, whom we met in chapter 1, is one such individual. He initially made use of a unique feature of China's socialist era policies, namely its official abhorrence of "wastefulness" in a rather wasteful system. His is a story of "swords into plowshares," for he obtained outdated field artillery ordnance from the People's Liberation Army and transformed it into plows that could be sold to surrounding rural areas. In following years, the CBE expanded into nonfarm products, most famously auto parts. Here Lu Guanqiu identified another gap in China's planning system—the ability to supply timely, high-quality provisions—and resolved it.

Within a decade, and now doing business as Wanxiang, Lu's company had developed a strong regional reputation. It ultimately won a place in the national state plan to produce universal joints for autos and trucks. It was only one of three firms out of hundreds to win a contract to supply China's state-owned automotive companies at the beginning of their expansion.

The firm's relentless focus on high-quality maintenance of local government support and an ability to translate gaps in the state provisioning system into market opportunities were core factors behind Wanxiang's success. Given its origins as a CBE, Wanxiang was not part of the system by which the state assigned workers and university graduates. Determined to recruit the best talent,

Wanxiang offered special bonuses to universities that directed their best students to the company, solving cash flow problem for universities and laying the foundations for the enterprise's long-term growth. In 2013, Wanxiang expected to reach $20 billion in global sales, with about $3 billion in the United States. It has about 40,000 employees—a figure that is changing all the time, according to Wanxiang America President Ni Pin—with 12,500 people under Wanxiang America. Wanxiang has been transformed into a dynamic holding company that has made acquisitions in China and around the world in sectors that complement the Chinese government's strategic goals (for example, clean energy) and allow the business to remain hugely competitive. Indicative of the company's scale and status, Lu Guanqiu was invited to join President Hu Jintao's delegation during Hu's 2011 state visit to the United States. Even before meeting the American president, President Hu Jintao visited Wanxiang's US headquarters in Chicago, with Lu beside him.

Establishment of Special Economic Zones

The central government established special economic zones (SEZs) with embedded utilities and other infrastructure to attract foreign companies doing export work, and with the broader intention of facilitating technology transfer and other positive spillover effects. SEZs have been critical to the incubation and emergence of many important Chinese companies.

The first nationally authorized trade zone was established in Shenzhen in 1980. Located near Hong Kong, it was an experiment to see how market capitalism could work in a socialist context. Its creation sparked the forces that enabled the Pearl River Delta area to become one of the world's great manufacturing zones. Shenzhen grew from a population of 310,000 in 1980 to nearly 10 million in 2011.

The model of the special economic zone was replicated across China with the support of both national and provincial authorities as Shenzhen and other early zones showed great results. SEZs have been established recently in interior regions to encourage growth where it has lagged behind the rest of the country. At the beginning of the twenty-first century, there were fifteen free trade zones, thirty-two state-level economic zones, and fifty-three high-tech zones.[2] These zones have been accompanied by the establishment of science and technology parks, which aim to provide the climate and infrastructure for advanced technology firms to emerge.

One firm to emerge from these gestation zones is UFIDA, which rode the wave of electronic accounting that was sweeping the government sector in the late 1980s.[3] Now a fourteen-thousand-employee company, UFIDA was launched in 1988 in the newly formed technology park—designed to replicate Silicon Valley's success in the United States—located between Tsinghua University and Peking University in Beijing. UFIDA's CEO, an employee in a government agency, took the risk, with the support of his superiors, to leave the government and establish the company.

Headquartered in Beijing (the destination for some of the best students in the country), UFIDA consciously built dormitories and high-quality office space to attract and retain graduates who didn't want to leave the city. As the needs of its government agency and SOE customers changed, UFIDA ensured that these demands were understood and appropriate adaptation made to its products and services. In addition to its customer-centric approach at home, UFIDA also tracked the product development and acquisition plans of its two large, global competitors, SAP and Oracle. With a firm foundation domestically, UFIDA could see where the industry was going internationally and race to offer competing products. Because indigenous innovation was a national priority, UFIDA had a natural edge over foreign competition, as the government and SOE customers largely favored it. Only in the case of the largest Chinese companies did SAP and Oracle beat UFIDA.

Location was such an important advantage for sales and staff recruiting for UFIDA in the information technology industry that Kingdee, UFIDA's Shenzhen-based competitor, ultimately moved offices and staff to Beijing to get a share of the Beijing SOE market and benefit from the city's rich human resources.[4] UFIDA also benefited from a well-timed, government-supported IPO on the Shanghai exchange that gave it considerable financial resources for multiple acquisitions and R&D.

In sum, UFIDA's success and growth have been a function of being located at the center (geographically and otherwise) of a robustly supported national priority. It was founded in the right industry at the right time, getting access to the best students and a variety of tax and other economic concessions, as well as having a very strong ex-government CEO. The core of its success, however, was a central government providing the context for the company to succeed.

Party and Government Shape the Possible

The Chinese Communist Party and the Chinese government can give (as in infrastructure investments) and they can take away (as in licensing and land access). To succeed, an entrepreneur needs their active support, or at least their benign neglect.

China's political system rules out certain classes of investments that are possible in other parts of the world (think newspapers, for example, and Rupert Murdoch's failure in China). No sector has experienced these limits more than the modern information industry.

Internet search engines such as Yahoo! and Google are the standard examples. Each company's leadership has had to contend with the ethical dilemma of whether or not to censor as dictated by the Chinese government.[5] Search terms like "June 4th Tiananmen" or "Jasmine Revolution" remain blocked. Foreign businesses must also contend with the government's demand for the search histories of individuals and organizations that it deems threatening to social stability.

Google resisted these policies. It made the decision to limit its activities in this market, and it made clear to China-based customers when they were searching for something "unavailable" in China. Chinese firms do not have the luxury of taking such a public stance, and some have benefited from the exodus of a range of foreign internet-based businesses. Google's local competitor,

Baidu, for example, now dominates the China search market with a 67 percent market share, though it remains unknown outside China. Google now serves its Chinese customers from Hong Kong, but Facebook, with its ability to create broad social networks, was unable even to enter China. Instead, a Chinese firm—Renren— has dominated this space, working closely with government monitors to ensure its continued operation. Similarly, in place of Twitter, China has "Weibo" microblogging sites where followers run in the millions, but under the ever-watchful eye of monitors.

Dorm99. An instructive case of a firm's failure to survive in this environment is Dorm99, a four-year-old start-up founded in 2007 by two HBS students during their second year in the MBA program.[6] One was a Chinese American who had already built two other ventures (and sold one). The other was a Chinese national, well connected politically, who had done his undergraduate years in the United States and then worked there for several years. Their concept was the creation of a university student Facebook-like site that would make it easier for students within and across universities in China to get to know another. It was a powerful idea for its time. The founders struggled to find the hook that would pull people to the website and entice them to register as users. Eventually, they conceived of putting a click-through ad on a non-governmentally owned and managed website that students accessed on a specific date to see if they had passed the national English examination administered twice a year to university students (passing this examination was a requirement for graduation). All the website told them was whether they had passed the test. However, if students signed up for Dorm99 by clicking on the Dorm99 icon and thus becoming customers, they could also find out their personal score as a percentile of both their university and their province, information that they could then share with potential employers. The founders believed this information would be of great interest to the students. They were right.

When the system was brought live, it was a great success. In the first four hours of operation, Dorm99 generated nearly two hundred thousand customers. Just as the founders started to savor success, however, they received a call from the Ministry of Education, demanding that this "unharmonious site" be closed down immediately. The founders thought they had covered their government political bases well enough, but they had not factored in the government's reaction to calls from angry parents, upset that their children had passed the test but only at the fifteenth percentile (information that had been previously unknown). This was just too much trouble for the Ministry, and a promising venture was derailed by political fiat. The company could not be revived in its planned form and eventually morphed into a university-sponsored student gaming platform, where it has languished.

The lesson here is that it can be very hard to understand the multiple interests of the Party and state at various levels, even for the well connected. The penalties are harsh if you get it wrong. The government and Party have life-and-death control over any business, making China a very nontransparent place to do business. Dorm99 is the poster child for this type of failure; great *guanxi* (connections) could not sustain this business.

Special Value to China

No point is more fundamental for a foreign organization seeking to do business in China than this: the goal of making a profit is an insufficient reason for the government to support you. You must show, at both the national and local level, how your organization provides value for the country and the province/city. If you facilitate technology transfer, improve the standards of living, extend life expectancy, and so forth, you are welcome. Your contribution may take many forms. For example, Blackstone's 20 percent minority investment in a large division of ChemChina was valued not just for the money it brought in but more importantly because of its transfer of sophisticated governance mechanisms to a Chinese company.[7]

The Esquel Group. An example of bringing special value to China is the Esquel Group, a $1 billion manufacturer of woven shirts for high-end international markets.[8] This firm is in the

fourth generation of a family textile business with a rich tradition of corporate social responsibility. It has brought the latest
textile manufacturing equipment and processes to its twenty-
three-thousand-employee plant in Gaoming City of Guangdong
Province, where it is a famously green, or environmentally sound,
company. It is also a large purchaser of cotton from the Xinjiang
Production and Construction Corps, in Western China. Esquel
is vertically integrated on every step of its supply chain, and it
controls quality relentlessly. It is vertically integrated, too, in its
necessary political and social relationships. It is involved in every
aspect of government, from running the local power plant to the
service of its chairman, Marjorie Yang, on the People's Political
Consultative Conference at several levels and also on two Chinese
university governing boards. More than 50 percent of the chairman's time is spent on these activities. The net benefit has been
the ability to gain access to material resources for the firm and the
ability to expand. Esquel is one of the best examples of bringing
special value to China beyond jobs.

Capital Rationing

Capital availability constrains the emergence of successful start-
ups. Foreign capital from overseas Chinese families and stock list-
ings has often been the only source for those firms. This is a result
of the government's policy to support financially major state-
owned enterprises and move those that cannot make it to relatively
soft landings through mergers or closures if necessary. To enable
an orderly reconfiguration of state-owned enterprises, the major
banks at government direction focus their lending activities on ful-
filling the liquidity needs of these enterprises. Consequently, much
of the medium- and larger-scale entrepreneurial sector has been
financed by a combination of foreign venture capital and the firms'
internally generated cash flows and, in recent years, flotation on
the Shanghai and Shenzhen stock exchanges. The establishment
of these two significant stock exchanges in 1990, post–Tiananmen
Square, has been critical. Their creation opened access to capital

from inside China to private firms for the first time, but only for firms approved by the government for listing.

These government-imposed capital scarcities shape the kind of entrepreneurial institutions that can survive (that is, those that have no need for externally supplied capital or can attract foreign capital or stock market support). This scarcity has also opened new business opportunities. An interesting example of a new organization that provides money to entrepreneurs is CreditEase.

CreditEase. CreditEase is a 2007 microfinance platform start-up that grew from thirty staff in 2009 to over seventeen thousand by the end of 2012. It operates in China's very inefficient capital market space for small loans. Normally, the only sources for loans for small business are family, friends, and local loan sharks (who charge exorbitant double-digit monthly interest rates). CreditEase's product strategy is aimed at this problem. It was founded by Ning Tang, a Chinese citizen who did two years as a math major at Beijing University, followed by two years at the University of the South in Sewanee, Tennessee, as an economics major. This was followed by tours in the New York offices of several financial houses, including DLJ Financial, before returning to China. As a result, he has a deep understanding of how the credit markets work. The company is currently backed by Kleiner Perkins Caufield and Byers and has expanded across more than fifty cities.

In the absence of a national credit history system in China (such as Equifax in the United States), CreditEase has developed a group of two hundred individuals who can do sufficient checking of various sources—employment, bank accounts, and the like—to become comfortable with an individual's risk of nonpayment. So far, the default rate has been well under CreditEase's budgeted 2 percent rate (of course, the company is young and has not yet been tested by a recession). Its business model is to find funding sources (high-net-worth individuals) who are looking for a high, relatively risk-free rate of return. CreditEase matches these sources of funds with people who need additional funds for their businesses and have the apparent capacity to repay them. CreditEase is the middleman providing the platform that enables the connection between the two parties. It bears no risk on the loan (it charges a fee for providing this service to both sides of the transaction).

CreditEase is an example of the opportunities that exist in the nooks and crannies of the Chinese infrastructure as the country moves to close a sixty-year-plus manufacturing and service gap with the West. This company's value is in creatively creating access to capital in a capital-starved environment in a way that has kept the government regulators comfortable to date. It provides capital for job creation in organizations that existing financial organizations are unable to serve. It lives, however, on a razor's edge. Like Dorm99, it could be stopped in an instant if it crossed people at the ministries, and so its leaders tread softly and carefully. The company's roster is filled with MBA graduates from prestigious American and Chinese universities. The company is truly exciting, but also vulnerable in a way a US firm would not be. CEO Ning Tang is also the head of the company's Communist Party and was recently named an "Outstanding Communist Party Member in Beijing"—important signs of how well he is managing those linkages.

In short, the role of the state and Party is all pervasive not only in state-owned enterprises but also in almost all foreign and private organizations of any scale. Mastery of Michael Porter's classic five forces analysis or his value chain simply is not enough to survive in this environment.[9] Government and Party in all their various aspects permeate every corner of corporate life. It is the invisible sixth force.

Local, State, and Party Alignment

China may be one country, but it is composed of multiple regions with different economies and capacities. The stories of the Charoen Pokphand Group (CP Group), the city of Kunshan, and ReSource Pro are instructive.

CP Group. The CP Group, one of the world's largest agribusinesses, has done much to transform Chinese commercial agriculture in recent decades by establishing an integrated supply chain "from farm to fork"; that is, from animal feed to animal husbandry to food processing to marketing in CP's own supermarkets.[10] In twenty-eight provinces, it has overseen an agricultural and commercial revolution without a land revolution. It has done so *province by province*, replicating and, as needed, "localizing" its approach in each setting, for there still are no easy national markets for pork, poultry, eggs, and seafood.

In close partnership with the municipal government of Cixi, in Zhejiang, south of Shanghai, the CP Group is experimenting with the future of Chinese agriculture. The local government has leased to CP nearly eighty square kilometers of land reclaimed from Hangzhou Bay. There it has invested $1 billion in a modern agricultural and ecological farm of enormous proportions. Hundreds of greenhouses nurture organic vegetables. Thousands of four-acre plots of formerly saline soil are planted mechanically for wheat, barley, and rice. The fields are fertilized by the manure of the thousands of chickens, which also lay 1 million eggs a year. The chickens, having done their work, are processed for soup, and some will find themselves recycled, sadly, to the alligator farm. Energy for the enterprise comes from multiple wind farms on site. The CP Group has a national and international reputation, but it needs local partners. Without the support and infrastructure given by Cixi, it could not succeed there.

Kunshan. One of China's greatest local success stories is that of the city of Kunshan.[11] When China reopened its doors to global economic interaction in 1978, Kunshan, in Jiangsu Province, possessed little promise of becoming a future hub of international trade. Its most famous modern businessman, An Wang, had made his career in America, inventing the Wang word processor. A small farming community approximately fifty kilometers west of Shanghai and thirty-seven kilometers east of Suzhou, Kunshan was more famous for its mitten (or hairy) crabs, which can be found in

Shanghai restaurants in season, than it was for its manufacturers. It had minimal resources to take advantage of its fortuitous positioning between two major cities in the Yangzi Delta. Through a combination of local government ambition, local entrepreneurs, and overseas investment (especially from Taiwan) in a little over two decades' time, Kunshan was transformed from an agricultural nowhere into a highly globalized urban tech cluster.

When the central government opened fourteen coastal cities as newly designated economic and technological development zones (ETDZ), Kunshan was not among them. Not wanting to wait for state recognition, the local government leaders decided to establish their own development zone in 1984.[12] The Kunshan Economic and Technological Development Zone was born in 1985 as the PRC's first high-tech industrial park. Even though it was established without permission, its success was such that it went unpunished. Over the last three decades, Kunshan has been home to many of the world's top information technology and communications manufacturers, including Foxconn, Compal Electronics, and Wistron Corporation, as well as consumer goods companies, including Giant Bicycles, and a local powerhouse that dominates global markets for children's goods, the Goodbaby Group.

In all of this, the key supporters of business have been Party officials; 86 percent of Kunshan government officials are Party members. Party Secretary Guan Aiguo described the role of Party and state in promoting Kunshan's business as follows: "We manage the stage, and the companies are the actors. By understanding our role and theirs, both are able to concentrate on success."[13] As Kunshan's leading native entrepreneur, Song Zhenghuan, president of the Goodbaby Group, described Kunshan's practice of shooting first and asking permission later: "When I was young, I worked on a farm. Each day I would pass a pond and notice that the ducks would often be walking around quacking loudly on the bank, until one duck jumped in. As soon as the first duck was in the water, the rest would follow. Looking at them, I decided that when I knew where I wanted to go, I would not wait for someone else to lead. This had guided my actions and seems to apply to Kunshan's government as well."

In 2011, the per capita GDP of Kunshan, counting only its 723,644 registered permanent residents, was approximately $52,000; even counting Kunshan's migrant workers, the per capita GDP of Kunshan's 2 million residents was $19,000. It is by any measure the wealthiest city in China. Chinese government is not always an opaque inflexible organism, but it adapts in unpredictable ways.

ReSource Pro. Another example of the enabling role of local government in helping a company of strategic importance to it is the case of ReSource Pro and the city of Qingdao.[14] ReSource Pro is a thousand-person outsourcing operation, only four years old, located in Qingdao on the southern coast of Shandong. Its business is to take portions of the back offices of US insurance brokers and move the activities to China, where they can be done more efficiently (75 percent labor cost advantage) and still be done in a timely fashion. Steadily growing in both revenues and profits, understanding the sources of ReSource Pro's success provides important lessons. First, it is a completely English-fluent office, since its staff must be in continuous contact telephonically and electronically with their English-speaking customers in the United States. The average age of its workforce is twenty-six, 85 percent are female, and all but two or three are Chinese citizens. They are mostly college graduates, the majority coming from Qingdao. Hiring is a highly focused process whose objective is to screen employees for ability, and especially for English skills. Overwhelmingly, men in the Qingdao schools and universities concentrate on math and science in college, while women focus on languages, explaining why this workforce is so skewed toward women.

ReSource Pro is a highly desirable employer from the viewpoint of the Qingdao government, which has given it many tax concessions and helped get it attractive office locations. These concessions were granted because the company provides a thousand good entry-level white-collar jobs for graduates of the local university, thus keeping them in Qingdao. The company also provides an opportunity for the staff to develop work histories and acquire new skills, and thus develops excellent staff for other employers in the region. High turnover of ReSource Pro's staff, though undesirable from the company's point of view, is a benefit for the city as it tries to attract new employers who need to build a quick nucleus of English-speaking local staff. This is an example of a foreign company being valued by the local government because it is bringing new skills to the area (in this case, opportunities for staff to learn to operate in English and thus helping Qingdao compete for other larger global employers). The manager, an American citizen, is fluent in Chinese and has a Chinese spouse, which blurs important tension points and helps to make the company feel appropriately local to the government. Its major global competitor is an Indian company. ReSource Pro competes effectively with its rival because its employees' English is so good that it is actually a positive differentiator. Key staff travel regularly to the United States, visiting clients, making the company more global in outlook—an advantage for Qingdao as well.

As these examples show, the Party-State at all levels is a critical influencer of success. With its active encouragement and supporting infrastructure, many things can become possible. When a firm creates jobs in a capital-starved world, alternative financing vehicles can be tolerated, at least for a while. But if a company threatens government control, even unwittingly, it is doomed. This is a state where management of information is key: that was Google's downfall. Finally, government *at all levels* is important.

Infrastructure

The rapid development of hard infrastructure and much slower development of soft infrastructure vis-à-vis the West creates both commercial opportunities and risks. We can see this in the examples of Sealed Air, Yili, and LongTop.

Sealed Air. By contributing to the development of soft infrastructure such as national standards, an organization can be seen as a good citizen of China. Sealed Air, the American packaging company, has built a successful operation of five hundred people in China on this basis.[15] Packaging in the meat products area offers the opportunity to significantly improve both the safety and the yield of meat products for the Chinese consumer. Its business is based on the assumption that urban supermarkets, not open markets, are the future, and that meat and other perishables have to be packaged for that purpose. It assumes, too, that instead of every fifth truck from Nanjing to Shanghai carrying live pigs (as was still the case in 2008), a modern refrigerated trucking industry will eventually be able to get Sealed Air's well-sealed packages to the supermarkets in good condition. Critical to the company's success has been its tireless work over a long period of time on various government standard-setting bodies to help China evolve and implement standards to catch up with global best practices in food quality and hygiene. In this context, Sealed Air is a desirable company to both the provincial and the national government because it is using its technology and skills to help an important industry in China to raise its standards to world level. By being in the center of this standard-setting process, Sealed Air is seen as improving the health and safety of the Chinese population and thus is welcome to grow and to make profits.

Yili. The absence of standards can have devastating consequences. Consider the case of Yili, a publicly traded state-owned dairy company located in Inner Mongolia.[16] Over the past fifteen years, the dairy industry's growth has been led by Yili, which had convinced tens of millions of lactose-intolerant Chinese, who historically have not liked milk, that only milk will help their children grow.

Yili invested in extensive research and development (with a staff of five hundred in R&D) and worked with medical experts to create additives to make milk more digestible to the Chinese. Its marketing platform took advantage of Chinese consumers' association of milk with Inner Mongolia's green grassland.

Yili also confronted the fact that milk had been considered a luxury product consumed only by the wealthy and the foreign. It wanted to make it a middle-class drink. But keeping milk fresh and affordable was a major challenge. The cold-chain process that kept pasteurized milk fresh for seven to ten days was costly in terms of both production and logistics, thus keeping prices high. To make milk available to a geographically wide range of consumers, Yili rapidly acquired smaller rivals, expanding its network. It also adopted the ultra-high-temperature (UHT) process, widely used in Europe, to dramatically extend the shelf life of its milk.

But Yili's success also rested on changes in the countryside, especially in the nature of dairy farming in China. Yili developed a new industry-transforming milk-collection system. It set up local milk-collection stations with milking machines to which farmers could bring their cows. This alleviated the previous system of collecting and transporting multiple barrels of milk from individual farms across multiple villages and also moved the industry from hand milking to automated milking. All of this was facilitated by the new infrastructure of railroads and highways. By 2008, Yili had seventy thousand employees and a nationwide distribution channel. In short, it industrialized and expanded enormously, and in the process enriched Inner Mongolia. In honor of its contribution, Yili was named the official yogurt of the Olympics. This story of innovation and marketing makes for a terrific MBA case.

But the rise of Yili and, especially, its competitors for the new milk market had hidden dangers and costs. Everything was suddenly put at risk by the systemic poisoning of children through the addition of melamine in milk products in 2008. Yili senior management was unaware of the problem in its own supply chain, and powerless to do much about its competitors. Either way, the damage to consumer confidence was done. Chinese increasingly favored imported dairy products, and especially baby formula. Two of Yili's competitors' key executives were sentenced to death, while others received life sentences. A belated result was the subsequent development and implementation of the same type of quality and inspection standards as in the Pure Food and Drug Act of 1907 in the United States. These standards are being rapidly adopted by this industry. Still, as Yili's case shows, it is easier to create the hard technology of distribution than the soft technology of standards and the processes for enforcing them.

LongTop. LongTop illustrates the absence of another type of soft infrastructure, that of reliable accounting and auditing. Long-Top was a Chinese software company that, in 2010, was the largest provider of banking software products to the Chinese banking industry. Founded in 1996 as a systems integration company, in 2001 it became a software and solutions provider and subsequently had very significant growth. Its clients included three of the four main state-owned banks as well as most of the thirteen national commercial banks and several large insurance companies. It provided both customer-designed and standardized software solutions. IDC, the independent research firm, named LongTop number one in performance in 2008 and 2009 in the banking solutions market. In October 2007 it became the first Chinese software company to be listed on the NYSE. In short, LongTop was a globally acknowledged start-up. Alas, its foundation was made of clay.

In June 2011, LongTop was delisted from the NYSE after its auditor, Deloitte (which had given LongTop four years of consecutive clean opinions), resigned the account after being unable to verify its cash balances, which were ultimately discovered to be almost entirely nonexistent. It turns out that the bank's branches were told by the company not to cooperate with Deloitte in the course of the audit. The banks were even told by LongTop that Deloitte was not the firm's auditor. When Deloitte asked LongTop's nonexecutive chairman how it happened and whose fault it was, after pausing for a moment, he said tersely, "Senior management!" The company is bankrupt as we write this.

In short, the institutions of financial and legal compliance are frailer in China than in the United States (even after acknowledging the realities of Enron and WorldCom). All is not what you read. It is our belief that these issues will be very hard to resolve.

Many Chinese companies listed on the NYSE are now delisting to escape onerous requirements like Sarbanes–Oxley. Others are being tarred by the China brush and, getting what they see as unacceptable multiples, are also delisting. They plan to go private and relist in China at higher multiples.

Understanding and managing the realities of soft infrastructure is hard. The gaps in habits and mind-sets are nonobvious and deep. It is the gaps here that will be the most enduring and hard to manage and leave us deeply concerned about China's ability to lead globally.

The New Chinese Consumer

Conventional wisdom holds that consumer consumption growth is key to China's future prosperity. Although real constraints impede entrepreneurial success (as noted in chapter 4), we believe conventional wisdom is right in this case. Two of the authors first visited China in 1979–1980, and a consumer-led demand explosion is the last thing either of us dreamed of at that time. At the airport bookstore, *The Selected Works of Mao Zedong* was the primary offering. The ever-present "Friendship Store" was stocked with tasteless piles of downmarket trinkets and clothing. Shanghai's Peace Hotel—once a palace on the Bund in the Republican era— was a relic. Meat hanging from the store ceiling as the flies buzzed around did not produce visions of cleanliness. State-owned restaurants filled every glass of beer before a single patron arrived, in the name of socialist efficiency. The concept of customer service seemed not to exist.

It is a very different world in 2014. Today, on the streets of China's leading cities, you can view Chinese and international elites as well as—and in much larger numbers—members of a new middle class that is as large as the entire population of the United States. Starbucks and KFC may be found not far from Michelin-starred restaurants. Although these changes are most evident in pace-setting cities such as Shanghai, Beijing, and Guangzhou, an entrepreneurial and consumption revolution can be found also in inland cities across the mainland. How fast and deep will this change run across China in the coming years? The answer is not clear. The need for personal savings to cover missing social infrastructure, the reemergence of state-owned enterprises as powerhouses, and the widening gap between the top and the bottom are real barriers.

Consumption in China is shaping and being shaped by a new generation of entrepreneurs and businesses, private and public. They are changing the clothes Chinese wear, the foods and beverages they consume, the homes they live in, and the means by which they travel across town and about the country. In only a decade, China has adopted all the trappings of a consumer economy. Every aspect of the marketing mix is in transition. Chinese consumption is being shaped, too, by the omnipresent role of Party and state in setting the rules and boundaries of private Chinese and foreign enterprise.

China's new middle-class consumers have become brand-conscious in an incredibly short period of time. Brand as a concept is now part of China's marketing mix, but with its short history, is still evolving in impact and complexity. In 1978, there were few national brands in China, just suppliers of items all manufactured in China by state-owned enterprises. (The best "brand" in those days was anything "made in Shanghai.") Nothing could be farther from this world in 2013. In selected categories, most major global brands are already in China, fighting the same battles as in other parts of the world. Coke and Pepsi, for example, backed by local advertising and product line extensions, are fighting nationwide for control of the bottled sodas categories. Product innovation, intense detail work, and creative advertising in recent years have all combined to give Coke an edge as the product categories continue to grow in size. Coke's chief Chinese competitor, the Hangzhou-based Wahaha Group, under its charismatic CEO, Zong Qinghou, has proven a canny competitor in secondary and tertiary cities. Its Future Cola is marketed with Chinese flags on the label as "the Chinese people's own cola" and is third in national market share, right behind Pepsi.

A similar battle is taking place in the athletic shoe sector, with Nike and Adidas having brought the full strength of their brands to this market in the leading urban centers. Initially satisfied with their position there, they have now pushed down to tier-two and -three cities where they are putting a domestic brand, Li Ning, under great pressure. Li Ning, a China-originated and -based apparel/shoe company, feels much like Nike when you visit its campus, except everything is half scale. The swimming pool is smaller, there are fewer basketball courts, and so on. Cofounded by the great Chinese Olympic gymnast Li Ning, its brand has been strongest in the tier-two and -three cities. Increasingly, despite Li Ning's appearance in the opening ceremonies of the 2008 Summer Olympics, the brand has been outgunned as the global resources of the others have been brought to bear on it.

Another example is the Ford/GM battle, where both firms are effectively competing and establishing their brand in the world's largest and fastest-growing automotive market. Ford, for example, has recently doubled its Chinese manufacturing capacity, while in 2011, with sales of over 2.5 million units in a market of 18.5 million, GM's China operation was a major contributor to the entire corporation's profits and recovery. The Buick brand, once fading fast in the United States, has been revived because of its popularity in China, where Buicks made in Shanghai combine quality and luxury at a high level—and, perhaps not the least, because Buick had set the standard for international luxury vehicles in *pre*-Communist China. Finally, fast food outlets like Starbucks, KFC, and McDonald's have also spread their presence through installation of thousands of outlets across the country.

As the cases of Wahaha and Li Ning show, there has been a steady emergence and strengthening of local brands in the consumer space. Other examples are Qingdao beer, the oldest but now also fastest-growing beer producer in China, and Haier, which is now the standard in white goods. Still others are firms in midmarket children's clothing, like the Zhejiang Semir Garment Company. Nurtured by advertising, internet promotion, and a softening of internal trade barriers, local and national brands for China are now emerging in significant numbers.

Finally, obsession with brands is taken to extremes in the realm of luxury goods, which are sought not only by the very wealthy but also by the brand-conscious. Today, whether in the French Concession in Shanghai or on Jinyu Hutong in Beijing, opulence and conspicuous consumption at the high end is overwhelming. The emerging practice of giving high-priced gifts to buy favor has helped support portions of the luxury markets. The focus of the new government leadership on corruption in 2013 temporarily chilled the sales of items like luxury watches. But the extent to which a "luxury culture" has permeated the best-off and better-connected is shown by the recent announcement that a Porsche can no longer be an official vehicle for the People's Liberation Army.

According to a report by Bain & Company, at the end of 2012, China surpassed the United States to become the world's largest luxury market.[17] Cartier, for example, has thirty-two stores in eighteen cities in China and hopes to double that number in the next four years; Cartier sees China as becoming its largest market. Tiffany & Co. has fourteen stores in China and expects its China sales to surpass those of the United States in the next five to ten years. Sales of BMW and Mercedes topped one hundred thousand cars in the first quarter of 2011, as China threatens to topple the United States as the world's largest luxury car market. The result is an extraordinary series of new markets at the high end with, of course, the potential of destabilizing the economy and triggering social unrest through the envy of the less fortunate. The opportunities for high-end goods and services may be the best in the world, as long as the pendulum of class-based resentment does not swing back.

Three Winners

The opportunity to build major organizations and brands for this market is extraordinary. What follows are the stories of three very different winners: China Merchants Bank, Grace Vineyard, and Haidilao.

China Merchants Bank. The story of China Merchants Bank is an important one. The five largest banks in China are all state-owned. Headquartered in Shenzhen, China Merchants Bank, a 1987 start-up and China's first joint-stock bank, is today the sixth largest bank in China (and roughly the same size as the fifth largest). China Merchants made use of available infrastructure and foreign technology while developing its brand and gaining bureaucratic support.

A Chinese law limiting joint-stock and private banks to no more than five new bank branches per year ought to have constrained China Merchants' growth. Instead, under the leadership of its former president, Ma Weihua, a longtime national banking regulator, China Merchants grew quickly. It did so initially by issuing credit cards, for which bank branches are unnecessary. Expecting one day to compete with large international competitors such as Citibank, China Merchants procured the necessary software from a small Taiwanese bank to support its expansion into this market. By 2003, China Merchants had a cardholder base of six hundred and twenty thousand. At the end of 2007, China Merchants had issued nearly 21 million cards, or 31 percent of all credit cards in China.

Despite the lack of consumer credit rating databases such as Equifax in the United States, personal knowledge of clients and rapid follow-up on delinquencies resulted in China Merchants Bank having credit write-offs that were much lower than global industry standards. Having established a dominant market share, China Merchants increased product profitability through expanded credit card functionality, online banking services, and wealth management services, keeping with its consumer-centered approach to growth. Although its market share fell to 21 percent (still the largest in the industry), cash flow soared. In turn, the bank was able to achieve stronger balance sheet ratios than other major financial institutions, despite initially having far fewer bricks-and-mortar branches.

Today China Merchants Bank has eight hundred branches, including one in New York City, and over sixty thousand employees. The company is an example of growth by serving unmet consumer demand in a way that aligned with government interests. Driven by a visionary and well-connected leader, China Merchants Bank prospered mightily, with $450 billion in assets reported in 2012. In May 2013, Tian Huiyu, who holds a master's degree in public policy from Columbia University, was named the new president of China Merchants Bank.

Grace Vineyard. A second example of innovation and changing tastes is that of Grace Vineyard, which is located in the middle of Shanxi Province, two hours south of the provincial capital of Taiyuan.[19] It was founded by C. K. Chan, a Chinese entrepreneur returned from Indonesia. Chan came of age in China and started his own company in Hong Kong, which he sold in 1994 for $80 million. Believing that China was becoming more consumer-oriented, he bet that the move to middle-class wine consumption that had occurred in much of the developed world was coming to China. In 1997, he invested $5 million to establish the wine-making operations of Grace Vineyard. Four years later, his first bottle of wine was produced. Grace Vineyard broke even in 2002 and won its first awards in 2003.

Land for the vineyard was acquired on a fifty-year lease from the local government of Taigu County, Shanxi, in a historically impoverished region. The company initially hired three hundred farmers, and rootstock was acquired from Australia. By 2008, there were four hundred and fifty farmers working in the vineyard and seven hundred thousand bottles per year were being produced, with roughly eighteen months' inventory being held for aging purposes. This was a very long-term investment, which required a decade or more for payout to the founding entrepreneur.

A family-owned company, Grace Vineyard has specialized in well-priced, high-quality wine in an industry previously dominated by SOE wineries that had been tempted to produce low-quality wines, which would create good financials short-term, but not exciting long-term results. This suited the SOE managers, who normally rotated out of a firm after four or five years to another company. As a consequence, an opening emerged in the market for well-capitalized strategic investors who had patience and an instinct for quality.

This case shows the opportunistic space that has been left for entrepreneurs to work in. In terms of quality, owner-operated vineyards have widely outperformed state-owned enterprises with much greater resources. Their wines are consistently of much higher caliber than Great Wall's ubiquitous products. Grace keeps its price point geared to international standards of quality. It also displays a trust in the government and local property rights systems, for Grace brings pride and prestige to its home province. It believes that fifty-year leases can be counted on. You cannot build a growing investment that realistically can be cash flow negative for more than a decade if you are concerned about expropriation or the government reneging on commitments. It is a consumer-oriented company that is prospering from emerging middle-class affluence and desire to reach a higher quality of life.

Grace Vineyard is now run by the founder's intrepid daughter, Judy Chan, and operates boutique shops in leading Chinese cities. Its wine is served in first-class in Cathay Pacific Airlines, is private-labeled by Hong Kong's Peninsula Hotel, and is at the leading edge of a resurgent Chinese wine industry. In fifty years, the *New York Times* reported in its annual "Year in Ideas," Chinese wine could rival the finest Bordeaux. "Grace Vineyards," the *Times* noted, "points to the country's potential."[20]

Haidilao. Our third example, Haidilao, began in central China with the creation of a six-table hotpot restaurant run by a high school dropout on a part-time, after-hours basis with the aid of his family.[21] Built around meticulous quality-control processes, overwhelming focus on service and friendliness (in a country once not known for either in the restaurant business), and driven by the owner's passion, it was soon drawing long lines of waiting customers. Today, it ranks twentieth in China's one hundred top dining enterprises and has fifty large hotpot restaurants across the country, including Beijing, that run twenty-four hours a day, seven days a week. Haidilao is prospering mightily in 2014 and currently has fourteen thousand employees. It has recently opened a US branch.

Haidilao's success is all built on the personal touch and a quality of caring from the bottom to the top. Not a single MBA works there. Quality control and friendliness dominate the sites, which often have three generations of workers from a family from a rural village toiling side by side. Families are queuing up from the home villages to get jobs at Haidilao (which takes care of their every need in the city from housing to schooling). Capital is its only major growth constraint. Haidilao cannot get bank loans, and it does not sell franchises. The owner expressed his strong personal bias toward retaining control in discussions with one of the authors. Selling stock is not an option for him—this is a one-person corporate vision. It is a company in which the government has no strategic interest (apart from standard questions of public health). Quality of its service and product, a deep network of relationships to attract and retain staff, careful attention to cash flow, and a deeply committed and driven CEO have been the drivers of success.

In summary, much of China's growth over the past thirty years has depended on an extraordinary cadre of entrepreneurs who have led the way toward building the foundations of a consumer-led economy. Important needs of consumers have not and will not be filled by the state-owned enterprises that have been so important in the infrastructure renovation and build-out. They can be filled only by the energy and creativity of private entrepreneurs and the companies they build and grow to deliver new products and services.

As we have seen, the life of an entrepreneur is not easy in China, and that of a foreign entrepreneur can be more challenging still.

But the reality today is that more than 50 percent of the economy, and much more of the growth, comes from the private sector. In short, the long-term growth and health of the Chinese economy depends on entrepreneurs. At every step along the way, however, there are hidden government hurdles at the local, provincial, and national levels as well as infrastructure opportunities and lags that must be understood and mastered by any entrepreneur who is to be successful.

Private Entrepreneurs in the Shadow of Goliath

The narratives above tell a story of a series of powerful successes along with instructive failures. Why then are Chinese private-sector CEOs so worried about the future? Why do they fear the state that has built so much of the infrastructure on which their success has been partly dependent? Why do so many seek to send their assets—and indeed, their children—abroad?

One answer lies in the observation of Chen Dongsheng, the chairman of Taikang Life Insurance Company and the cofounder of the Chinese Entrepreneurs' Forum, whom we met in chapter 1. Noting that the first decade of the twenty-first century had been a "golden decade" for private firms, he also noted that it had witnessed a powerful resurgence of state-owned enterprises at every level.

The main competitor for the CP Group, for example, is not another private or foreign firm, but the vast state-run foodstuffs company COFCO, the China National Cereals, Oils, and Foodstuffs Corporation.[22] COFCO dates from the early Maoist period and is the nation's largest food processor, manufacturer, and merchant of agricultural products and one of China's largest state-owned enterprises. It provides competition to virtually every private player in agribusiness. Grace Vineyard, for example, must contend with the ubiquitous Great Wall wines produced in bulk by COFCO, 95 percent of which are bottled and labeled as of Chinese origin, but perhaps half of which contain unlabeled and undistinguished imported vat wines.

At the local level, small start-up firms can find themselves completely at the mercy of regional officials whose power is unchecked. A decade ago, remote Jingbian County in northern Shaanxi Province was the site of some four thousand small oil wells opened by private entrepreneurs and small-scale investors, producing 2 to 3 percent of China's output of crude oil. They had bought their drilling rights legally from the local government. But they were too successful. The monopolistic ambitions of the China National Petroleum Corporation and Shaanxi Yanchang Petroleum, the regional state-owned petroleum company, led to the abrogation of contracts and the confiscation of private wells. Local Chinese Communist Party leaders became executives of the regional state-owned corporation, and the entrepreneurs who sued to get their assets back were arrested and jailed for disturbing the peace. To paraphrase former premier Zhu Rongji again: *"Guojin mintui"*—the state advances, the private sector retreats."[23]

We conclude by quoting China's most visibly successful and innovative entrepreneur, Jack Ma of Alibaba.[24] At the 2011 annual gathering of his Taobao employees in Hangzhou, the capital of China's leading private enterprises, Ma talked about the difference between Alibaba and Taobao on the one hand, and state-owned enterprises on the other. "They are big because they are state-owned," he shouted. "We are big because we are *good!*" Then, in am imaginative play on words, he noted: "They are the so-called *guoying* [nationally run] companies. We are the truly *guoyou* [national] companies." The real public companies, serving the needs of the people, in other words, were private enterprises: "We are China's real national treasures."

Jack Ma is right. But will his be the vision of the future?

We conclude this chapter with a series of questions, the tone and shape of which should begin to seem familiar.

Doing Business in China

- Does my firm know key ministries and Party organizations that influence our success? Do we know the key people, and are we regularly interacting with them and their subordinates? Who are the up-and-coming leaders in the Party and government organizations with which we must deal?

- Does my firm know the key local municipal and government units and Party structure that influence our success? Are we interacting with key individuals and their subordinates?

- What unique contributions and technologies does my firm bring to China? Are we emphasizing them in all our Party and government conversations? What will our future contributions be?

- What unique contributions and technologies is my firm bringing to the province and city? Are we clearly communicating with them? What will our future contributions be?

- What emergent hardware or software infrastructures will impact our products and operations? Are we prepared for them?

- Is my firm building a competitive brand? Is it both nationally and regionally focused?

- Does my firm have appropriate regional marketing strategies? Are they evolving?

6

GLOBAL CHINA

The Limits of Power

China now stands as the second-largest economy in the world, earlier surpassing Germany in volume of manufacturing exports, and with a presence in all parts of the globe. A geographic and not a political entity before 1912, China moved in the mid-twentieth century from being a ward, if not semicolony, of the great powers to being a great power in its own right. While from Chinese perspectives, the history of China's globalization has often been told as a story of invasion and degradation, today much of the world sees China as actively contending for global power and influence.

China's global rise can been seen in the rapid growth of Chinese firms and their exports. Seventy-six of the *Fortune* Global 500 companies in 2012 are Chinese firms, second in number only to those of the United States (see table 2-2 for a list of the top twenty Chinese firms). China's balance of trade with the United States has been massively in China's favor (see figure 6-1 for the history of the past twenty-seven years), and despite steady revaluation of the RMB in recent years (see figure 6-2), this pattern has furthered accusations that China's growth has damaged mainstays of American manufacturing, such as textiles and steel, as well as new industries, including solar power and other clean energy technologies.

In sum, while modern China has always been deeply involved in the global economy, today Chinese firms are trading, investing, and buying companies around the world from a position of increasing strength.

FIGURE 6-1

US trade with China (1985–2012)

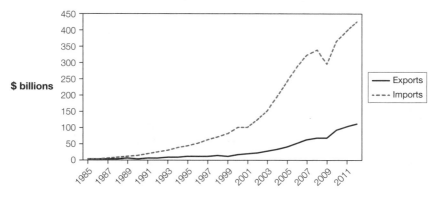

Source: US Department of Commerce, Bureau of the Census, Foreign Trade Division, http://www.census .gov/foreign-trade/balance/c5700.html#1985.

FIGURE 6-2

Revaluation of the Chinese RMB

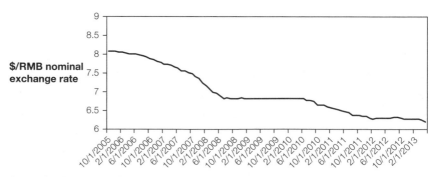

Source: OANDA rates, http://www.oanda.com/currency/historical-rates/.

China in the World: Tools of Engagement

At the start of the new millennium, Chinese businesses were encouraged to go global, and they have done so on a large scale. General Secretary Jiang Zemin stated at the 2002 sixteenth Party Congress that overseas expansion would give rise to "strong multinational enterprises and [Chinese] brand names."[1]

Three government institutions helped Chinese firms to expand operations internationally while preserving the government's supervisory oversight of business activities.

- *Export-Import Bank of China:* The Export-Import Bank of China (Ex-Im Bank), established in 1994, offers credits to exporters and their buyers, facilitating the entry of Chinese businesses into new markets. With lines of credits in billions of US dollars, Chinese telecommunication companies such as Huawei and ZTE have been able to compete successfully in both Africa and Asia. According to its annual reports, the Ex-Im disperses funds to a wider range of firms and industries than does the Export-Import Bank of the United States. The US policy bank lends overwhelmingly to the air transportation industry—47 percent of its $75 billion portfolio in 2010.[2] That same year, the Ex-Im disbursed a roughly similar amount of loans amounting to RMB 426 billion, worth about $64 billion at the time.[3]

- *China Development Bank:* The China Development Bank (CDB), also established in 1994, was initially under a mandate to support improvements in China's domestic infrastructure and the upgrading of key industries. In 1998, Chen Yuan was named head of the bank. He is the son of Chen Yun, a founding father of the People's Republic of China who held leading positions in economic policy. Chen Yuan transformed the China Development Bank into a financial success, partly by taking the Bank beyond its original domestic mission. By 2010, the CDB had $678 billion in outstanding loans on its books, more than twice those of the World Bank.[4] Of these, nearly 25 percent were foreign currency loans, an indicator of the volume of support available to Chinese firms and their customers.

- *State-Owned Asset Supervision and Administration Commission:* The State-Owned Asset Supervision and Administration Commission (SASAC), established in 2003, was intended to oversee the modernization of the public enterprise system through oversight of the hundred-plus central government–controlled state-owned enterprises and their subsidiaries. While SASAC does not directly control these operations, it nonetheless successfully pushed through a number of corporate governance reforms, including mergers and acquisitions within strategic sectors. In 2006, it also mandated that all central government–controlled state-owned enterprises issue corporate social responsibility reports. This requirement indicated interest not only in improving government oversight but also in enhancing the global reputation of China's increasingly global state-owned businesses. China has now among the largest number of corporate signatories to the United Nations Global Compact, a voluntary code of conduct for global enterprises aiming to align business practices with best practices relating to labor, economic, and social rights.

COSCO is a paradigmatic example of a state-owned firm that has prospered through the government's embrace of globalization. The second-largest shipping company in the world today, it was little known a few decades ago.[5] Even then, however, the company was taking steps to become globally competitive. Its expansion began with a drive to obtain knowledge of global best practices. In 1979, COSCO signed a crewing contract with one of Japan's leading shipping companies, allowing COSCO employees to improve their training. That same year, one of its merchant ships sailed to Seattle, the first Chinese ship to do so since 1949.

Beginning in the late 1990s, under the leadership of chairman and CEO Wei Jiafu, the company shook up its internal operations and built up its overseas partnerships, including a 49 percent stake in one of Singapore's port terminals, the second-busiest in the world. COSCO also took stakes in several US ports, in addition to Belgium's Antwerp and the Suez Canal Container Terminal in Egypt.[6] COSCO today employs eighty thousand people around the world.

Other Chinese state-owned companies have followed a similar pattern, enhancing global competitiveness first by seeking technology transfers from abroad and later through foreign acquisitions made possible through the support of China Ex-Im, the China Development Bank, and SASAC. The results are hard to miss. Of the seventy-six Chinese firms on *Fortune*'s Global 500, three have made it to the top ten. These new global giants are overwhelmingly state-owned businesses. Their success is attributable to many causes, but government financial support for global expansion has been a key factor.

How Did This Happen? Forces from the Past, 1912–1978

China was a new country, albeit with a proud tradition, when the Republic was founded in 1912. The definition and defense of the new Chinese state took place in an environment of inescapable internationalization at home. This was most obvious in the cities, such as Shanghai, with its paved streets, electric lights, public parks, and big movie houses showing mostly Hollywood films, not to mention the thousands of foreigners who lived there. But internationalization was also evident across the country, wherever rail lines were laid with foreign financing; or in the skies, where Pan American and Lufthansa introduced civil aviation to China in partnership with the Chinese government.[7] Even remote areas could be changed overnight by the force of the international economy.

Take the case of Dayu County, in southwestern Jiangxi Province, which in the twentieth century enjoyed dramatic incorporation into global markets. This former prefectural seat had for centuries been a major trading depot on one of the most frequented trading routes linking Canton to east central China. As French historian Jean-Baptiste du Halde described the city in 1736, it was "as large as Orléans [ca. one-hundred thousand], populous and handsome, has a great trade, and is a place of much resort."[8] Dayu prospered during the era when all Chinese foreign trade went in and out of Canton (Guangzhou), trafficking in tea, silk, and opium. But by the mid-nineteenth century, Dayu's decline had begun. The expansion of the treaty-port system and the growth of Shanghai turned Dayu into a backwater.[9]

Then tungsten was found at Dayu. It was discovered in the late nineteenth century by a foreign missionary who owned property at nearby Xihua Mountain, which, it turned out, held the largest concentration of wolframite—the ore from which tungsten is mined—in the world. In 1906, a frenetic land rush ensued; the mountain was subdivided into hundreds of smallholdings, with twenty thousand miners extracting the world's most valuable strategic ore.[10] Dayu became a boomtown. It developed a thriving market for delicate silks, imported Western woolens, and even Western cosmetics. Teahouses and wine houses thrived. Dayu enjoyed two decades in the sun as the center of the world's tungsten trade—with an extraordinary boom during World War I, since tungsten, from which some of the hardest steels are made, was central to Western armaments industries. From the 1930s onward, Chinese governments owned the mines and controlled the exports of this first generation of rare earth elements, of which China had 85 percent of the world's reserves. Government tungsten mining largely funded China's international aid in World War II and subsequent imports from the Soviet Union in the People's Republic's First Five-Year plan.[11]

The silk industry illustrates a different set of issues and challenges. Inferior Chinese quality and marketing had endangered one of the nation's most important export industries. In 1932, the national and provincial governments worked with the Silk Reform Association of private industrialists to set national quality standards for silk manufacture that were designed above all to meet international standards.[12]

These reforms—largely successful—were first steps not just toward the nationalization of these industries but also toward their internationalization.[13] The Chinese state internalized international standards and made them its own. This strategy continues today, not just in mining and textiles but also in telecommunications and other sectors where Chinese state planners and industry associations hope to reap benefits from the scale of Chinese production and markets, compelling foreign and local manufacturers to adhere to a "China standard."

Cultural and Economic Internationalism

Internationalization went well beyond mining and manufacture. In education, for example, as noted in chapter 4, the first half of the twentieth century was an era of vibrant, initially uncoordinated, international educational exchange. The campuses of many of China's great universities today—Peking University, Tsinghua University, Nanjing University, Fudan University—were built on the physical and intellectual infrastructure of Sino-foreign colleges and universities that had begun to flourish a century ago.

The greatest international schools of all were simply the treaty ports. Those great cities were multicultural arenas of learning, meeting, and Nationalist conflict. Their heyday coincided with Chinese capitalism's first "golden age" and the rise of China's first middle class and of an internationally oriented intelligentsia. Just as today's great Chinese cities house business and cultural sojourners from around the globe, the treaty ports gave us the best examples of the world of pre-Communist China's "private" foreign relations.[14] Then, as now, almost all important Chinese businesses had vital international connections, even as almost all had Nationalistic ownership.[15]

The Rong family (introduced in chapter 2) established a series of successful light industries. Founder Rong Zongjing became the richest man in pre-Communist China. His sons and sons-in-law were sent abroad for education to keep abreast of the business and technical challenges in the global textile industry.[16]

The Esquel Group, introduced in chapter 5, shows the endurance of international connections over generations in a Chinese family business. Today's Esquel is a Hong Kong–based, $1 billion company that manufactures high-end shirts and other apparel. It is the direct descendent of the Mayar Silk Mills of Republican-era Shanghai. Its founder, Tsai Shengbai (or Cai Shengbai), was educated at the American-funded Tsinghua College and at Lehigh University. He "westernized" industrial practices and technology in the silk industry and made Mayar one of the earliest Chinese firms to gain substantial export markets for light industrial products. His successors in the family businesses combined international education in China (St. John's University in Shanghai) and abroad (Lowell Textile Institute) and, more recently, Harvard Business School and Harvard College. Now in its fourth generation as a leading international textile firm, Esquel is an international company still rooted in China.[17]

National Models

Internationalization has been at the heart of Chinese politics, too. The new Chinese republic experimented with a multiplicity of foreign political models: parliamentary democracy, military dictatorship, and Communism, among them. It sought to learn directly from two foreign mentors, first Germany, then the Soviet Union.

Under the Nationalist regime of Chiang Kai-shek in the decade from 1927 to 1938, China's closest relations were with Germany. A German military mission reorganized the Nationalist army, and its leading members served as Chiang's personal political and economic advisers. In the mid-1930s, Sino-German trading, credit, and technical assistance agreements laid the foundation for China's nationalized industries. At the same time, a German industry program subsidized the education of Chinese technical manpower.

Returning students from Germany increasingly staffed Chinese agencies in control of industrial and military modernization.

The Chinese-German relationship was undone in the late 1930s by politics. Hitler's "world policy" of conquest and his determination to forge an alliance with Japan led China to seek other partners.

With regard to the Soviet Union, we must always recall that without the Soviet Union there would be no Chinese Communist Party. Given Mao Zedong's strenuous efforts to brand his own form of communism, it is easy to forget how strongly Chinese Communism was connected to international forces in its youth and how deeply it internalized Soviet forms of political discipline and organization.[18] Indeed, the rituals of Communist rule in today's People's Republic would be instantly familiar to any citizen of the former Soviet Union.

After the Communist seizure of power, the Chinese-Soviet alliance defined the political economy of the early People's Republic. This was an alliance of (initially) shared ideology and built on decades of Soviet mentoring of the CCP. It was the most fully articulated military alliance in China's history. It was also a cultural and educational alliance, with thousands of Chinese studying in the USSR and thousands of Russians teaching in China. And it was an economic alliance of greater depth and complexity than any of modern China's foreign economic relationships. China was the beneficiary of the largest planned transfer of technology in world history, giving the People's Republic a new core of state industries.

The scope of the Sino-Soviet exchange is still breathtaking: the construction of over two hundred industrial projects, mostly as turnkey (fully finished) installations, which became the core of the Communist state industrial sector; the transfer of thousands of industrial designs; the visit of perhaps ten thousand Soviet and East European specialists to China and of over fifty thousand Chinese engineers, trainees, and students to the Soviet Union and its European allies.[19] The concept of intellectual property was so alien to the Soviet bloc that scientific-technical documentation, including blueprints, was provided without direct compensation. China was charged for the physical machinery, but the technology was basically free. (Perhaps this explains the rather cavalier attitudes toward intellectual property in today's China!) As with Sino-German relations a generation earlier, the tensions that ultimately undid the Sino-Soviet alliance emerged in politics, not economics, particularly Mao Zedong's attempt to become Stalin's successor as the leader of international Communism.

The United States, of course, played a central role in China as well, especially during the four years of their anti-Japanese alliance from 1941 to 1944. They were strategic partners with a common enemy. But unlike the cases of Germany and the Soviet Union, there was no strong, preexisting foundation for this alliance (not in trade, ideology, or personal relationships) before it was forged by the Japanese attack on Pearl Harbor. Perhaps that is why it foundered so quickly after the war.[20] In fact, until this wartime alliance, Chinese-American relations were of central importance to neither nation. From 1949 to 1972, China and the United States became antagonists on different sides of the global cold war.

Unintentional Internationalization: Nixon in China

In returning to global political and economic engagement near the end of the Cultural Revolution, China was assisted by an unlikely source—US president Richard Nixon, an ardent anti-Communist. Nixon traveled to China in 1972. While few events in the world of international politics deserve to be called "Diplomatic Revolution," this was one (see "Key Moments in US-China Diplomatic Relations" for the history of US-China relations since Nixon's visit). The anti-Soviet entente that emerged from his visit gave both Washington and Beijing welcome leverage against a mutual adversary, the Soviet Union. As was true of the Chinese-American alliance of 1942–1945, Chinese-American relations in the 1970s were defined almost exclusively in terms of what they were against: a common enemy.

Key Moments in US-China Diplomatic Relations

April 1971: A US Ping-Pong team visits China, the first US delegation to receive an invitation to visit China since 1949. The visit signals the mutual desire to restore China-US contacts after more than two decades of enmity.

February 1972: US president Richard Nixon conducts a state visit to China, resulting in the Shanghai Communiqué that sets the foundation for diplomatic relations between the two countries.

January 1979: China and the United States officially establish diplomatic relations at the ambassadorial level. The United States announces it will sever diplomatic relations with the Republic of China on Taiwan, withdraw its troops from that island, and terminate the US-Taiwan Mutual Defense Treaty by January 1980. Weeks later, Chinese vice premier Deng Xiaoping becomes the first leader of the People's Republic of China to visit the United States.

August 1982: China and the United States issue the August 17 Communiqué, which aims to gradually reduce US arms sales to Taiwan.

June 1989: The massacre in Tiananmen Square leads the United States, together with its allies, to impose a series of diplomatic and economic sanctions against China.

March 1996: China conducts military exercises in the Taiwan Strait, apparently to intimidate the Taiwanese electorate before pending presidential elections. The move triggers the third Taiwan Strait Crisis. The United States dispatches two aircraft carrier battle groups to the region. Subsequently, tensions in the Taiwan Strait diminish and relations between the United States and China improve.

(continued)

October 1997: Chinese president Jiang Zemin visits Washington. Jiang and US president Bill Clinton agree to establish a regular consultation mechanism for defense. Two months later, senior defense officials hold the first-ever bilateral defense consultations.

April 1999: Premier Zhu Rongji signs a joint statement with President Clinton on China's accession to the World Trade Organization (WTO). Five months later, China and the United States sign a bilateral agreement on China's accession to the WTO.

August 2005: Chinese vice foreign minister Dai Bingguo and US deputy secretary of state Robert Zoellick co-chair the first China-US Strategic Dialogue in Beijing. In subsequent years it is held regularly in rotation between China and the United States.

August 2008: President George W. Bush attends the opening ceremony of the Beijing Olympic Games.

April 2009: Chinese president Hu Jintao and US President Barack Obama hold a meeting in London, the first of this kind for the two leaders. During the meeting, they decide to expand the strategic dialogue as the "China-US Strategic and Economic Dialogues."

June 2013: Chinese president Xi Jinping and US President Barack Obama carry out a two-day informal "summit" (no ties required) in Rancho Mirage, California. Cybercrime is a major theme.

What were Chinese-American relations *for* during and after President Nixon's visit? We always ask this question when we assign our students the minutes of the meeting between Nixon and Mao Zedong of February 21, 1972. We ask them what Nixon and Mao had discussed related to trade. They are silent, for good reason. Mao and Nixon made no mention of trade and had no vision of the world in which we now live. Nonetheless, China's extraordinary economic growth, predicated on its reentry into global systems of trade, has made it today what it clearly was not in 1972: an economic power of the first rank. The United States and China are now economically interdependent and interculturally connected as never before.

If the American government had known how unstable China was in the autumn of 1971, when Nixon's visit was planned (its knowledge of the Lin Biao incident—an apparent *coup d'état* attempt, followed by a purge—was sketchy at best), and how unsound, medically and mentally, Mao Zedong himself was at that time, or if it had known the full scope of the disasters wrought under CCP leadership, the American president would never have gone to China. But bad intelligence has never deterred American foreign policy. So Nixon went, and a diplomatic revolution ensued.

Re-engagement: The New US-China Relationship

When Mao Zedong died in 1976, Maoism died with him. In late 1978, Deng Xiaoping succeeded Mao as China's "paramount leader" and permitted a decade of openness and experimentation, including with the United States.

For the first time, US-China relations became of preeminent importance to both nations. American businesses dreamed, as their forefathers had, of a vast "China market." Chinese firms—all state-owned enterprises at first—sought foreign investment and expertise. Between 1979 and 2011, trade volume between the United States and China increased from $2 billion to $503 billion, and decidedly in China's favor.[21] With this growth came an infusion of well-known Western brands into China and cross-cultural mixes that included weddings in KFC and a Starbucks in the Forbidden City (for a time). Buicks were also driven on Chinese streets for the first time since 1949, but they were now "Made in China."

In 1980, China was granted preferential access to the US market. The most-favored-nation or normal-trade-relation status allowed China to export goods to the United States at tariff rates lower than nations lacking this privilege. In turn, China promised US businesses fertile partnerships and strong commitments. Several large US businesses rapidly entered the market. In some cases (AIG, Coca-Cola), they were returning to a market they had been forced to leave in 1949.

For old and new entrants in the early days of renewed Sino-American trade, China's business climate was challenging. The foreign and Chinese sides entered into partnerships with different goals. The first wave of foreign investors aimed to sell to what they hoped would be a huge Chinese domestic market. The Chinese partners, however, wanted American technology more than American consumer products. The paradigmatic case here is Beijing Jeep, a joint venture between two struggling firms, the American Motors Corporation (AMC) and Beijing Automotive Works (BAW).

To this day, the Beijing Jeep case, nicely chronicled by James Mann, is an important example of how not to structure market entry to China.[22] Not only was the foreign investor stunned to find that it had little real say in the business development strategy of its joint venture with BAW, but over time, the US company faced exit-related problems, foremost among them repatriation of its profits. AMC wanted to export the Jeep Cherokee in kits for assembly in China and for sale to Chinese businesses and consumers. BAW wanted to build the traditional Jeep—the kind soldiers could easily jump out of—for the People's Liberation Army.

There were, in short, fundamental disagreements about product, customers, and strategy, all of which led to disastrous results. Beijing Jeep, born as a symbol of Sino-American cooperation, became a metaphor for the mutual incomprehension that marked many of the deals of the 1980s.

At the (re)start of their relationship, the governments of China and the United States aimed to defend their own domestic political interests. In the early 1980s, the CCP waged a campaign against "bourgeois liberalization" even as American goods and films were making their way to Shanghai ports. China-bashing became an expected part of every US presidential campaign after 1980. The greatest challenge, however, came in 1989, when Chinese leaders proved themselves, in the eyes of disillusioned Americans, to be—as Bill Clinton later put it—"butchers of Beijing." The government's assault on civilian demonstrators in Tiananmen Square appalled the world. Particularly shocked were American friends of China who had allowed their aspirations for Deng Xiaoping's rule to cloud their understanding of the regime's determination to retain its grip on power.

Many foreign companies left China. Most returned in due course. Since 1989, Chinese-American business, cultural, and educational relations have all deepened significantly, but political relations still bear the strain of the very different belief systems that underlie the two political systems. Instead of the antagonisms of the Cold War era or the easy good feelings of the immediate post-Mao period, relations between the two governments grew more professional, more sober, and more predictable in the 1990s.

Since the early 1990s, major American companies have argued the virtues of constructive engagement with China. Opposing this have been interests representing organized labor, human rights activists, Taiwan and Tibet supporters, anti-Communists, and low-end US producers, among others, in fear of the "Made in China" phenomenon.

Microsoft, a strong supporter of engagement, eventually came to embody a spirit of "all-in" commitment to the Chinese market. This emerged only after a history of frustration. Shortly after its 1992 arrival to China, the company was vocal in its unhappiness with intellectual property rights (IPR) violations occurring there. Nonetheless, its Chinese country manager dissuaded headquarters from its continuing legal threats against IPR violators. Microsoft stayed in China but pursued a strategy of engagement. It built an R&D center in Beijing in 1998 and established relations with several Chinese universities, signaling a spirit of collaboration instead of raw competition. It also forged closer links with its government partners through an agreement to share its software code in exchange for improved enforcement of Microsoft's IPR within their respective offices.

Other US firms also ventured deeply into Chinese markets in anticipation of trade normalization. None were more anxious to take on this role than US automakers and the American aerospace industry. Both had been active within China before 1989. Promising to change China through economic commitment, these firms devoted considerable resources to lobby US politicians, arguing that anything less than "engagement" with China would give Japanese and European competitors an advantage in the China market.

At the same time, China learned how to engage in American politics. Periodic "Buying from America" campaigns in the run-up to congressional hearings helped to ensure that its most-favored-nation status remained secure. Also working in China's favor was the fact that the bulk of "Chinese" exports to the United States came from American firms manufacturing there. A strike against China thus was also a hit on American stock portfolios. These factors helped thaw the economic frost imposed in the wake of 1989's tragic events. In 1991, the Chinese government contracted to buy over $130 million of auto parts and cars from Chrysler, General Motors, and Ford.[23]

Less than a year later, McDonnell Douglas received a $1.6 billion contract to supply forty new jetliners, all to be made in China. The company had already been coproducing MD-82 jetliners in Shanghai. Now, however, it promised to allow its China partners a hand in airplane design. While the Chinese government used the lure of an enormous market to win concessions from American businesses and gain access to new technologies, the US government used the same dynamic to advance its line of strategic political and economic interests.

In 1992—more than a decade after the first US-China trade agreement had been signed—the United States and China signed their first memorandum of understanding on intellectual property rights. Much like agreements to follow, each memorandum was preceded by a US threat of trade sanctions. The intricate play of business contract signings and political threats yielded results. China gradually opened its market to a wider range of American goods, while US politicians stood on principles that they ultimately bent. Finally, in 2000, China was granted permanent normal trade relations with the United States, setting it on course to enter the World Trade Organization (WTO).

On October 10, 2000, President Clinton signed legislation granting China permanent normal trade relations with the United States. US exporters, especially in the agricultural sector, were thrilled. Those directly investing in China also expected a positive return. Textile and other light industrial manufacturers foresaw decline, and the bargaining position of US organized labor in protecting American jobs was diminished.

China's Accession to the World Trade Organization

China's leaders saw China's accession to the WTO as a way to open further the Chinese economic system without venturing into the impossible zone of political liberalization. No one better represented this sentiment than Premier Zhu Rongji, who used China's WTO negotiations as a wake-up call to expand political and economic domestic reforms. None was more controversial than moving the Chinese state from a central planning role to that of a regulator. This move meant banning government ministries from running their own businesses, leading to huge restructurings and spin-outs of new companies. The reality of global competition inside China permitted Zhu Rongji to begin the first major reform of state-owned enterprises.

While seemingly everywhere, many Chinese state-owned enterprises were going nowhere. In China's northeastern rust belt, for example, many firms could not adapt to market pressures and survived only through state recognition of their role as employers. The subsidies provided to these firms deeply indebted local governments.

In 1998, Zhu Rongji called for China to "grasp the big and let go of the small" state-owned enterprises. This was followed by a wave of privatization, mergers, and outright closures of businesses. One hundred state-owned industries in key sectors were separated from the ministries that controlled them and were permitted to draw up their own economic plans and financing, as well as participate directly in foreign trade. The list gradually expanded, reaching 520 top state-owned enterprises in 1999, of which 196 central-level enterprises were identified as critical to the country's national development goals. These companies were corporatized, with the state retaining a role as a majority shareholder. The firms were given latitude to design their own development path as long as they could emerge within a few years as China's "national champions" that could compete globally.

The Chinese government took the position that the competitiveness of Chinese businesses had to begin with reform of its own internal systems. In the context of China, this took great courage, as many sacred cows of socialism would no longer be worshipped. Foremost was the elimination of the "iron rice bowl," a birth-to-grave social welfare guarantee offered to urban citizens. Guarantee of employment also ended for this privileged segment. In their place, real estate, insurance, and health care businesses emerged, all willing to tend to the people of China—for a price. The government chose to retreat or abstain from these roles.

These moves reflected considerable faith in the global economic system to ultimately pull China forward. China acceded to the WTO after fifteen years of negotiation, in December 2001. Its membership signaled a new stage in economic development as well as enhanced global status. Tariffs and other trade barriers had to be gradually dismantled. In return, China was promised equal treatment in other markets and an end to annual scrutiny of its domestic political situation as a price of doing business. Not all Chinese businesses welcomed the advent of additional domestic competition, but the promise of equal treatment going overseas opened new opportunities.

Catching Up in the Race for Resources

The first Chinese firms to go global were those in search of raw commodities to feed the booming economy back home. Hitherto, Chinese companies were compelled to buy their products from non-Chinese multinational firms that had gained control of global resources over the past century. This made for an uneven playing field.

China's desire to rebalance things can be seen in its frustration with the existing system of iron ore purchase pricing. This system enabled the big three producers—Vale do Rio Doce, BHP Billiton, and Rio Tinto—to maintain enormous leverage in global pricing, leaving China with little negotiating space.[24] As China's balance sheet improved, there has been a strong push to obtain these resources directly through acquisitions.

Over the past ten years, China has acquired iron ore reserves in Brazil and South Africa; copper reserves in Afghanistan, Peru, and Chile; zinc and iron ore in Australia; and platinum and gold in spots across Africa. China Guangdong Nuclear Power Corporation's acquisition of Rio Tinto's stake in Kalahari Minerals illustrates the growing, global conception of Chinese economic security.[25] With this deal, the Guangdong-based company controlled the world's second-largest uranium mine, Namibia's Husab uranium project, in which Kalahari holds a 43 percent stake.[26]

Acquisition, however, was not always possible, especially with respect to the state-owned industries of other countries. China's ample financial resources, however, have ensured a steady supply of raw commodities through other means. For example, in 2006, Chile's Codelco agreed to provide 836,250 metric tons of copper over a fifteen-year period to Minmetals, its long-term Chinese trading partner, in exchange for $2 billion funding from the China Development Bank (CDB) to aid the Chilean firm's expansion plans.[27]

In 2009, the CDB gave a $10 billion line of credit to Petrobras, Brazil's national oil corporation. This deal was completed on the condition that Petrobras offer ten years of guaranteed oil shipments to Sinopec, one of China's leading national oil companies—this included 150,000 barrels in the first year, and 200,000 barrels per year for the remaining nine years.[28]

The ability of Chinese businesses to draw on the CDB and other policy banks allowed them to secure raw commodities and gain greater control over critical intermediate inputs, foremost among them petrochemicals and organic materials, critical components for the chemical manufacturing industry.[29] For example, ChemChina, described in chapter 4, achieved much of its growth through strategic acquisitions, giving it global controlling shares of products such as methionine and silicone.[30] As noted in chapter 5, other Chinese firms used overseas acquisitions to secure proprietary technologies. These in turn increased their value-added share within major global value chains, including those for auto parts (Wanxiang), wind turbines (Goldwind), and heavy equipment (SANY).

Chinese state financial support and desire for corporate growth extended to Chinese food security. In 2010, Chinese companies started to provide credit to Brazilian farming communities in exchange for guaranteed supplies of soybean. This move made China less dependent on its other major supplier, the United States.[31] A similar deal was concluded in 2011 between the Beidahuang Group, located in Heilongjiang Province, and the provincial government of Rio Negro, in Argentina. In this case, Chinese funding was used to cultivate unused land and upgrade a nearby port in exchange for the province's guaranteed soybean exports over the next two decades.[32] Most recently, in May 2013, Shuanghui International Holdings announced the largest US acquisition agreement—$4.7 billion for Smithfield Foods, Inc., the world's largest hog farmer and pork producer, located in Smithfield, Virginia.

While Chinese businesses are not unique in their pursuit of overseas farmland and other natural resources, some ventures are of sufficient scale to raise concerns about the Chinese government's desire for enhanced geostrategic control of trade channels.[33] The Gwadar Port deal is particularly instructive here.

In May 2001, Premier Zhu Rongji visited Pakistan to celebrate the fiftieth anniversary of PRC-Pakistani relations. On this occasion, he announced that the Chinese government would underwrite the port's construction, offering $248 million in loans for Phase I of the project, $50 million of which was earmarked as a grant. The Chinese Development Bank played a role in this deal. Once operational, the port, along with supporting road routes, will allow

Western China easier access to sea routes and create an alternative channel by which China may ship goods currently coming through the Straits of Hormuz, including oil. It will also permit the Chinese government to monitor maritime activities in the Arabian Sea.[34] The negotiations survived local opposition in Baluchistan Province, where the Gwadar Port is located, and where several Chinese engineers were killed in 2004.[35] The final obstacle standing in the way of Chinese control of the port was Singapore's PSA International's role as port operator. In August 2012, the Pakistan government negotiated that company's exit, clearing the way for a Chinese investor to assume this role and gain full control of a vital port.[36]

China and the Developing World

Nowhere has the impact of the global expansion of Chinese business been felt more deeply than in Africa and Latin America. For much of the twentieth century, African and Latin American nations made common cause with China in support of political independence and economic development. No global group was more excited about China's rise. Today, no group feels more threatened. China was one of them—a developing country but it has evolved into a formidable competitor.

These tensions were illustrated in the lobbying efforts surrounding elimination of the global Multi-Fiber Arrangement (MFA) in January 2005. Dating to the early 1970s, this agreement divided up the globe in terms of preferential tariffs awarded through quotas to developing world countries to facilitate their export of garments and textiles to developed countries. The system was controversial from the start. For pro–market advocates, a global system of trade quotas went against market forces, inducing countries to continue in an industry where they no longer held a natural comparative advantage. For pro–developing country advocates, the system was unjust because quotas were being granted both with political considerations in mind and with terms of conditionality related to labor, environment, and other items.

As the end of the MFA approached, developing countries campaigned to keep it in place. Complex algorithms predicted how many more Chinese shirts would hit the market and the negative impact on places like Lesotho and Cambodia. Indeed, once China secured its accession to the World Trade Organization, it was developing countries, not the developed world, that brought the largest number of antidumping cases against Chinese businesses.[37]

Many developing countries expected expanded benefits from Chinese aid and investment. The Tanzania Railway, funded by China in the early 1970s, was still running. This $500 million aid project reflected how China viewed its role in the world at that time. China had taken particular interest in countries where it had a "special friendship," a phrase dating back to Maoist era diplomatic discourse. The bonds with many developing world countries were "special" to China because of the pivotal role played in aiding China to unseat Taiwan in the United Nations.

In the 1990s, the country again looked to old friends, only now to help secure resources and markets for its burgeoning economy. China's trade volume with Africa leapt from $3 billion in 1995 to $123 billion in 2010 (see table 6-1 for growth of China's Africa trade over the past decade).[38] Concurrently, many of China's largest

TABLE 6-1

China's trade with Africa (in $ billions)

	2000			2010		
	Exports	**Imports**	**Total**	**Exports**	**Imports**	**Total**
Total	4.9	5.2	10.1	56.0	63.7	119.7
Agricultural products	0.5	0.6	1.1	1.8	2.9	4.7
Fuels and mining products	0.1	4.2	4.3	1.3	57.3	58.6
Manufactures	4.3	0.4	4.7	52.9	3.4	56.3

Source: WTO Trade Statistics. Table generated using the Time Series Statistical Program from the International Trade and Market Access data of the World Trade Organization: http://stat.wto.org/StatisticalProgram/WSDBStatProgramHome.aspx?Language=E.

state-owned enterprises entered Africa through direct investments and aid projects.

Africa remains one of the most difficult places to do business, owing to its limited road network, inadequate electricity grid, corruption, and need for improvements in human capital. Chinese-led infrastructure development projects, financed by concessional lending and aid to partner governments, have focused heavily on lowering these transaction costs. Other projects include housing development, antimalarial centers, biofuel research and development, as well as the provision of doctors, nurses, and teachers across forty-eight African states. Much of this aid is *tied*, meaning that recipient countries must source subsequent procurements through an approved list of Chinese firms.

It is too soon to tell how well these Chinese investments in infrastructure will stand tests of weather, politics, and time. There is little doubt, however, that China's strategy has made an impression. Leaders from the developing world do not hesitate to draw comparisons between Chinese dignitaries who visit their countries for days versus their American counterparts who often stay only a few hours. China has also largely ignored "best practices" put in place by the World Bank, USAID, and IMF to ensure sustainable economic development through anticorruption efforts, stakeholder dialogues, environmental impact assessments, and other measures.

Instead, the Chinese government and firms have vowed not to mix politics and business. This approach allows Chinese deals to move quickly from blueprint to execution, resulting in both the perception and the reality that China is doing more for Africa. Between mid-2008 and mid-2010, China lent $110 billion to Africa and other developing countries.[39] This amount is greater than the commitment of the World Bank to the entire world during the same period. In short, China's direct investment in Africa continues to increase but remains concentrated within the raw commodities and energy sectors.

The Chinese global presence, as illustrated by the examples above, embodies a different model of international development than that of the United States. China chooses to partner with governments rather than looking to nongovernmental organizations and private entrepreneurs to foster development. The Chinese government continues to stress the role of state sovereignty, political stability, and infrastructure conditions as the best means of improving economic welfare. By channeling its aid through its own procurement network, the Chinese government also has avoided the worst forms of aid corruption: the grant that never leaves a developing country's minister's office.

There has also been a long list of Chinese missteps across the African continent—workers shot by Chinese bosses, partnerships with dictators, environmental degradation, fake medicines, demand for banned animal products (especially ivory), and bribery of government officials. None of this has played well in the local and international press, particularly because of the close links between the Chinese state and Chinese business overseas. China has been portrayed as colonialist, mercantilist, and clueless about its profound global impact.[40]

China's diplomatic blunders in Africa highlight a growing schism between how China sees itself and what is expected of it as a major global economic power. On the one hand, China has a growing need of commodity resources, and Chinese leaders believe that only the worst of the world's resources map has been left to them. Prime oil fields, better mines, and fertile farms are largely under contract with conglomerates from the United States and elsewhere, or they are simply not for sale. China feels (and is) at a disadvantage.

On the other hand, Chinese firms often invest abroad with seemingly little self-awareness of their impact or that the Chinese government may be held accountable for the global activities of its state-owned enterprises. Take the case of China in the Sudan. Shortly before the 2008 Olympics, the American actress Mia Farrow accused China of supporting genocide and exposed its role in the provision of small arms to local militia. Despite its stated reluctance to meddle in the internal affairs of other governments, China had become involved in one side of a civil war. The phrase "No Blood for Oil," originally coined in reaction to the first US-Iraq conflict, was now aimed at

China.[41] In 2006, universities such as the ten-campus University of California system and Yale began to divest from the publicly traded arms of Chinese companies doing business in Sudan, such as Petro-China and Sinopec.[42] In 2007, activists began to go after the financial industry itself, pressuring Fidelity and Berkshire Hathaway, among others, to weed out companies with activities in Sudan.[43]

In its involvement in Sudan, China missed multiple opportunities to exert international leadership. For years, it resisted sanctions against the Sudanese government or the authorization of United Nations peacekeepers. The massive violence witnessed against noncombatants in Sudan's civil wars was depicted as an "internal matter." When Sudan officially broke into two parts, in 2011, China found itself on the wrong side, as the now-independent South Sudan took with it the bulk of Sudan's oil riches.[44]

China is also subject to the constraints imposed by African states seeking to control foreign investment. In 2004, Sinosteel was confronted with the Black Empowerment Act, a law that required all South African companies to turn over at least 26 percent equity stake to a local "black" partner. Since Sinosteel initially acquired control of its mines through a joint venture, it meant that successful implementation of the empowerment rule would result in the South African side acquiring a majority share of a business— something that did not sit well with Chinese state-owned company heads back in Beijing.

China and the Developed World

The global impact of Chinese firms is not confined to the developing world. Direct investment in the United States, Canada, and Europe, partly through acquisitions, is growing as well, but often with resistance and adverse publicity. Additionally, Chinese firms have been accused of dumping their products in these markets.

A particularly interesting case has to do with new energy— wind and solar. A decade ago, no one considered Chinese firms to have a lead in these sectors. By 2012, in terms of market share by installed capacity, four Chinese wind turbine manufacturers had made it into the global top ten: Goldwind, Sinovel, United Power, and Ming Yang.[45] Threats of trade sanctions against Chinese wind and solar manufacturers quickly appeared in the United States and European press. US senator Charles Schumer called the Chinese government to task for unfairly subsidizing exports in these sectors even as Chinese firms leapt ahead of their competitors. Sinovel was also accused of stealing proprietary wind turbine technology from its American main supplier. Although firms such as Germany's Siemens and Japan's NEC Corporation have pursued a different strategy vis-à-vis rising Chinese competition—seeking strategic alliances with Chinese counterparts in their home countries, similar to Sino-foreign joint ventures within China—other governments (including India and the United States) have challenged these collaborations, citing national security concerns.

The US government regulates foreign investments through CFIUS (the Committee on Foreign Investment in the United States), to ensure that there is no threat to US national security. CFIUS has prevented Chinese telecommunication companies, such as Huawei and ZTE, from penetrating the US market. In 2013, however, it did approve Wanxiang's acquisition of A123 Systems Inc., the Waltham, Massachusetts–based electric car battery manufacturer, for $250 million in bankruptcy. Wanxiang's record of investing in US auto parts companies (and saving jobs in the process) has given it a strong platform from which to grow.

Chinese acquisitions have hit roadblocks elsewhere, however, and mostly with no predictable pattern. For example, Sinochem's effort to acquire Canada's Potash Corporation, the largest global supplier of this critical agricultural nutrient, never got very far out of concerns that it would upset the dynamics of a market-based economy.[46] Conversely, in July 2012, CNOOC, one of China's national oil companies, was able to acquire Nexen, one of Canada's leading upstream oil and gas companies, for $15 billion.[47]

China Construction America, a subsidiary of the Chinese State Construction Engineering Corporation, one of China's largest state-owned construction companies, has been successfully active in the United States since the mid-1980s, employing unionized American workers, and often for work on local government projects.[48] After it began operations in the United States, CCA slowly built partnerships. Consequently, when it moved to become a more high-profile figure in the real estate and construction industries, it had strong supporters in multiple quarters advocating on its behalf.

It is tempting to think that a well-oiled system exists to align Chinese government interests with the activities of Chinese businesses at home and abroad. Closer scrutiny, however, shows a more complex, often confusing picture of divergent interests not only between government and business but also across government ministries, state-owned enterprises, and private Chinese firms. What is clear is that China's internationalization, measured in the nineteenth and twentieth centuries by the influence and activities of foreigners within China, has taken a new turn as Chinese businesses invest and acquire across the globe.

Global Soft Power

The internationalization of China has been a century and more in the making. As a new country after 1911, China experimented with numerous foreign political models and, at different times, modeled itself after specific foreign nations. Briefly, in the 1960s, it was in fact an international model itself—of an anti-Soviet "people's revolution" that inspired self-styled Maoists from Nepal to Peru. More recently, some describe today's China as a new model of an authoritarian developmental state.

For the first two decades after China's reopening in 1978, the government worked diligently to signal the country's slightness instead of its global significance. But today, China has changed from being a major source of global supply to a major source of global demand. The economic well-being of many developing countries hinges on whether China continues to hunger for their resources. As the Chinese government becomes more involved on the world stage, it has taken on greater global responsibilities in international institutions. (See "China's Growing Leadership in International Organizations"). It and the actions of its firms around the world will also, inevitably, be held to a high standard.

China's Growing Leadership in International Organizations

More Chinese than ever have held key positions in international organizations in recent years, broadening developing countries' influence on the world stage:

United Nations

Wu Hongbo: Under-Secretary-General for Economics and Social Affairs in the United Nations since May 2012. He replaced Sha Zukang, another Chinese official. Wu was formerly the Chinese ambassador to Germany.

He Changchui: Deputy Director-General of the Food and Agriculture Organization (FAO) of the UN from 2009 to 2011. He worked his way up the ranks in the Asia office of FAO.

International Monetary Fund

Zhu Min: In 2011, Zhu Min became the first Chinese to hold the position of deputy managing director of the International Monetary Fund.

World Bank

Justin Yifu Lin: World Bank chief economist and senior vice president who concluded a four-year term in June 2012.

World Health Organization

Margaret Chan: Director-General of the World Health Organization since November 2006. She joined the Hong Kong Department of Health in 1978 and joined the WHO as an expert on communicable diseases in 2003.

International Telecommunications Union

Zhao Houlin: Two-time Deputy Secretary-General of the International Telecommunications Union, elected for a second four-year term in October 2010.

Foreign investments in China, or Chinese investments around the world, have seldom foundered only for business or economic reasons. Political issues have played an important role. This is why China's potential to acquire and exercise what our colleague Joseph Nye would call "soft power," as a complement to its international economic strength, is so important for its future global role.[49] A rising nation with sharp elbows (as in recent disputes in the South China Sea) will also find partnerships more difficult to forge.

The pursuit of soft power is now at the heart of China's public diplomacy, that is, its diplomatic and cultural outreach to nonstate actors. The initial success of some four hundred Confucius Institutes, which teach Chinese language and culture, may be promising, but certainly they are not sufficient. Even less reassuring are the assumptions and insecurities that underlie the pursuit of public diplomacy. As the *People's Daily* wrote in June 2012: "China urgently needs to carry out more effective public diplomacy if it is to overcome the misunderstandings, prejudice and suspicions that people in other countries have toward it."[50]

Soft power is more than favorable newspaper coverage. After all, a main purpose of newspapers in countries with a free press is to print *bad* news and to monitor and criticize government performance. The continued blocking of foreign press and websites in China and the marketing of cheery, boosterish editions of *China Daily* abroad are unlikely to advance the Chinese government's cause, nor is the fact that all 550 publishing houses in the country are arms of the government.

Soft power is rooted in values that others share, or wish to share. In imperial times, Chinese civilization spread throughout East Asia, not primarily by conquest but by emulation. In more recent times, China's emulation of foreign models was rooted in part in its admiration of foreign values, for example those of the Soviet Union.

But what are "Chinese values" today? Is the China model of the engineering and infrastructure state enough? Will the reintroduction of the Chinese humanities to university curricula bring about, in time, a more nuanced sense of the distinguishing features of what it means to be Chinese in the twenty-first century? These are fundamental and difficult questions.

Doing Business in China

- Who are and will be my firm's major Chinese competitors? What are their strengths? Can my firm survive, or should it sell? Does it need new strategic alliances to fend these competitors off?

- Are Chinese companies likely to enter my industry *de novo*? By acquisitions?

- Does my firm possess technologies or natural resources critical to China? If yes, how do we deal with that reality? Do we just sell the firm to a Chinese firm? What are our survival strategies?

- Can my firm be protected through lobbying or calling for governmental intervention? What ethical steps are available to the firm? What are the lines the firm won't cross (e.g., ugly, scorched-earth defense campaigns)?

7

CHINA 2034

The Future in the Light of the Past

They take the long view. They see history on their side.

—Henry Kissinger, on Chinese leaders (1972)

The Mandate of Heaven does not last forever.

—Sun Yat-sen

Beijing, 1900

On the twenty-fifth day of the fifth month of the twenty-sixth year of the reign of the Emperor Guangxu, or June 21, 1900, the Empress Dowager of the Great Qing Empire declared war on the world. Qing forces besieged the foreign legations in Beijing. Thus the first world war of the twentieth century took the form of an extended hostage drama—the famous *Fifty-five Days at Peking*, as Hollywood would later film it—when Charlton Heston and Ava Gardner held out against 450 million Chinese before an international expeditionary force could ride to their rescue.

An international force of only twenty thousand men made quick work of the regular Qing forces as well as of the "Boxer" irregulars who had incited the Qing's ill-fated crusade. They sacked and plundered Beijing, occupied its ancient palaces, and devastated the surrounding countryside with punitive expeditions. The Celestial Court, which had fled the Forbidden City in disguise, in donkey carts, finally submitted to terms that included an enormous indemnity—four times the Qing's annual revenue—to be paid through the year 1940.

How the world changes. Little more than a century earlier, at the time of the American Revolution, the Qing empire had presided over the strongest, richest, and most sophisticated civilization on the planet. It was supremely self-confident. It ruled China and dominated East Asia by a combination of power and cultural prestige. Its civil service, wherein the most learned men in the realm joined the government, was the envy of Europe. The imperial economy was the largest in the world. The richest men in the world lived in China.

By 1900, however, China had been invaded, defeated, and degraded first by Western nations and then by Japan. The Boxer War was a final, futile act of resistance by a government, and indeed an entire system of governance, that would be blown away. When the Qing finally fell eleven years later, an imperial tradition of more than two thousand years came to an end.

Beijing, 2014

A little more than a century after the Boxer War, China is again a great power. Beijing is once more the capital of a multiethnic empire that dominates East Asia. Its leaders live and work in the shadow of the Forbidden City. Beijing no longer threatens foreigners; it welcomes them, recently as the proud host of a magnificent Olympic Games. Foreign students flock to Beijing and elsewhere in China to study, live, and work. They disembark at stunning airports, the likes of which they may never see in their own countries. They travel across the land by high-speed train lines at some three hundred kilometers per hour. They study at new and renewed Chinese universities, which are rising in world rankings and boast facilities of which many foreign universities can only dream. They can shop anywhere from Huaihai Road in Shanghai to Liberation Square in Chongqing at a wealth of international and Chinese stores catering to an increasingly affluent Chinese middle class.

That middle class has visions of a prosperous country not unlike those widely held in the United States in the 1950s: owning a home (80 percent of Chinese middle-class families do, and mostly without a mortgage) and a car (30 percent do, and the rest want one); a national network of modern highways on which to drive; and a college education for one's child.[1] For them, the "China Dream" of which President Xi Jinping has spoken looks much like the "American Dream" of the twentieth century. This middle class lives in a country that seems strong, has a powerful government, appears respected in the world, and for the first extended time in its modern history faces no real external threats to its security. How can this not be the "prosperous age," the *shengshi*, of the People's Republic of China, the high point of all successful Chinese dynasties?

Chinese models of economic development, education, and infrastructure are studied, and sometimes envied, the world over. Chinese language and culture are spread in part by more than three hundred Confucius Institutes in one hundred countries. China is the second-largest economy on earth, and within fifteen years will again be the first. Leading Chinese entrepreneurs are renowned at home and abroad. An increasing number of the world's richest people are again Chinese. As noted earlier, many of the world's largest companies are Chinese. The prospects for China seem limitless. Its return to preeminence seems assured. How can China *not* lead?

The Western plunderers of the Boxer War in 1900 could not have imagined the unified and increasingly prosperous China of 2014.

Neither could China's poor and malnourished population of the Maoist era ever dare dream of the prosperous and mobile society emerging today. The past, in short, is much easier to predict than the future.

We began this book by quoting the titles of many others that predict that the twenty-first century will be the "Chinese century": *The Dragon Awakes*; *China's Rise*; *The Rise of China*; *China's Ascent*; *As China Goes, So Goes the World*; and *When China Rules the World*. So, will China "rule the world"? By this, we don't mean political dominion, but broad, compelling influence in global politics, economics, and culture in a manner that made the twentieth century, by some measures, the "American century."

We have reviewed in this book stories of remarkable success and stunning setbacks; of bottom-up private entrepreneurship and top-down bureaucratic capitalism; of an unmatched and unchecked culture of engineering ambition; of rote learning and educational experimentation; of sophisticated tastes and basic concerns with food safety; of a China at once cosmopolitan and confused in its new global roles. How do we now imagine the China we will encounter twenty years from now?

Beijing, 2034

Beijing is, of course, not China, though it is often a metaphor for it. This northernmost outpost on the North China Plain became a capital city under the Mongols, and for much of past seven hundred years it has been a center of political and cultural power. It is an open question, however, whether Beijing will remain the capital in 2034. Will it physically be sustainable, or will it be a casualty of China's economic growth and environmental degradation? Will its ministries continue the infrastructure state of the twentieth century well into the twenty-first? Will its universities lead China to international leadership in education? Will it be a center of global influence? And will the current regime, or some semblance of it, still be in power? And if not, what does that mean for the rest of us?

Environment

Beijing *is* a metaphor for China when it comes to environmental issues. Its notoriously bad air, caused by local and regional pollutants, as well as inner Asian sandstorms, improved only temporarily during the 2008 Olympics. Water for this municipality of 20 million is increasingly in short supply. Once-famous springs have disappeared and reservoirs have run dry, as have many of the streams still listed on Beijing maps: in late 2011, the China Ministry of Water Resources found that only 22,909 rivers still existed in China, compared with its estimated 50,000.[2] Two-thirds of the city's water comes from groundwater, which is being consumed much faster than it can be refreshed, and it too is being polluted. Current plans call for even more groundwater use, together with a major diversion of water from the Yangzi River in central China. To critics, these solutions are "like trying to quench thirst by drinking poison."[3] In the "airpocalypse" of early 2013, Beijing's air exceeded 2010's "crazy bad" levels, according to the unofficial estimates of the US Embassy in Beijing.[4] Those levels were far off the already-scary scales of reference for atmospheric pollution.

Nationwide, China has sixteen of the twenty dirtiest cities in the world, a mostly befouled freshwater system, and growing desertification.[5] Nevertheless, this is an area in which we feel progress is likely, even if we have doubts about the implementation of the most extravagant plans, such as the Yangzi water diversion. This is because no one is hurt more by environmental degradation in China than the Chinese people themselves. Even the government quarters of Zhongnanhai are shrouded in noxious haze. Environmental remediation is becoming a matter of national priority. Both economic growth and public health depend on continued improvement in this area. In recent years, we have seen remarkable investments being made in every environmental asset class, from nuclear power stations to wind farms, solar panels, and hydroelectric facilities.

Unlike in the United States, there is both a broad perceived need from the top of the government in Beijing to the provinces and the villages on the importance of these issues and a willingness to act on them. There is little debate on either the scope of environmental challenges or the underlying science. Global climate change is not an area of controversy in China. Chinese experience it and believe it.

This is a case where China's engineering state may actually be an asset. (Perhaps we may someday be able to speak of "environmental action with Chinese characteristics.")

With significant government subsidies, it is also an area of opportunity for Chinese business. We expect that over the next two decades Chinese firms will emerge as the global leaders in clean energy. Effective investment in the electric automobile is less likely to happen in the United States than in China. (Self-interest in harvesting old investments and lack of risk capital will limit the Americans.) Thus our old friends at the Wanxiang Group, having mastered the universal joint, dominated the Chinese auto parts industry, and acquired multiple American auto parts firms, are poised to be the leaders first in batteries for electric vehicles and then as a manufacturer of "green" cars. As noted in chapter 6, in 2013, Wanxiang acquired the American lithium-ion battery maker A123 and its state-of-the-art technology.[6] A visitor today to its Hangzhou headquarters is whisked immediately to see "Wanxiang EV," the site of electric battery and future electric automobile manufacturing.

Goldwind Science and Technology Limited, another of our case studies, made its way from far-west Xinjiang Province to Beijing in the 1990s.[7] A Beijing-based firm, it is now a global corporation and one of the largest wind turbine manufacturers in the world. Both Wanxiang and Goldwind are private businesses. Different from China's state-owned corporations, they hire talent from around the world to advance their continued growth and innovation as global corporations. For this reason, the Taiwan experience gives us hope. In its political economy the PRC today mirrors the Taiwan of the 1970s: authoritarian politics coexisting with a large degree of market economy. Taiwan in the 1970s had bad air, bad water, and extraordinary levels of pollution even in rural rivers. Today, after two decades of environmental protests followed by remediating policies, Taiwan is a place that once again can display its great natural beauty, with clearer skies, cleaner rivers and streams, and a broad public commitment to environmental sanity. It was also a place where small entrepreneurs had trouble competing against the government's favored big businesses and gaining entry into certain sectors. Global economic integration, however, opened new doors and opportunities for them, forcing the government to pay greater attention to their contributions to economic well-being.

From Infrastructure State to Consumer Society

Nothing has been more consistent and sustained in the past thirty years than the huge investment in Chinese infrastructure. Plans dating back to Sun Yat-sen began to be realized on a massive scale only in the 1980s. This investment continues with ever more ambitious projects. At this writing, China has just opened the world's longest high-speed rail line (from Beijing to Guangzhou); there are forty-five airports planned for the next five years; and Beijing is rumored to be planning a new, third airport—the world's largest—that will be the size of Bermuda.[8]

Still, in the end, there will be limits to the number of roads, railroads, airports, electric lines, and amount of telecommunications bandwidth that can be delivered. This engine will likely begin to run out of steam by 2033, as the current migration from country to city begins to slow. In the next twenty years, however, there will be new needs as the population living in cities passes 60 percent and roads expand to support the cars that an anticipated production rate of 32 million units per year will bring.[9] This will create a sustainable need for many more middle- and lower-income housing units, as well as all the necessary "old-fashioned" elements of urban infrastructure such as water, sewers, and high-quality schools for all citizens, including the children of rural migrants.

The cornerstone of our forecast for the future, however, rests on China's ability to raise sharply levels of domestic consumer spending both in aggregate terms and as a percentage of disposable income. This outcome assumes a drop in the country's high domestic savings rate, and for most Chinese people this fundamental shift hinges on dramatic improvements in the pension and medical system safety nets. The recent extension of rudimentary health insurance to 95 percent of the rural population is a step in the right direction, but still covers only basic care.[10] Out-of-pocket expenses remain extremely high—and, for many poor people, unaffordable. If this coverage increases to cover catastrophic illnesses, which are a certainty for many families in a society in which 60 percent of the men smoke, it will make a big difference.[11] These issues will not be resolved overnight, and the timing and extension of benefits will vary significantly by city, region, and province.

In more affluent urban areas, younger generations have already taken to the credit card economy, and luxury consumer goods consumption has grown in the tier-one and -two cities. We see the continued growth of these consumption patterns in the coming years both in the tier-one through -three cities and then moving steadily into the countryside. Universally accessible television and internet advertising will combine to bring higher common material aspirations across the country in what is becoming a deeply networked society.

Our work on credit card companies shows a growing appetite for consumer debt among the young and urban, and we see this dramatically spreading over the next ten years.[12] The government has shown a willingness to let peer-to-peer lenders, such as CreditEase and China Risk Finance, enter the market to help satisfy the credit needs of small job-generating organizations at the base of the pyramid. If (and this is a huge *if*) there is a serious reform of the Chinese banking system, including an end to the singular focus of China's large state-owned banks on funding state-owned enterprises and large-scale private enterprises, and if interest rates are permitted to increase sufficiently to dampen the dramatic rise of China's shadow banking sector, the situation would change.

The recent drive to license existing informal bank networks is a start, but without allowing the large banks to lend on prudent rather than policy grounds, existing weaknesses will only deepen, and the likelihood of small and medium-sized firms obtaining formal bank credit will remain small. The rise of poorly regulated wealth management products and the explosive growth of local government debt are but two indicators of a financial system in need of change.

The net of new infrastructure, a new generation of single children, lower savings rates, and government investment in special economic zones in tier-two and tier-three cities all argue for an expanding consumer economy over the long term. But without a sound financial system, all is under threat. In 2011, Li & Fung, the large Hong Kong trading company, doubled its staff from fifteen thousand to thirty thousand to focus on the opportunity of China's rising consumer economy. The wisdom of this move depends on the evolution of a sounder financial system.[13]

An Innovation and Education Economy?

In chapters 3 and 4 we explored the dramatic growth of technology in China as it has moved from emulating or mimicking Western practices to making modifications and extensions to existing technologies, and then to the development of some fields of new technologies. We noted that China is making extraordinary investments in education, particularly in science and technology, at precisely the time when American universities are retrenching. More than half of Chinese university students concentrate in science and technology, while their American counterparts focus on *financial* engineering and accounting. In addition, the hundreds of thousands of Chinese students who pursue undergraduate and graduate education abroad also concentrate overwhelmingly on applied science and technology. Moreover, an increasing number of these students are now returning to China, where they are finding significant opportunities for their new skills in university and corporate laboratories. If investment were a sufficient cause of innovation, there could be no doubt that

China would be a global leader in disruptive technologies. The fact that America produced Alexander Graham Bell and Steve Jobs is no guarantee that it will continue to develop a disproportionate share of these creative, restless individuals in the future. This is a subject for another book, but our concerns about the United States are deep in this area.

Yet as we noted in earlier chapters, there is to date little confidence in China itself for its indigenous innovative capacities. One reason that Chinese parents send their children to American schools—and in ever-increasing numbers—is a seeming lack of confidence even in China's most elite educational institutions. It is this competitive challenge, as much as it is the idea of becoming the Harvards or Berkeleys of the East, that has prompted so many leading Chinese universities to reintroduce the humanities to higher education and to aim to educate *leaders*—who are more broadly and deeply educated than the engineers and soldiers who run the country today. It used to be that the students who went abroad for undergraduate study were those who could not get into leading Chinese universities. Today, even Peking University and Tsinghua University—the most prestigious and connected of institutions—lose students to leading American, British, and Hong Kong universities. Even though many of these students will return to China, their choice of university is telling. The jury on China's efforts at innovative programs of general education remains out, in part because Chinese universities are themselves so hamstrung by bureaucratic and political constraints.

There is a great disconnect between those who oversee Chinese universities (the Party-State at various levels) and those who have to run them. From the state's perspective, a "Chinese model" of higher education takes as its goal the building of *national* strength, developing talent for the collective good, not primarily for individual merit; to serve national strategies; to make the best, strategic use of the enormous funding now coming from central, provincial, municipal, and local governments; and to be under the guidance of Party and state. Closer to the ground, however, the local and provincial officials who are the main funders of universities often have a much shorter-term, utilitarian viewpoint: to spur economic growth; to enhance the job opportunities of people in their late teens and twenties; and to take advantage of the unbelievably cheap credit offered by state banks for the expansion of higher education. In this light, universities are themselves state-owned enterprises, tethered to government banks. Too often lost in all this is that the basic idea of liberal education, which is valued so highly in leading American institutions and is now the subject of experimental programs in China, is to liberate and educate the *individual* to be a critical thinker and active citizen.

In 2000, the standard tuition at public universities was RMB 5,000 per semester. Today, it ranges from RMB 16,000 to RMB 27,000. This figure is not high by American standards, but it is about 150 percent of the disposable income of rural residents. In private Chinese universities, tuition can be far higher, leading to a situation in which the poorest students often end up at the most expensive institutions, while the better off and better connected have greater access to the less expensive elite institutions.

We can see this in statistics of rural students attending Chinese universities. Nationwide, about 50 percent of university students hail from rural families (with a generous definition of what constitutes a rural family), but at the elite universities of Peking and Tsinghua, only about 20 percent of the student body is made up of students from rural areas. Today, the army and public security offer better means of social mobility to China's rural and poor than do China's now mass universities.

Educational inequality can also be measured in regional terms—for in this industry, as in others, there is no single, national market. In recent years, the gross enrollment ratios of college-age students in Beijing, Tianjin, and Shanghai all surpassed 50 percent. This is much higher than the national ratio of 23 percent. Indeed, Shanghai is already above 60 percent. But in Yunnan, Guangxi, Guizhou, and Tibet, the (unlikely and unrealized) *goal* is for a gross enrollment ratio of 15 percent. In higher education, the disparity between regions is not decreasing, but increasing.

Finally, take the case of entrance and admissions. The *gaokao*, or higher-level examination, persists because, like the old imperial examinations, it has the *appearance* of fairness and meritocracy—in principle, only the best, determined by competitive examination, are admitted. But the limitations of the *gaokao* have long been known, and elite universities are the leaders in setting patterns for alternative portals of entry: through additional tests, interviews, special achievement awards, and other mechanisms that privilege those of means and position who went to the best schools.

At the end of the day, the question of potential Chinese leadership in this, as in other areas, is comparative: who leads whom? Leadership in higher education means overtaking the Americans. As we have seen, in international rankings, the American system appears to be the most formidable. But that was not the case a century ago, and there is no reason to assume that the United States will remain in a leadership position without constant reform, reinvestment, and reinvention. In terms of extending access to higher education, the American system is itself in a crisis of stagnation. The great public systems of American higher education are in deep trouble financially. Recent years have witnessed the slow-motion self-destruction of the University of California system. For this, the American aversion to pay taxes for anything is partly to blame. As the president of one famous American public university once told us: "This is a much better university than the citizens of this state deserve." Then there is the question of governance. It is easy to criticize Chinese universities for the Party committees that oversee and limit them, but how much transparency is there, really, in the governance of America's leading private universities?

Having said all this, however, our judgment is that, for all the problems facing the American system, China is not yet poised for leadership in education and, by extension, innovation. This is in spite of the fact that no country is counting more on education for its future than China.

The Chinese World Order

Historically, there was no clear demarcation between domestic and foreign affairs in imperial China. The internal and external were a continuum. The values of civilization did not have hard borders. Good governance of the empire led naturally to submission and emulation abroad. This is no longer the case.

The new Chinese nation-state inherited two burdens from the Qing empire. The first was the defense of a large and diverse empire, which became a modern nation-state. The borders have indeed been well defended, even by weak governments, and the process of making China into a modern country has been ongoing for more than a century.

This burden of national defense has led inevitably to a militarization of the Chinese state in the early twentieth century, to a militarization of society during the anti-Japanese and civil wars, and finally to an attempted militarization of the soul in the Cultural Revolution, when the army was to be the model for society. The military has played a decisive role at every major turning point in modern Chinese political history. China's borders, however, are now secure from external forces. China's territorial ambitions, if we may call them that, in the East and South China seas, were largely inherited from the claims of the Nationalist government. Even the issue of Taiwan, over which China claims sovereignty, has been put on a back burner in recent years as Taipei and Beijing have agreed to a fuzzy consensus of "one China, two interpretations." Why then have Chinese military budgets risen in recent years, far above a pace that seems warranted? Why, we asked a leading officer of the People's Liberation Army, does the PLA ask for 10-plus percent increases year after year in its budget? "Because we can," was the very honest answer we received. Given its past history and current resources, it is not surprising to see Chinese military budgets rise.

Does this mean, then, that China is inevitably on a military collision course with the United States, which outspends the rest of the world combined on matters military? We do not think so. Now that China is again an important maritime trading nation, it should share concerns with the Americans on the freedom of sea-lanes, the combating of piracy, and other issues. China's boom since 1978 has been predicated on an era of peace in East Asia, the likes of which has not been seen since the first Opium War. To be sure, there will be tensions in strategic policy between China and the United States, and miscalculation is always possible, but it is massively in the interest of both countries to avoid conflict. To the extent there is a Chinese-American competition, we believe it will be primarily economic, not military, in nature.

The second burden inherited by modern China from the Qing is less easily defined: it is a desire to embody, in some form, universal values of civilization. It was a set of broadly shared values—of how families, communities, and states are organized—that defined the governance of the Empire over the centuries and was a primary reason that Chinese civilization spread across East Asia over time. Chinese civilization had an enormous amount of soft power.

The concept of soft power is taken seriously in China as it seeks to improve its image abroad. Why, Chinese visitors sometimes ask us, is the coverage of China in the *New York Times* so negative? What can China do to improve it? We usually respond along the following lines. First, there is *more* coverage of China in the *New York Times* than of any other country outside the United States because China is so important. Second, *most* of the news in American newspapers is bad news. Only in China is all the news good. Third, if the Chinese government did not so routinely harass and intimidate global opinion makers—its own leading intellectuals and the international journalist corps in China, for starters—its image might be rather better.

Historically, at least until the nineteenth century, the values by which the empire was ruled were those that could be broadly shared by others with whom it came into contact. That is not the case today. When was the last time you read of someone seeking asylum in China?

China has been a responsible member of many global organizations, but not a leader of them in the broadest sense. Instead, when China seeks to project values abroad—as recently in the Libyan and Syrian crises—it has been in defense of a narrow conception of national sovereignty and of noninterference in the domestic affairs of others (and, by extension, of China). It is easy to forget that China is also a signatory to the Universal Declaration of Human Rights, of which Nationalist China was a coauthor.

And so the world today respects China for its growing hard power—the infrastructure state with a military at its core—but not its soft power. China has the hardware, but not yet the software, for global leadership.

Can China Lead?

Will China "rule the world"? We don't think so. And neither, we believe, do those who rule China today.

One of the great contradictions in contemporary China is the juxtaposition of official power and wealth with transparent anxiety. Why, one may ask, after decades of Chinese economic growth and now in a period of enduring economic crisis in the West, is the Chinese Party-State still so insecure? Why does it feel the need to spend more, at least in publicly announced expenditures, on domestic public security than it does on national defense?

One answer is that, for the first extended time since the middle of the nineteenth century, China's borders are not aggressively threatened by any external enemy: not Japan, Russia, India, Vietnam, or the United States. Rather, all of the dangers facing the Chinese regime today are internal: from artists and essayists; from Uighurs and Tibetans; from advocates of human rights to proponents of environmental rights; from hundreds of millions of migrant workers who are second-class citizens in the cities and towns in which they work and live; from all those at the bottom of the income scale in a "socialist" land that has become, in terms of income, one of the most unequal on earth; and (at present indirectly) from a vibrant private sector that is the historic engine of Chinese economic growth and yet faces increasing restrictions at every turn by the state and its state-owned enterprises.

In its incapacity to brook dissent, the Chinese Communist Party has managed to have two Nobel Peace Prizes conferred on its self-selected enemies: first the Dalai Lama of Tibet, and more recently a courageous writer, Liu Xiaobo. How could the great and powerful Chinese Communist Party so fear a single critic such as Liu Xiaobo? Here again history may be some guide.

In the first half of the sixteenth century, the Portuguese established a foothold on Macau, then an island (now a peninsula) of southern Guangdong Province. The Portuguese were there some years before the Ming court knew of their presence, but when it found out, it severely limited Portuguese access to any place beyond Macau. Why, one wonders, would the Ming empire, in its day the most powerful and sophisticated in the world, fear a small band of Europeans off its coast? The answer is provided by the historian John Wills: "To outsiders, Chinese exclusion of foreigners, fear of spies, invasion, and conquest sometimes seemed overdone, irrational, and pathological. After all, China is so huge and so densely populated; why should it fear foreign conquest? The Chinese [rulers] knew better ... The Chinese people could not be trusted."[14] This lack of trust still exists and has profound implications.

Today the Chinese people cannot be trusted to communicate with one another without official supervision. The "Great Firewall of China" seeks to limit certain external sources of information. More important is the role of domestic electronic surveillance and censorship. The Harvard political scientist Gary King recently led a team to study internet restrictions in China, which he calls "the most extensive effort to selectively censor human expression ever implemented." His research team found that the Chinese Party-State does not, at least in the first instance, censor criticism of itself. It suppresses instead two areas: criticism of the censors, who appear to be quite thin-skinned, and, above all, any critique that may lead to collective action.[15] What kind of collective action does it fear? Surely it is not a sign of confidence that Wang Qishan, elected to the Politburo's Standing Committee in 2012 to oversee Party discipline, is recommending that comrades read Alexis de Tocqueville's *The Old Regime and the French Revolution.*[16]

So the people cannot be trusted in the People's Republic. At times they can be diverted, for example to Nationalist fury over the tiny (try to find them on a map) and inconsequential Diaoyu islands, the site of a recent spat with Japan, but they cannot be trusted.

Perhaps it is in recognition of this that people with means and influence want to send their children and their money out of China. Chinese presence in American universities has increased dramatically. According to the Institute of International Education, during the 2001–2002 academic year, there were 63,211 students from China studying in the United States. One decade later, the number had practically tripled: during the 2011–2012 academic year, there were 194,029 Chinese students enrolled in American universities.[17] Capital flight from China is growing. Polls show that half of Chinese millionaires (in dollar terms) have contemplated emigration.[18] Ordinary people voice their anger on the web at the astonishing levels of corruption that are the hallmark of a one-party system without any checks on its authority: the Shanxi provincial official who fathered ten children with four wives (this in the country of the one-child family) or the opium-smoking official in Yunnan who has twenty-three homes, six of them abroad.[19] These are provincial stories; the wealth of China's ruling families in Beijing is believed to be greater still by orders of magnitude. There are of course periodic, top-down, Party-led crackdowns on corruption, but in the absence of an unpoliticized police force; an honest, independent judiciary; and a press truly free to criticize authority, these crackdowns will come and go without systemic effect.

The point here is that China does not necessarily need the electoral democracy of the American system (itself hardly a model for action today) in order to significantly increase honesty, transparency, and confidence in government and thus inspire trust. China's economy has leapt far ahead of its processes of governance. High-tech business parks coexist with low-tech surveillance and old-fashioned thuggery.

An area of particularly needed change is the judiciary. At present, the judiciary is an integrated part of the executive line structure of the Party-State. Since 1949, it has had no tradition of judicial independence, and we see little evidence of forces that would push it in this direction. This is bad news for foreign investors, who have scant hope of litigating successfully in local Chinese courts. It is worse news for Chinese citizens, who can find in the law and the courts no checks on arbitrary authority. To be sure, when a high-profile case of abuse of public trust emerges, penalties can be both speedy and massive, but there is no such thing as due process to get to this result. Take, for example, the melamine poisoning of children that arose several years ago. There was a convulsive action by officials to do something immediate and visible to prevent civil disorder. There was, however, little or no due process for the individuals involved as death sentences and life-imprisonment sentences were handed out. Neither were there mechanisms to avoid the problem in the first place nor to channel constructive civil dissatisfaction in its aftermath. Like the military, the judiciary is in the service of the Party; unlike the military, the judiciary has no influence of its own. Unless the judiciary becomes truly professional and apolitical, without Party oversight, all this will remain a chilling reality in the China of 2034.

The Chinese Communist Party rules China today not on the basis of revolutionary thought or Marxism-Leninism but because of a promise of prosperity and stability. It delivered neither growth nor stability in the first three decades of its rule before presiding over the Chinese economic miracle that was made possible above all by abandoning the dysfunctional policies of the Maoist era, and it still has done little to institutionalize political change.

We have just witnessed what journalists too easily have called China's "once-in-a-decade" transition—this despite the minor detail that the People's Republic of China managed exactly one routinized transition of power in its first sixty-two years. There have been many more coups d'état than peaceful transitions. The transition of 2012, with the purge of Bo Xilai and evident tensions within both the Party and the military, was anything but smooth. Those among China's leadership elites who feared chaos in that transition may now be relieved; those who had hoped that the events of 2012 might offer the prospect of political reform may now be disappointed. We have seen a closing—for now—of ranks. The seven men (still all men) who marched to their prescribed spots on the stage in Beijing in November 2012 promised order and stability, not change. Foreigners interested or invested in China can expect no major initiatives soon, no quick rollback of state-owned enterprises or deep reform of the banking system, no early experimentation in political reform, and no major change in Chinese-foreign relations.

Will this be the last such transition? We do not know, but we do know that the rule of authoritarian systems is not endless. Here is a simple rule of history: no political party, anywhere, rules forever. The question is not if it will lose power, but when and how. And the question for the leaders of the Chinese Communist Party and its military is if, or when, they will choose to act in the long-term interests of *China*, and not simply of the Chinese Communist Party, in moving toward a more enduring political structure. The question for China today is less whether the CCP can succeed, like the Guomindang in Taiwan, in overseeing a process of political change that allows legitimate competition, but rather whether it has any wish to do so. Sun Yat-sen, after all, believed that some form of democracy was the final goal of his revolution. Mao Zedong never did.

Like the Nationalist Party-State that preceded it (and the Manchu conquerors that preceded that), the People's Republic of China came to power as a military conquest regime over sixty years ago. Unlike the Manchus, and indeed unlike every success-ful ruling house in Chinese history, by the second decade of this century the CCP conquerors have yet to show that their power can be transferred to civilian political and legal institutions with enduring legitimacy. Civilians can serve the Party-State if they are lucky, but never can they govern separately from it.

As the successor in our century to the old imperial system, the Chi-nese Party-State has shown that it can do many things better: it can organize, it can industrialize, it can militarize, and it can terrorize. But unlike the system that disappeared in 1912, it has not yet shown that it can *civilize*. We use that term in two senses: to establish a last-ing system of *civil* service—of civilian rule—using the great talent of the Chinese people, and, second, to stand for something enduring in human values, for a civilization that goes beyond political con-trol, material development, and martial strength. This was the great strength of the old empire, whose influence and models radiated across East Asia. Perhaps this will be the quest of political struc-tures still unformed, once the Party-State has finally had its day.

Let us be clear. We *do* believe that China will fare extraordi-narily well in many domains in the coming decades. But we believe that it will do better still if it can move beyond a political model that has already run its course.

To sum up: What does it take to contend for global leadership today?

- Economic dynamism is a necessary but not sufficient condition.

- One's most successful citizens do not seek to emigrate with their wealth.

- One's most successful citizens do not educate their children abroad.

- One needs the rule *of* law, not just the rule of order or rule *by* law.

- One's currency cannot be blocked.

- One cannot mistrust citizens so profoundly that every blog is monitored.

- One cannot lead and yet fear to recognize one's own Nobel Prize winners.

- One must have the capacity for moral leadership, at home and abroad.

———————

Will the twenty-first century be *the* Chinese century? Not at this stage, in our judgment, absent the addressing of the above issues in ways not yet seen. If addressed, however, the twenty-first century could be a century not just for China, but for all of us, in an interconnected world of shared aspirations and common problems.

Americans still believe in the American Dream. President Xi Jinping has articulated a vision of a China Dream. It used to be said, of the Chinese-American relationship, that we were *tongchuang yimeng*—"sleeping in the same bed, while dreaming different dreams." Today Chinese and Americans are embedded together as never before in a bilateral relationship that will do much to define their common future. They dream many—but not all—of the same dreams.

In 2034, we expect China will be richer, its people more prosperous, its military more powerful, its polity less centralized. If it can get to these stages without a political explosion, then China and the rest of East Asia will thrive.

But until the big political questions are answered—what political form, what kind of society, what relationship between state and society will ultimately replace those of the old empire, with its two-thousand-year-old roots—and until a political system of enduring legitimacy and confidence is erected, China will thrive, but it will not lead.

As we end, we would like to leave with some broad questions, which are much easier to pose to the businessperson than to answer. Some are so sensitive, it is hard to articulate them.

Doing Business in China

- How can my firm operate where there is such limited rule of law? How much capital can my firm put at risk in this environment? How big should my firm's reserves be?

- Is my firm big enough and well connected enough to mobilize home country, government, and political support if we feel we are being abused?

- Is my firm's China risk profile adequately hedged?

- What indicators do we monitor on the stability of the political environment? Are we confident in them?

- Are my firm's regional and national networks broad enough to hedge risks of major political change?

APPENDIX A

SELECTED MACROECONOMIC
DATA ON CHINA

The Chinese economic miracle of the past thirty years has been well discussed in other publications, and we do not propose to go into all of the aspects here but simply provide some key overview economic data. This appendix contains selected data for readers to understand the scope of what has happened since 1979.

Figure A-1 shows China's average annual real growth rate from 1979 to 2012. A quick reading indicates a steady nearly double-digit annual growth, with only 1989–1990 being below 6 percent per year.

Figure A-2 tracks the growth of the GDP of the PRC in 2011 US dollars from 1960 to 2011. The explosive growth of the economy leaps out from this data, particularly in recent years, as GDP jumped from $1.2 trillion in 2000 to $7.3 trillion in 2011.

Figure A-3 shows the gross regional product per capita in selected Chinese provinces. This shows the vast differences in standard of living between high-end Beijing and Shanghai, and low-end Tibet and Ningxia. Not all regions of the country have prospered uniformly. To date, the major growth has been in the eastern seaboard provinces.

FIGURE A-1

China's average annual real growth rate (%)

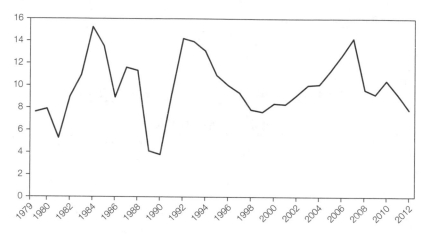

Source: Wayne M. Morrison, "China's Economic Conditions," Congressional Research Services, December 4, 2012, http://www.fas.org/sgp/crs/row/RL33534.pdf.

FIGURE A-2

GDP of the People's Republic of China (USD 2011)

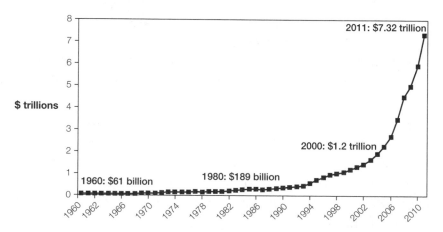

Source: Data sourced from The World Bank, World Development indicators, and Global Development Finance, http://data.worldbank.org/.

FIGURE A-3

Gross regional product per capita in selected Chinese provinces

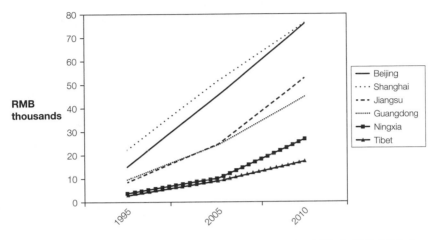

Source: All data from China National Statistics Bureau. 2010 data from chart 2-15 in the 2011 statistical yearbook; 2005 data from chart 3-9 in the 2006 statistical yearbook; 1995 data from chart 2-11 in the 1996 statistical yearbook.

APPENDIX B

CASES REFERENCED IN
CAN CHINA LEAD?

Alibaba.com

F. Warren McFarlan, Carin-Isabel Knoop, and David Lane

(Boston: Harvard Business School, 2001), Case 301-047

> This case focuses on the early-stage strategic issues of an emerging dot-com in the rapidly emerging internet nation—China. Alibaba, based in Hangzhou, China, was trying to carve out a niche in the B2B e-commerce world. The issues are surprisingly similar to those confronting companies in Western Europe and the United States.

Alibaba (B)

F. Warren McFarlan and Fred Young

(Boston: Harvard Business School, 2001), Case 302-073

> The largest Chinese electronic commerce company faced many challenges at the end of 2001. This case describes its strategy reorientation to become a B2B.

Appellation Shanxi: Grace Vineyard

Michael Shih-ta Chen, Keith Chi-ho Wong, and William C. Kirby

(Boston: Harvard Business School, 2011), Case 309-075

> A family-owned, private winery in China, Grace Vineyard is set on establishing itself as a world-renowned quality vintner

in 1997. Its wines were rapidly growing a strong following and had won international awards. The key issue is: how can the company capitalize on this success? Should it expand its operations to multiple Chinese provinces, continue as a premium boutique winery serving a growing market in China, or seek to make a mark internationally?

Beyondsoft Co. Ltd. (A)

Donghong Li, F. Warren McFarlan, and Hong Zhang
(Beijing: Tsinghua University School of Economics
and Management, 2011), TU0001

Beyondsoft Co. Ltd., established in 1995, is a leading software outsourcing company. In the past two decades, the Chinese software and outsourcing industry has risen from almost nothing to real significance. It is currently growing much faster than the world market. This case describes Beyondsoft's challenges for future development following the world financial turmoil of 2008–2009.

Beyondsoft Co. Ltd. (B)

Donghong Li, Hong Zhang, and F. Warren McFarlan
(Beijing: Tsinghua University School of Economics
and Management, 2012), TU0030

This case focuses on the strategic path of Beyondsoft during 2010–2011 and the market environment faced by the company in early 2012, when Beyondsoft did an IPO, as it sought to broaden its footprint.

Boardroom Battle Behind Bars: GOME Electrical Appliances Holdings—A Corporate Governance Drama

William C. Kirby and Tracy Yuen Manty
(Boston: Harvard Business School, 2012), Case 312-025

Despite widespread news of the incarceration of GOME Electronics' CEO, Huang Guangyu, Bain Capital felt that it had carefully undertaken due diligence before making a significant investment in the company. Bain was confident that it and the current management could work together to revamp the fortunes of China's leading electronics retailer. However, it did not anticipate the power Huang had behind bars. As the majority shareholder, Huang managed to manipulate shareholder meetings, current management decisions, and structure. The case surfaces important issues on corporate governance.

The Challenges of Launching a Start-Up in China: Dorm99.com

William C. Kirby, F. Warren McFarlan, and Tracy Yuen Manty
(Boston: Harvard Business School, 2008), Case 307-075

An internet start-up, Dorm99 had received venture capital investment and prepared a product launch for its social net-working website. On the day of the launch, it faced an unex-pected setback from China's Ministry of Education and was forced to withdraw the product. The case highlights both the challenges posed to firms by China's government ministries and the numerous opportunities available to entrepreneurs in China.

ChemChina

Donghong Li, Hong Zhang, Lei Li, and F. Warren McFarlan
(Beijing: Tsinghua University School of Economics
and Management, 2012), Case TU0028

ChemChina is China's largest basic chemical manufacturing firm. In the 2012 *Fortune* Global 500, it ranked 402. A represen-tative of "big but less strong" companies, ChemChina lags far behind the world's leading chemical giants in terms of technol-ogy and management. Nevertheless, its evolution to becoming a *Fortune* Global 500 giant and a leading chemical enterprise in China in less than thirty years, through both internal prod-uct innovation and global acquisitions of technology-based companies, makes it an important story. New opportunities exist, as Blackstone has become a strategic partner.

China in Africa: The Case of Sudan

Regina Abrami and Eunice Ajambo

(Boston: Harvard Business School, 2010), Case 308-060

> The case highlights the tensions between China's demand for natural resources like oil and the political risks that come with securing them. China's approach to business ethics, environmental issues, and government relations in third-world countries are described.

China Construction America (A): The Road Ahead

Regina Abrami and Weiqi Zhang

(Boston: Harvard Business School, 2011), Case 911-408

> The case examines the US market entry strategy of the CSCEC (China State Construction Engineering Corporation), China's leading state-owned construction company. The company strikes deal after deal in South Carolina (despite political backlash) and in New York, where well-established competitors dominate. These deals enable exceptional growth of the company, despite a major slowdown in the US construction industry.

China Construction America (B): The Baha Mar Resort Deal

Regina Abrami, Malcolm Riddell, and Weiqi Zhang

(Boston: Harvard Business School, 2011), Case 911-411

> This case describes how CSCEC beat out Harrah's and other contenders for a stake in the Baha Mar Project in the Bahamas. It shows the role of project financing by China's Export-Import Bank and highlights the competitiveness of China in encouraging the growth of its companies outside China.

The China Entrepreneurs Forum

William C. Kirby, Tracy Yuen Manty, and G. A. Donovan

(Boston: Harvard Business School, 2012), Case 312-095

> Some of China's most successful entrepreneurs and founders of private enterprises share insights and tactics for growth of

successful private firms in China. The group expands its role to advocate government policy changes to improve the environment for private business in China.

China Merchants Bank: Here Just for You

F. Warren McFarlan, Chen Guoqing, Zhu Hengyuan, Michael Shih-ta Chen, Bin Yang, Yan Yang, Wai Shun, and G. A. Donovan
(Boston: Harvard Business School, 2009), Case 307-081

China Merchants Bank (CMB) is a pioneer in the use of technical innovation and IT as a competitive tool in the rapidly evolving Chinese banking sector. Its IT-driven products enabled CMB to become the number-six Chinese bank in terms of assets. Critically, by April 2006, CMB had captured one-third of the Chinese credit card market.

China Merchants Bank in Transition

Guoqing Chen, Ziqian Zhao, and F. Warren McFarlan
(Beijing: Tsinghua University School of Economics and Management, 2011), TU0017

China Merchants Bank underwent a second strategic transformation post-2006. In the 1990s and early twenty-first century, CMB used IT to expand nationwide by credit card differentiation. In a changing government policy environment, the company changed its market share strategy focus dramatically to become a profit-driven firm by 2009.

China Mobile's Rural Communications Strategy

William C. Kirby, F. Warren McFarlan, G. A. Donovan, and Tracy Yuen Manty
(Boston: Harvard Business School, 2011), Case 309-034

The world's leading mobile communications service provider, China Mobile had over 400 million customers at the time of the case. It planned further investment in new products and value-added services to make its mobile phone network more valuable to the lifestyles of China's rural population.

China Netcom: Corporate Governance in China (A)

Regina Abrami, William C. Kirby, F. Warren McFarlan,
Ning Xiadong, and Tracy Yuen Manty
(Boston: Harvard Business School, 2008), Case 308-027

> Listed on the Hong Kong stock market and New York
> Stock Exchange, state-owned enterprise China Netcom
> must develop the corporate governance practices to meet
> exchange-mandated corporate governance standards. The
> company hoped that its commitment to developing globally
> accepted governance would help capital markets and potential
> investors understand that the company was a true, modern
> corporation, even with the state as a majority owner.

China Netcom: Corporate Governance in China (B)

Regina Abrami, William C. Kirby, F. Warren McFarlan, and Tracy Yuen Manty
(Boston: Harvard Business School, 2008), Case 308-091

> Description of progress in the company's approach to
> developing globally accepted governance structures and
> processes.

China Risk Finance: Riding the Wave of China's Financial Services Industry

Regina Abrami, Weiqi Zhang, and Matthew Shaffer
(Boston: Harvard Business School, 2012), Case 912-417

> As China shifts toward a consumer-led growth model, non-
> bank lending plays an ever more important role. The case
> focuses on the promises and pitfalls of this industry. The com-
> pany's approach to trying to navigate them is identified.

China and the WTO: Doing the Right Thing?

Regina Abrami
(Boston: Harvard Business School, 2004), Case 704-041

> The People's Republic of China joined the World Trade Orga-
> nization (WTO) in late 2001. The case describes why business,

organized labor, and other governments either favored or opposed China's entry into the WTO. It provides historical background on Chinese foreign economic relations, especially trade relations with the United States.

A Chinese Start-Up's Midlife Crisis: 99Sushe.com

William C. Kirby, F. Warren McFarlan, and Tracy Yuen Manty

(Boston: Harvard Business School, 2009), Case 309-060

In its third year, the original Dorm99 has morphed from a social networking site to an online gaming business. Having an entirely new staff and established new partnerships, it now urgently needs new funding. No longer a start-up, it faces the ramifications of midlife.

Cisco China

F. Warren McFarlan, Guoqing Chen, and David Kiron

(Boston: Harvard Business School, 2001), Case 302-069

The case describes how Cisco has taken its US-based infrastructure and adapted it to its China operations and highlights how so much of Cisco's US intranet practices have been made operational in China.

COSCO

F. Warren McFarlan, Guoqing Chen, and David Lane

(Boston: Harvard Business School, 2002), Case 302-051

The case identifies the IT challenges facing COSCO, one of the largest shipping companies in the world. COSCO must aggressively deal with the internet and modern information technology to compete effectively as a Chinese company in a globally IT-intensive industry. It highlights the role the state can play in energizing a laggard state-owned enterprise in a critical sector.

The Comeback: Baosteel Stays in Brazil (C)

Regina Abrami and Iacob Koch-Weser

(Boston: Harvard Business School, 2011), Case 912-413

> Baosteel's efforts at building a steel mill in Brazil continue to
> face regulatory approval problems. This is compounded by the
> global financial crisis that is impacting global steel demand.

CP Group: Balancing the Needs of a Family Business with the Needs of a Family of Businesses

William C. Kirby and Tracy Yuen Manty

(Boston: Harvard Business School, 2011), Case 312-059

> CP is the leading Thai agribusiness corporation in Thailand.
> It is a diversified conglomerate expanding its business in
> Southeast Asia and China. The case highlights a business
> culture that combines the closeness of a family business with
> the strategic vision, innovations, and transparency of a pro-
> fessionally run company—complicated by the fact that many
> business units are public companies.

CSCEC: Transformation and Development

Donghong Li, Hong Zhang, and F. Warren McFarlan

(Beijing: Tsinghua University School of Economics
and Management, 2011), TU0019

> In 2001, CSCEC (China State Construction Engineering
> Corporation), the largest residential building constructor
> in China, appointed Sun Wenjie as general manager. In the
> next decade, Sun transformed CSCEC from a bureaucratic to
> a highly competitive firm. In 2010, Yi Jun, Sun's close asso-
> ciate, took over and reviewed potential adjustments in the
> corporation's strategic goals, business structure and mix of
> business, and internal management controls to bring them
> into alignment with the new competitive landscape.

Digital China Holdings Ltd.: Managing the Transition from a Product-Oriented to a Service-Oriented Company

F. Warren McFarlan, Guoqing Chen, and Kai Reimers

(Boston: Harvard Business School, 2007), Case 307-093

> The history and current strategy of China's largest indepen-
> dent systems integrator (IBM and HP are larger) is described.
> A seven-thousand-seven-hundred-person company, it is rapidly
> growing. It is largely unknown outside China.

Digital China Holdings Ltd.: ERP as a Platform for Building New Capabilities

F. Warren McFarlan, Guoqing Chen, Kai Reimers, and Xunhua Guo

(Boston: Harvard Business School, 2002), Case 302-080

> This case analyzes a complex enterprise resource planning
> implementation that takes place in one of the leading com-
> panies in China. The issues are indistinguishable from those
> facing a US organization trying to do similar things.

Enterprise Culture in Chinese History: Zhang Jian and the Dasheng Cotton Mills

Elisabeth Köll

(Boston: Harvard Business School, 2010), Case 308-068

> One of the earliest and most successful industrial enter-
> prises in prewar China, Dasheng was founded by the famous
> entrepreneur Zhang Jian (1853–1926). It became a state-
> owned enterprise in 1953. In 1996, it was restructured as the
> Jiangsu Dasheng Group Co. Ltd. Issues of corporate gover-
> nance, legal environment, government relations, and the
> role of family business structures are discussed in the con-
> text of how they shaped the business environment in prewar
> China and continue to influence Chinese enterprise culture
> today.

Esquel Group: Integrating Business Strategy and Corporate Social Responsibility

William C. Kirby, F. Warren McFarlan, and Tracy Yuen Manty

(Boston: Harvard Business School, 2011), Case 307-076

> This case highlights the experience of China's largest shirt manufacturer in managing government relations at multiple levels in China. It identifies a wide variety of social initiatives Esquel has undertaken as part of being a good citizen in China.

Fiyta: The Case of a Chinese Watch Company

Regina Abrami, William C. Kirby, F. Warren McFarlan, Luc Wathieu,

Fei Li, Gao Wang, and Tracy Yuen Manty

(Boston: Harvard Business School, 2008), Case 308-025

> Fiyta has long been one of China's foremost watch brands. As China's economy improved, however, Chinese consumer tastes began to change. Exposed to more luxurious foreign brands, many Chinese now strive to purchase a Swiss or Japanese watch. The case highlights the challenge Fiyta faces in rebuilding its brand image for the more sophisticated Chinese consumer.

Goldwind USA: Chinese Wind in the Americas

Regina Abrami and Iacob Koch-Weser

(Boston: Harvard Business School, 2012), Case 912-416

> Renewable energy is a fledgling, high-risk market. Goldwind USA, a leading producer of wind turbines, is trying to overcome the odds and succeed in this market. The case examines the strategic challenges the Chinese company Goldwind faced in establishing its first major overseas subsidiary. These included building a local team around a US CEO, bridging cross-cultural differences among management, overcoming regulatory hurdles, sourcing from local suppliers, and facilitating turbine sales through innovative deal structures.

GOME Electronics: Evolving the Business Model

Regina Abrami, William C. Kirby, F. Warren McFarlan, Gao Wang,

Fei Li, Tracy Yuen Manty, and Wai Shun Lo

(Boston: Harvard Business School, 2008), Case 308-026

> After twenty years of expansion, GOME Electronics has
> become China's largest consumer electronics retailer. It
> has opened stores in almost every province in China, has
> acquired some of its competitors, and went public in Hong
> Kong. However, it has begun to experience a slowdown in
> growth as sales per square meter have declined. The company
> is now being challenged to develop new ideas for growth,
> including experimenting with its product mix, renegotiating
> its relationships with suppliers, and developing new business
> models to maximize profitability.

The Haidilao Company

Ziqian Zhao, Zheng Xiaoming, and F. Warren McFarlan

(Beijing: Tsinghua University School of Economics

and Management, 2011), Case TU0021

> This restaurant chain's workforce is mostly composed of
> young employees. Instilled with the founder's unique entrepre-
> neurial values, they are enthusiastic and motivated to deliver
> extraordinary service to customers creatively. This case
> depicts the founder's entrepreneurial experience and values.
> It also shows a firm that was built on entirely internally gener-
> ated funds.

Heavy Metal (A): Baosteel Enters Brazil

Regina Abrami and Iacob Koch-Weser

(Boston: Harvard Business School, 2011), Case 912-411

> Baosteel, a top Chinese steelmaker, responds to the Chinese
> government's "go global" policy and a possible rise in iron
> ore input costs by building a plant in Brazil. Steel mills are
> complex, capital-intensive projects, and Brazil is an emerging
> market that poses manifold risks to foreign investors. Baosteel

evaluates if Brazil is the right country, partner, and site for its first overseas greenfield investment.

Heavy Metal (B): Baosteel Struggles in Brazil
Regina Abrami and Iacob Koch-Weser
(Boston: Harvard Business School, 2011), Case 912-412

Baosteel has built a steel mill in Brazil with Vale do Rio Doce, the world's leading iron mining company. Regulatory obstacles and unexpected costs have placed the project in jeopardy. Outside Brazil, however, Baosteel has been growing rapidly, and market trends favor an overseas plant. Baosteel is deciding whether or not to continue in Brazil.

HNA Group: Moving China's Air Transport Industry in a New Direction
William C. Kirby, F. Warren McFarlan, and Tracy Yuen Manty
(Boston: Harvard Business School, 2008), Case 309-029

The parent company of Hainan Airlines is positioning itself to go global as the largest private airline in China. Positioned behind the "Big Three" state-owned carriers, Hainan Airlines seeks to create a world-class business by following modern management practices, keeping sharp attention to cost control, and making aggressive entries into international markets.

Information Technology at COSCO
F. Warren McFarlan, Guoqing Chen, and David Lane
(Boston: Harvard Business School, 2005), Case 305-080

The second largest container shipping company in the world, COSCO, is developing new IT applications. The case shows a series of organizational and application choices it must make in the future. As a subtext, it highlights the growing IT sophistication of large, state-owned enterprises in China.

Inner Mongolia Yili Group: China's Pioneering Dairy Brand

Regina Abrami, William C. Kirby, F. Warren McFarlan, and Tracy Yuen Manty
(Boston: Harvard Business School, 2011), Case 308-052

> Setting the goal to become one of the top twenty enterprises
> in the world dairy industry by 2010, the Inner Mongolia–based
> Yili Group had ambitious plans. To set itself apart, Yili focused
> on R&D and innovative ways to improve the industry. Proving
> that it could shift industry standards and lead a country not
> accustomed to dairy consumption to a point where demand
> outpaced supply, the Yili Group hoped to go global. When milk
> was poisoned with melamine, all these plans were put at risk.

International Agribusiness in China: Charoen Pokphand Group

William C. Kirby, Michael Shih-ta Chen, Tracy Yuen Manty, and Yi Kwan Chu
(Boston: Harvard Business School, 2011), Case 910-418

> The leading Thai agribusiness corporation and largest agri-
> business investor in China, Charoen Pokphand Group (CP)
> faces a crossroads in China as the country starts to undergo
> rural reform. CP is trying to balance its place as a key investor
> in China's burgeoning agriculture market with its obligation
> to provide guidance and expertise in food safety, technology,
> and jobs for rural farmers.

Jiamei Dental: Private Health Care in China

William C. Kirby and G. A. Donovan
(Boston: Harvard Business School, 2011), Case 910-404

> Founded in 1993, Jiamei Dental Medical Management Group
> ("Jiamei") rode the wave of China's rapid economic develop-
> ment and is China's largest private dental chain, with eighty-
> four clinics in Beijing and seven other major cities. In 2009,
> Jiamei planned to open dozens more clinics. At the same time,
> it faces stiff competition from regional and international
> private dental clinic competitors, high-end private hospitals,
> and possibly the government.

Journey to the East: Natcore Technology in China

Regina Abrami, Weiqi Zhang, and Matthew Shaffer

(Boston: Harvard Business School, 2012), Case 912-414

A US solar technology firm is manufacturing in China instead of the United States. Both the company and the US government are assessing this decision. The case examines the making of a new joint venture in China at a time when both the US and the Chinese governments are eager to expand and develop their clean-tech sectors.

Juner New Materials: On the Road to IPO

Donglin Xia, Ning Jia, Ziqian Zhao, and F. Warren McFarlan

(Beijing: Tsinghua University School of Economics

and Management, 2012), Case TU0003

A private China-based company, Juner develops, produces, and distributes modified plastic compounds. Founded in 1995 by serial entrepreneur Chen Xiaomin, Juner has exhibited strong performance and growth potential. The company has a workforce of more than three hundred employees and is an icon of high-technology ventures in Zhejiang Province. The board of Juner has concluded it is opportune to take the company public. This decision has led to several issues: (1) the choice of stock exchange, (2) the "justified" valuation, and (3) the methods Juner should adopt to maintain its growth rate after the IPO.

Kingdee

Ziqian Zhao, Jin Zhang, and F. Warren McFarlan

(Beijing: Tsinghua University School of Economics

and Management, 2011), Case TU0005

The competitive strategy of Kingdee, the number-two management software company in China, is laid out. The Shenzhen-based firm is competing with Beijing-headquartered UFIDA and major international firms SAP and Oracle for position in the Chinese market. Given its young non-*hukou* (household registration)-bearing staff in Shenzhen, the company has focused heavily on its internal culture as a competitive weapon.

Kingdee in 2011: Stranding or Dormancy?

Jin Zhang, Xiaohui Li, and F. Warren McFarlan

(Beijing: Tsinghua University School of Economics and Management, 2012), Case TU0041

In 2011, reacting to competitive pressure, Kingdee made strategic investments, expanded its business, and suffered a net profit decline despite operating revenue growth and changes in top management.

Kunshan Incorporated: The Making of China's Richest Town

William C. Kirby, Nora Bynum, Tracy Yuen Manty, and Erica M. Zendell

(Boston: Harvard Business School, 2013), Case 313-103

The city of Kunshan in 1980 was mere countryside, registering neither on the Chinese government's nor on the international business community's radar. By 2010, Kunshan was the richest city per capita in China and a global technology powerhouse. The case describes its entrepreneurial self-starting development, strategic location, and high levels of local government support. A key question is: would the founding of an international joint venture campus with Duke and Wuhan University keep the city of Kunshan innovative and ahead of the curve?

Li & Fung 2012

F. Warren McFarlan, Michael Shih-ta Chen, and Keith Chi-ho Wong

(Boston: Harvard Business School, 2012), Case 312-102

This case describes the opportunities and strategy facing a large global supply-chain company ($20 billion sales and twenty-nine thousand staff) and the strategy it has chosen to deal with the expanding demand for its services. It tries to do supply-chain orchestration faster and more accurately than anyone else with the aid of a sophisticated information system. Midway through its current three-year plan, Li & Fung is assessing the path it is taking in extending its distribution network business in Asia.

Li & Fung: Internet Issues (A)

F. Warren McFarlan and Fred Young

(Boston: Harvard Business School, 2005), Case 301-009

The issues facing a Hong Kong–based trading company in an electronic age are highlighted. The firm links hundreds of factories in India and Asia with major customers like Gap and The Limited in Europe and in the United States. It hopes its dot-com operation will allow its extraordinary network of factories in Asia to target much smaller retail chains in Asia and Europe.

Qingdao TGOOD Electric Corporation

Hong Zhang, Zheng Xiaoming, Chen Hao, and F. Warren McFarlan

(Beijing: Tsinghua University, 2012), Case TU0035

The largest specialized developer and producer of cubicle-type transformation and distribution equipment in China, TGOOD sells its products mainly to the railway, coal-mining, and power industries. In seven years, TGOOD developed into an enterprise with net annual operating revenue of RMB 600 million and employment of around one thousand. In 2011, the stepping down of railway minister Liu Zhijun (for corruption) and the HSR (high-speed rail) accident of June 2011 caused China to slow down its railway construction, leading TGOOD to rethink the strategic direction of the company.

Real Blue? Viagra and Intellectual Property Rights Law in China

Regina Abrami and Tracy Yuen Manty

(Boston: Harvard Business School, 2010), Case 910-409

Pfizer's China team received disappointing news on July 5, 2004. China's patent review board had just invalidated the company's existing patent on one of its most successful drugs,

Viagra. Making matters worse, a Guangdong-based pharmaceutical company laid claim to Viagra's street name *Wei Ge* (Great Brother), arguing that the term was not a well-known trademark in China. Pfizer is left to wonder whether trade politics or the rule of law will prevail.

ReSource Pro
Elisabeth Köll, Lynda M. Applegate, William R. Kerr, and David Lane
(Boston: Harvard Business School, 2011), Case 812-031

An insurance agency back-office outsourcing firm, ReSource Pro employed 250 people, of whom only four were US-based. With aggressive growth plans, they were examining potential cities in China for expansion.

The Rong Family: A Chinese Business History
Elisabeth Köll
(Boston: Harvard Business School, 2010), Case 308-066

Using the example of the Rong family, China's most prominent industrialist family in pre-1949 China, the case analyzes the organizational structure and transformation of Chinese family firms in terms of managerial hierarchies, kinship alliances, and local networks. It highlights the response of family business to major political crises and interprets the success of overseas Chinese family business as well as the revival of family business networks in the wake of China's economic reforms.

Sealed Air China
Regina Abrami, William C. Kirby, F. Warren McFarlan, and Tracy Yuen Manty
(Boston: Harvard Business School, 2011), Case 308-051

The US-based packaging company Sealed Air China bet on China to help propel its growth as a global company. The company identified China as one of the initial investments in the company's global manufacturing strategy that aimed to create

efficiencies in its operations across the globe. It opened its new
Shanghai plant in 2008.

Shenzhen Stock Exchange

F. Warren McFarlan, Guoqing Chen, Iris T. Li, and David Kiron
(Boston: Harvard Business School, 2002), Case 302-070

The Shenzhen Stock Exchange is the second-largest stock
exchange in China. It shows a surprising sophistication for so
young a company. This case describes the Exchange's growth
and underlying technology as Chinese financial markets
slowly mature.

Taikang Insurance: Standing Out in China's Crowded Insurance Market

William C. Kirby and Tracy Yuen Manty
(Boston: Harvard Business School, 2012), Case 312-109

As a joint-stock insurance company in China, with both state-
owned enterprises and foreign firms as investors, Taikang
Insurance was becoming an important player as an entrepreneurial upstart. It competes with well-entrenched state-owned
rivals. Taikang has had to be innovative to maintain its place
as the fourth-largest insurer in China in an ever more competitive insurance landscape.

UFIDA (A)

Bin Yang, E. Chen, and F. Warren McFarlan
(Beijing: Tsinghua University School of Economics and
Management, 2011–2012), Case TU0007

The six-case UFIDA series describes China's largest supplier
of management/ERP software, its twenty-year evolution, and
current strategic challenges. The (A) case introduces the
company's history, strategic turning points, current market
position, and competition.

UFIDA (B)

Bin Yang, E. Chen, and F. Warren McFarlan

(Beijing: Tsinghua University School of Economics and

Management, 2011–2012), Case TU0009

This case highlights the leadership, cultural, and organizational structure dimensions of UFIDA. The case focuses on the people and their values. From different angles, students can feel Chairman Wang Wenjing's management style and his personal impact on UFIDA.

UFIDA (C)

Bin Yang, E. Chen, and F. Warren McFarlan

(Beijing: Tsinghua University School of Economics and

Management, 2011–2012), Case TU0011

The evolution of UFIDA's management control system is documented over a decade as it grew fivefold from RMB 325 million in sales to RMB 1.66 billion in sales, while its staff grew by more than threefold.

UFIDA (D)

Bin Yang, E. Chen, and F. Warren McFarlan

(Beijing: Tsinghua University School of Economics and

Management, 2011–2012), Case TU0013

The financing decisions of the company are described as it passes through different stages of development. Started in 1988 as an individual business under the umbrella of China's "Reform and Opening" policy, the firm has experienced tremendous growth and became the leading publicly listed software company in China. It had more than RMB 2.3 billion revenue from business product sales in 2009.

UFIDA (E)

Bin Yang, E. Chen, and F. Warren McFarlan

(Beijing: Tsinghua University School of Economics and

Management, 2011–2012), Case TU0015

> UFIDA began internationalization in 2004. In the subse-
> quent six years, UFIDA entered Hong Kong, Singapore,
> Japan, Thailand, Vietnam, and other overseas Asian markets.
> Nonetheless, UFIDA's overseas business footprint was still
> very limited. Overseas revenue accounted for only 0.43 percent
> of UFIDA's total sales in 2009. The case highlights UFIDA's
> launch of its 2010–2012 internationalization strategy and notes
> the barriers to its success.

UFIDA (F)

Bin Yang, E. Chen, and F. Warren McFarlan

(Beijing: Tsinghua University School of Economics and

Management, 2011–2012), Case TU0037

> An extension of UFIDA (A–E), UFIDA (F) looks at the major
> steps UFIDA has taken during 2010–2011. It identifies accom-
> plishments, major future opportunities, and challenges.
> UFIDA's core strategy has shifted from being the leading
> accounting software vendor in China to becoming the largest
> management software vendor in Asia and eventually a world-
> class cloud service provider.

Wanxiang Group: A Chinese Company's Global Strategy

Regina Abrami, William C. Kirby, F. Warren McFarlan,

Tracy Yuen Manty, and Keith Chi-ho Wong

(Boston: Harvard Business School, 2008), Case 308-058

> For nearly forty years, the Wanxiang Group has navigated
> through the significantly different political and economic
> changes in China to succeed as a global leader in the auto parts
> industry. Beginning in 1994, when it first began its operations
> in the United States, Wanxiang expanded as a parts supplier by

being a discerning acquirer of distressed US companies, with specific management strategies to deal with US sensitivities.

Wanxiang Group: A Chinese Company's Global Strategy (B)
William C. Kirby, Nancy Hua Dai, and Erica M. Zendell
(Boston: Harvard Business School, 2013), Case 313-096

Wanxiang has just won the bankruptcy auction for A123, a leading developer and manufacturer of advanced lithium-ion batteries. A key issue is how to handle the international political factors that could jeopardize the deal. A secondary issue is Wanxiang's strategy to ensure this battery technology will become mainstream.

Xiamen PX Project: The Rule of Contract or Citizens in China Today
Regina Abrami and Weiqi Zhang
(Boston: Harvard Business School, 2009), Case 808-123

Focusing on the petrochemical sector, this case examines the effect of environmental activism on China's investment climate. It shows how tensions between a country's national economic development goals and political constraints make for a more unpredictable investment climate, despite evolution in the rule of law within China.

Xi'an International University: The Growth of Private Universities in China
Michael Shih-ta Chen, William C. Kirby, Tracy Yuen Manty, and Keith Chi-ho Wong
(Boston: Harvard Business School, 2009), Case 309-074

Xi'an International University (XAIU) was founded as a private institute of higher education in 1992. Throughout its ensuing years, it met the demand of students who did not test into one of China's public institutions. In 2008, it was seeking to grow by aggressively pursuing opportunities in other provinces and municipalities. Its plan was to franchise the university throughout China. A core concern was whether franchising or expanding into tier-two and tier-three cities would compromise the ground-work that had already been laid and jeopardize XAIU's funding opportunities and academic quality and integrity.

Xinxing Ductile Iron Pipes: Transforming the Management Control Process in Time of Crisis

Ning Jia, Xiaohui Li, and F. Warren McFarlan

(Beijing: Tsinghua University School of Economics

and Management, 2011), TU0023

A Chinese state-owned enterprise that manufactures cast pipe products and steel products, the company is the dominant player in the ductile iron pipe industry, holding more than 40 percent domestic market share and nearly 20 percent global market share. Historically, Xinxing Pipes' management control system was based on standard costs, which worked well until the global financial crisis in 2008, when market demand for steel declined rapidly, resulting in intense price fluctuations in both upstream and downstream operations. The existing management control system failed to respond in a rapid and efficient manner, and Xinxing Pipes tried to reform it.

Zhejiang Semir Garment Co., Ltd.

Jie Jiao, Yuren Fang, and F. Warren McFarlan

(Beijing: Tsinghua University School of Economics

and Management, 2012), TU0039

With the rapid growth of China's economy and China's increasing integration into the global economy in the past two decades, China's leisure clothing and garment enterprise has achieved a rapid rise and become an important competitive force confronting foreign brands trying to enter the Chinese market. Zhejiang Semir Garment Co., Ltd. was founded in 1996 and currently owns two brands. Both occupy a leading position in the Chinese market. Intensified market competition, changes of cost elements, and new sales channels, however, have caused the two brands to come under significant pressure.

NOTES

Chapter 1

1. Aage Krarup-Nielsen, *The Dragon Awakes* (London: J. Lane, 1928); Min-ch'ien T. Z. Tyau, *China Awakened* (New York: Macmillan, 1922); James Cantlie, *Sun Yat-Sen and the Awakening of China* (New York: F.H. Revell, 1912); William F. Burbidge, *Rising China: A Brief History of China and a Biographical Sketch of Generalissimo and Madame Chiang Kai-shek* (London: J. Crowther, 1943); Arthur Judson Brown, *New Forces in Old China: An Unwelcome but Inevitable Awakening* (New York: F.H. Revell, 1904).

2. Lawrence E. Grinter, ed., *The Dragon Awakes: China's Military Modernization Trends and Implications* (Montgomery, AL: United States Air Force University, 1999); C. Fred Bergsten et al., *China's Rise: Challenges and Opportunities* (Washington, DC: Peterson Institute, 2008); Minqi Li, *The Rise of China and the Demise of the Capitalist World Economy* (London: Pluton Press, 2008); Robert S. Ross and Zhu Feng, eds., *China's Ascent: Power, Security, and the Future of International Politics* (Ithaca, NY: Cornell University Press, 2008); Karl Gerth, *As China Goes, So Goes the World: How Chinese Consumers Are Transforming Everything* (New York: Hill & Wang, 2010); Martin Jacques, *When China Rules the World: The End of the Western World and the Birth of a New Global Order* (New York: Penguin, 2009).

3. Carl Crow, *400 Million Customers: The Experiences—Some Happy, Some Sad, of an American in China, and What They Taught Him* (New York: Halcyon, 1937).

4. Ichisada Miyazaki, *China's Examination Hell: The Civil Service Examinations of Imperial China*, trans. Conrad Schirokauer (New York: Weatherhill, 1976).

5. "Overseas Chinese Population Count," *Overseas Chinese Affairs Council*, 2012, http://www.ocac.gov.tw/english/public/public.asp?selno=8889&no=8889&level=B.

6. Sun Yat-sen, *The International Development of China* (London: G.P. Putnam's Sons, 1922), 20.

7. Sun, *The International Development of China*; Michael R. Godley, "Socialism with Chinese Characteristics: Sun Yat-sen and the International Development of China," *Australian Journal of Chinese Affairs*, no. 18 (July 1987): 109–125.

8. William C. Kirby, Tracy Yuen Manty, and G. A. Donovan, "The China Entrepreneurs Forum," Case 312-095 (Boston: Harvard Business School, 2012).

9. Regina Abrami, William C. Kirby, F. Warren McFarlan, Tracy Yuen Manty, and Keith Chi-ho Wong, "Wanxiang Group: A Chinese Company's Global Strategy," Case 308-058 (Boston: Harvard Business School, 2008).

Chapter 2

1. John Lee, "China's Rich Lists Riddled with Communist Party Members," *Forbes*, September 14, 2011, http://www.forbes.com/2011/09/14/china-rich-lists-opinions-contributors-john-lee.html.

2. "China Communist Party Members Exceed 82 Million," *Xinhua*, June 30, 2012, http://news.xinhuanet.com/english/china/2012-06/30/c_131686357.htm.

3. Ibid.

4. William C. Kirby, "Continuity and Change in Modern China: Chinese Economic Planning on the Mainland and on Taiwan, 1943–1958," *Australian Journal of Chinese Affairs*, no. 24 (July 1990): 121–141.

5. For example, Sherman Cochran, "Capitalists Choosing Communist China: The Liu Family of Shanghai, 1948–1956," in *Dilemmas of Victory: The Early Years of the People's Republic of China*, eds. Jeremy Brown and Paul J. Pickowicz (Cambridge, MA: Harvard University Press, 2010).

6. Willy Kraus, *Private Business in China: Revival between Ideology and Pragmatism* (London: Hurst, 1991), 57; Mao Zedong, "Don't Attack on All Fronts" (Mao Zedong's Speech at the Third Plenum of the Seventh Central Committee, June 6, 1950), in *The Writings of Mao Zedong: 1949–1976, Volume 1, September 1949–December 1955* (Armonk, NY: M.E. Sharpe, 1986).

7. Regina Abrami, "Naming Progress, Finding Vice: Class Labeling, Credible Commitment, and the Making of Private Entrepreneurship in Vietnam and China," unpublished manuscript, 2013.

8. Kraus, *Private Business in China*, 53.

9. Abrami, "Naming Progress."

10. Frank Dikötteer, *Mao's Great Famine: The History of China's Most Devastating Catastrophe, 1958–1962* (New York: Walker & Co., 2010).

11. Henry Yuhuai He, *Dictionary of the Political Thought of the People's Republic of China* (Armonk, NY: M.E. Sharpe, 2001), 351.

12. "Shadow Banks on Trial as China's Rich Sister Faces Death," *Bloomberg*, April 11, 2012, http://www.bloomberg.com/news/2012-04-10/shadow-banks-on-trial-as-china-s-rich-sister-faces-death.html.

13. For a book-length study on early practices, see Kellee S. Tsai, *Back Alley Banking: Private Entrepreneurs in China* (Ithaca, NY: Cornell University Press, 2002).

14. "China's Cash-Strapped Small Firms Ring Alarm Bells," *Xinhua*, October 10, 2011, http://news.xinhuanet.com/english2010/china/2011-10/10/c_131181749_2.htm.

15. Edward Wong, "China's Court Overturns a Young Tycoon's Death Sentence," *New York Times*, April 20, 2012, http://www.nytimes.com/2012/04/21/world/asia/china-court-overturns-death-penalty-for-tycoon-in-fraud-case.html.

16. "Premier Wen Says to Handle Ex-Tycoon Death Sentence Based on Facts," *Xinhua*, March 13, 2012, http://news.xinhuanet.com/english/china/2012-03/14/c_131466718.htm; "China Suspends Death Sentence for Wu," *Bloomberg*, April 21, 2012, http://www.businessweek.com/news/2012-04-20/china-s-top-court-orders-new-trial-for-rich-sister-wu-ying.

17. "Shadow Banking in China: The Wenzhou Experiment," *The Economist*, April 7, 2012, http://www.economist.com/node/21552228.

18. "China Has More Than 4,000 Micro-finance Companies," *Xinhua*, January 9, 2012, http://news.xinhuanet.com/english/china/2012-01/10/c_131350905.htm.

19. Regina Abrami, Weiqi Zhang, and Matthew Shaffer, "China Risk Finance: Riding the Wave of China's Financial Services Industry," Case 912-417 (Boston: Harvard Business School, 2012).

20. Cheng Li, ed., *China's Emerging Middle Class: Beyond Economic Transformation* (Washington, DC: Brookings Institution Press, 2010).

21. "China Rich List," *Forbes*, October 11, 2012, http://www.forbes.com/china-billionaires/.

22. Kraus, *Private Business in China*, 24.

23. See table 3 in Kraus, *Private Business in China*, 64.

24. Zhao Ziyang, "Advance Along the Road of Socialism with Chinese Characteristics" (report delivered at the Thirteenth National Congress of the Chinese Communist Party, October 25, 1987), *Beijing Review*, no. 45 (November 9–15, 1987).

25. Chris Hogg, "China's Reluctant First Entrepreneur," *BBC*, April 5, 2010, http://news.bbc.co.uk/2/hi/asia-pacific/8487888.stm.

26. Louisa Lim, "China's Capital of Capitalism Weathers Recession," *National Public Radio*, March 17, 2010, http://www.npr.org/templates/story/story.php?storyId=124740579.

27. Wayne Morrison, "The Growth of the Private Sector in China and Implications for China's Accession to the World Trade Organization," *Congressional Research Services*, March 28, 2001.

28. Wan Runnan, "My College Upper Classman, Hu Jintao," *China Times*, August 2012, http://www.thechinatimes.com/online/2012/08/4701.html.

29. Katherine Forestier, "Chinese Troops Turn on Computer Pioneers," *New Scientist*, no. 1671, July 1, 1989; Thomas B. Gold, "Urban Private Business and Social Change," in *Chinese Society on the Eve of Tiananmen: The Impact of Reform*, eds. Deborah Davis and Ezra Feivel Vogel (Cambridge, MA: Council on East Asian Studies, 1990).

30. "China's Private Entrepreneurs Gain More Clout," research paper, *Xinhua*, January 9, 2007, http://news.xinhuanet.com/english/2007-01/09/content_5585156.htm.

31. Ibid.

32. China Department of Industry and Transport Statistics, via CEIC.

33. Ross Garnaut and Ligang Song, eds., *China's Third Economic Transformation: The Rise of the Private Economy* (London: Routledge, 2004), 34.

34. Garnaut and Song, *China's Third Economic Transformation*, 35.

35. "Laid-Off Workers Protest en Masse," Associated Press, March 18, 2002, http://www.weijingsheng.org/doc/labor/Laid%20%20Off%20Chinese%20Protest%20en%20Masse.htm.

36. Garnaut and Song, *China's Third Economic Transformation*, 89–90.

37. Liu Hua, "Zong qinghou fankong daneng lujing diaocha" [After Zong's rebuttal, Danone only deepens its investigation] *Sina*, April 12, 2007, http://finance.sina.com.cn/chanjing/b/20070412/09073494827.shtml.

38. Fang Xuyan and Lea Yu, "Government Refuses to Release Gini Coefficient," *Caixin*, January 18, 2012, http://english.caixin.com/2012-01-18/100349814.html.

39. Shen Hu, "China's Gini Index at 0.61, University Report Says," *Caixin*, December 10, 2012, http://english.caixin.com/2012-12-10/100470648.html; for other countries, see "Country Comparison: Distribution of Family Income—Gini Index," *CIA World Factbook*, Central Intelligence Agency, 2013, https://www.cia.gov/library/publications/the-world-factbook/index.html.

40. Dwayne Benjamin et al., "Income Inequality during China's Economic Transition," in *China's Great Economic Transformation*, eds. Loren Brandt and Thomas G. Rawski (New York: Cambridge University Press, 2008), 755; Willy Lam, "The 'Latin-Americanization' of China's Domestic Politics," *China Brief* 6, no. 21 (May 9, 2007), http://www.jamestown.org/single/?no_cache=1&tx_ttnews%5Btt_news%5D=3991.

41. Chun Liao, *The Governance Structure of Chinese Firms: Innovation, Competitiveness, and Growth in a Dual Economy* (New York: Springer, 2009), 99.

42. "China's Billionaire People's Congress Makes Capitol Hill Look Like Paupers," *Bloomberg*, February 26, 2012, http://www.bloomberg.com/news/2012-02-26/china-s-billionaire-lawmakers-make-u-s-peers-look-like-paupers.html.

43. "The Perils of Private Enterprise: There Was Blood," *The Economist*, August 4, 2012, http://www.economist.com/node/21559950.

Chapter 3

1. "Car Sales Set to Double in China by 2020," *Powder Metallurgy Review*, March 21, 2012, http://www.ipmd.net/news/001631.html.

2. William C. Kirby, Nora Bynum, Tracy Yuen Manty, and Erica M. Zendell, "Kunshan, Incorporated: The Making of China's Richest Town," Case 313-103 (Boston: Harvard Business School, 2013).

3. "铁道部:全国铁路营业里程9.8万公里居世界第二" [Ministry of Railways: national railway operating mileage of 98,000 kilometers ranks second in the world], *chinanews.com*, January 17, 2013, http://finance.chinanews.com/cj/2013/01-17/4496731.shtml.

4. Elisabeth Fischer, "China's High-Speed Rail Revolution," *railway-technology.com*, November 21, 2012, http://www.railway-technology.com/features/feature124824/.

5. "339,700 Chinese Choose to Study Abroad in 2011," *Xinhua*, February 11, 2012, http://news.xinhuanet.com/english/china/2012-02/11/c_131403850.htm.

6. Institute of International Education, "Fields of Study of Students from Selected Places of Origin, 2011/12," *Open Doors Report on International Educational Exchange*, http://www.iie.org/opendoors.

7. Loren R. Graham, *The Ghost of the Executed Engineer: Technology and the Fall of the Soviet Union* (Cambridge, MA: Harvard University Press, 1993), 42.

8. Zhong Shaohua, "Zhongguo gongchengshi xuehui jieshi" [Brief history of the Chinese Society of Engineers], manuscript; Ralph Heunemann, *The Dragon and the Iron Horse* (Cambridge, MA: Council on East Asian Studies, Harvard University, 1984), 69–70.

9. Sun Yat-sen, *The International Development of China* (London: G.P. Putnam's Sons, 1922), 191.

10. T'ang Leang-li, *Reconstruction in China* (Shanghai: China United Press, 1935).

11. Sun, *The International Development of China*, 192.

12. Ibid., v; generally, see Michael R. Godley, "Socialism with Chinese Characteristics: Sun Yat-sen and the International Development of China," *Australian Journal of Chinese Affairs*, no. 18 (July 1987): 109–125.

13. For a review of Republican-era research on Sun's plans, see Zhong Shaohua, "Zhongshan shiye jihua yu Zhongguo xiandaihua" [Sun Yatsen's *Industrial Plan* and China's modernization], *Zhongshan shehui kexue jikan* [*Sun Yatsen Social Science Quarterly*] 5, no. 4 (December 1990): 134–148.

14. Richard Louis Edmonds, "The Legacy of Sun Yat-sen's Railway Plans," *China Quarterly*, no. 111 (September 1987), 442.

15. Sun, *The International Development of China*, 66–67; Hong Qingyu, "A Review of the Work during the Early Stages of the Three Gorges Project," in *Megaproject: A Case Study of China's Three Gorges Project*, eds. Shiu-hung Luk and Joseph Whitney (New York: M.E. Sharpe, 1993).

16. See Johnson, *MITI and the Japanese Miracle: The Growth of Industrial Policy, 1925–1975* (Stanford, CA: Stanford University Press, 1982), 17ff; Douglas Reynolds, *China, 1898–1912: The Xinzheng Revolution and Japan* (Cambridge, MA: Council on East Asian Studies, 1993); on the Nationalist Party-State as the political precondition of its Communist successor, see Robert E. Bedeski, *State-Building in Modern China: The Kuomintang in the Prewar Period* (Berkeley: Center for Chinese Studies, University of California, Berkeley, 1981).

17. Maryruth Coleman, "Municipal Politics in Nationalist China: Nanjing, 1927–1937" (PhD diss., Harvard University, 1984), 252.

18. Coleman, "Municipal Politics in Nationalist China," 18.

19. Guodu sheji jishu zhuanyuan banshichu [Office of Technical Experts for Planning the National Capital], compilers, *Shoudu jihua* [Plan for the capital] (Nanjing: Guodu sheji jishu zhuanyuan banshichu, 1929).

20. Ibid., 25–32.

21. Ibid., passim. The quotations are from Min-Ch'ien T. Z. Tyau, ed., *Two Years of Nationalist China* (Shanghai: Kelly and Walsh, 1930), 389–394.

22. Coleman, "Municipal Politics in Nationalist China," 254.

23. City planners and public works officials tended to be young university graduates, "enthusiastic and generally honest." See Christian Henriot, *Shanghai, 1927–1937* (Berkeley: University of California Press, 1993), 170.

24. Tyau, *Two Years of Nationalist China*, 389, 396–398.

25. Barry Till, *In Search of Old Nanjing* (Hong Kong: Joint Publishing Company, 1982), 203; *Xin Nanjing* (New Nanjing) (Nanjing: Nanjing shi zhengfu, 1933); Chen Jimin, ed., *Minguo guanfu* (Republican government offices) (Hong Kong: Jinling shu chubanshe, 1992); and "Nanjing shi zhi jingji jianshe"

[Economic development of Nanjing], in *Shinianlai zhi Zhongguo jingji jianshe* [China's economic development in the past ten years], compilers, Zhongyang dangbu guomin jingji jihua weiyuanhui [Commission on national economic planning of the Central Committee] (Nanjing, 1937).

26. V. I. Lenin, "Report of the All-Russia Central Executive Committee and the Council of People's Commissars on the Home and Foreign Policy to the Eighth All-Russia Congress of Soviets," December 22, 1920, reprinted in *V. I. Lenin: Selected Works in Three Volumes*, vol. 3 (Moscow: Progress Publishers, 1977), 461.

27. For a selection of Sun's comments on the topic, see Wang Shuhuai, "Jianshe weiyuanhui dui Zhongguo dianqi shiye de guihua" [The National Reconstruction Commission's planning for China's electric power industry] (paper presented to the Conference on the Centennial of Sun Yatsen's Founding of the Kuomintang for Revolution, Taipei, 1994), 3–4.

28. Yun Chen, "Dianqi wang" [Electrical power network], *Jianshe yuekan* no. 9 (October 1930): 37.

29. Sun, *The International Development of China*, 192.

30. See A. Viola Smith and Anselm Chuh, *Motor Roads in China*, US Department of Commerce Trade Promotion Series, no. 120 (Washington, DC: US Government Printing Office, 1931), 2–3, 7, 20ff.

31. Société des Nations, General 50/R5669-71, "Engineering Mission of the League of Nations in China," Report no. 7, September 7, 1932, p. 3.

32. Ibid., Report no. 8, October 19, 1932, p. 4 and appendix.

33. Ibid., p. 1; Report of December 10, 1932, appendix, "Highway inspection trip to Hunan province"; Chin Fen, "The National Economic Council: History, Organization, and Activities" (March 1935), 6–14.

34. See William M. Leafy Jr., *The Dragon's Wings: The China National Aviation Corporation and the Development of Commercial Aviation in China* (Athens: University of Georgia Press, 1976), 13–16; Bodo Wiethoff, *Luftverkehr in China* (Wiesbaden: O. Harrassowitz, 1975), 104–131; Jack C. Young, "Joint Venture and Licensing in Civil Aviation: A Sino-American Perspective," *Stanford Journal of International Studies* 15 (1979): 253.

35. Academica Historia, Taiwan, 2–12.02.I, file, "Zhongguo hangkong qicai zhizao gongsi" [China Air Materials Construction Company] (1934–37); *Zhongguo jindai gongyeshi ziliao* [Materials on the modern history of Chinese industry], vol. 3, ed. Chen Zhen (Beijing: Sanlien shudian, 1961), 921.

36. Shanghai Academy of Social Sciences Documentary Collection, Ministry of Industry file, "Gongye zhongxin" [Industrial center]: "Guoying gangtiechang" [State-run iron- and steelworks] Ministry of Industry report, August 1932; "Benbu yinianlai choushe guoying gongye gaikuang" [Overview of this ministry's preparations for state-run industry in the past year], March 1933; "Shiyebu chouban guoying gongye" [Ministry of Industry preparations for state-run industries], 1936; *Zhongguo jindai gongyeshi ziliao* [Materials on the modern history of Chinese industry], vol. 3, ed. Chen Zhen (Beijing: Sanlien shudian, 1961), 790–793.

37. Chen Guofu, "Gaige jiaoyu chubu fangan" [Draft plan for the reform of education], in *Chen Guofu xiansheng quanji* (Taipei: Zheng Zhong shuju, 1952), 169.

38. William C. Kirby, "The Chinese War Economy: Mobilization, Control, and Planning in Nationalist China," in *China's Bitter Victory: The War with Japan, 1937–1945*, eds. Steven I. Levine and James C. Hsiung (New York: M.E. Sharpe, 1992).

39. "Ziyuan weiyuanhui gongbao" [Resources Committee Bulletin] 13, no. 4 (October 1947), 40; Chu-yuan Cheng, *China's Economic Development: Growth and Structural Change* (Boulder, CO: Westview Press, 1982), 138; Su Hsing Hsueh and Lin Tse-lin Mu-ch'iao, *The Socialist Transformation of the National Economy in China* (Beijing: Beijing Foreign Language Press, 1960), 20; Thomas G. Rawski, *China's Transition to Industrialism* (Ann Arbor: University of Michigan Press, 1980), 30.

40. Chu-yuan Cheng, *Communist China's Economy, 1949–1962* (South Orange, NJ: Seton Hall University, 1963), 9.

41. See ibid. for details.

42. The group was also named in part because it was formed in the thirty-first year of the Republic.

43. The following is based largely on extensive interviews in the PRC and on Taiwan with living members of this group, and with the NRC officials who supervised them.

44. William C. Kirby, "China's Internationalization in the Early People's Republic: Dreams of a Socialist World Economy," *China Quarterly* (December 2006): 870–890.

45. Leo A. Orleans, *Professional Manpower and Education in Communist China* (Washington, DC: US Government Printing Office, 1961), 67ff.

46. "2013 年上海市统计局、 国家统计局上海调查总队统计数据信息发布计划" [2013 Shanghai Municipal Bureau of Statistics, National Bureau of Statistics Survey Organization Shanghai Information Dissemination Plan] Shanghai Municipal Bureau of Statistics, http://www.stats.sh.gov.cn/data/release.xhtml.

47. William C. Kirby, F. Warren McFarlan, Tracy Yuen Manty, and G. A. Donovan, "China Mobile's Rural Communications Strategy," Case 309-340 (Boston: Harvard Business School), 2011.

48. Data taken from the China Premium Database from CEIC Data, www.ceicdata.securities.com.

49. Regina Abrami and Weiqi Zhang, "Xiamen PX Project: The Rule of Contract or Citizens in China Today," Case 808-123 (Boston: Harvard Business School, 2009).

50. "Three Gorges Dam Has Caused Urgent Problems, Says China," *The Guardian*, May 19, 2011, http://www.guardian.co.uk/environment/2011/may/19/china-three-gorges-dam.

51. Wiethoff, *Luftverkehr in China*, 318.

52. See *Rising Above a Gathering Storm: Energizing and Employing America for a Brighter Future* (Washington, DC: National Academy of Sciences, 2007). Other studies have indicated a smaller number of graduates at the BA level or higher, and point to the fact that the United States grants more such engineering degrees per million residents than does China. See Gerald W. Bracey, "Heard the One About the 600,000 Chinese Engineers?" *Washington Post*, May 21, 2006, http://www.washingtonpost.com/wp-dyn/content/article/2006/05/19/AR2006051901760.html.

Chapter 4

1. The China Europe International Business School, the Wenzhou Chamber of Commerce, the Benelux Chamber of Commerce, and Booz & Company, *Innovation: China's Next Advantage? 2012 China Innovation Survey*, July 2012, http://www.booz.com/media/uploads/BoozCo_2012-China-Innovation-Survey.pdf.

2. Jason Lim, "Why China Won't Be Innovative for at Least 20 More Years," *VentureBeat* (blog), March 26, 2012, http://venturebeat.com/2012/03/26/why-china-doesnt-innovate/.

3. Ichisada Miyazaki, *China's Examination Hell: The Civil Service Examinations of Imperial China*, trans. Conrad Schirokauer (New York: Weatherhill, 1976).

4. Elisabeth Köll, "Enterprise Culture in Chinese History: Zhang Jian and the Dasheng Cotton Mills," Case 308-068 (Boston: Harvard Business School, 2010).

5. Elisabeth Köll, "The Rong Family: A Chinese Business History," Case 308-066 (Boston: Harvard Business School, 2010).

6. Eliana Johnson, "NSA Chief: Chinese Cyber-Theft 'Most Significant Transfer of Wealth in History,'" *National Review Online*, June 23, 2013, http://www.nationalreview.com/corner/351786/nsa-chief-chinese-cyber-theft-most-significant-transfer-wealth-history-eliana-johnson.

7. Regina Abrami, William C. Kirby, F. Warren McFarlan, Ning Xiadong, and Tracy Yuen Manty, "China Netcom: Corporate Governance in China (A)," Case 308-027 (Boston: Harvard Business School, 2008).

8. Ibid.

9. Regina Abrami, William C. Kirby, F. Warren McFarlan, and Tracy Yuen Manty, "China Netcom: Corporate Governance in China (B)," Case 308-091 (Boston: Harvard Business School, 2008).

10. F. Warren McFarlan, Guoqing Chen, and David Lane, "COSCO," Case 302-051 (Boston: Harvard Business School, 2002).

11. F. Warren McFarlan, Carin-Isabel Knoop, and David Lane, "Alibaba .com," Case 301-047 (Boston: Harvard Business School, 2001).

12. Lydia DePillis, "A Lot of CEOs Get Taken Hostage in China," *Washington Post*, June 25, 2013, http://www.washingtonpost.com/blogs/wonkblog/wp/2013/06/25/a-lot-of-ceos-get-taken-hostage-in-china/.

13. What follows is drawn from Micah Springut, Steven Schlaikjer, and David Chen, *China's Program for Science and Technology Modernization: Implications for American Competitiveness*, report prepared for the U.S.-China Economic and Security Review Commission, CENTRA Technology Inc., January 2011, pp. 26–32, http://china-us.uoregon.edu/pdf/uscc_report.pdf.

14. Richard P. Suttmeier, Cong Cao, and Denis Fred Simon, "China's Innovation Challenge and the Remaking of the Chinese Academy of Sciences," *Innovations* (Summer 2006), 78–97.

15. The Ministry of Science and Technology replaced the Science and Technology Commission in 1998.

16. See http://genychina.com for descriptions of these and other such ventures.

17. "Research and Development," Huawei website, 2013, http://www.huawei.com/en/about-huawei/corporate-info/research-development/index.htm.

18. Eli Lake, "Beijing Spying Feared in Telecom Proposal: Chinese Firm Would Make Parts," *Washington Times*, October 20, 2010, http://www.washingtontimes.com/news/2010/oct/20/beijing-spying-feared-in-telecom-proposal/?page=all.

19. Leslie Kwoh, "Huawei, A Rising Chinese Tech Firm, Aims to Penetrate the U.S. Market," *Star Ledger* (Newark, NJ), July 31, 2011, http://www.nj.com/business/index.ssf/2011/07/chinas_huawei_the_biggest_comp.html.

20. Ashlee Vance and Bruce Einhorn, "At Huawei, Matt Bross Tries to Ease U.S. Security Fears," *Bloomberg Businessweek*, September 15, 2011, http://www.businessweek.com/magazine/at-huawei-matt-bross-tries-to-ease-us-security-fears-09152011.html.

21. Ibid.

22. "Global R&D Network," Haier, 2013, http://www.haier.net/en/research_development/rd_System/global/.

23. "SANY America," SANY Group, 2013, http://www.sanygroup.com/abroad/america/en-us/about/america.htm; "SANY America," SANY Group, 2013, http://www.sanygroup.com/abroad/america/en-us/about/america.htm.

24. Aaron Kirchfield, "Sany Will Buy Biggest Cement-Pump Maker Putzmeister in Biggest China-German Deal," January 27, 2012, http://www.bloomberg.com/news/2012-01-27/sany-will-buy-cement-pump-maker-putzmeister-in-biggest-china-german-deal.html.

25. Xiao Wan, "ChemChina Develops through Acquisitions," *China Daily*, October 24, 2008, http://www.chinadaily.com.cn/cndy/2008-10/24/content_7136469.htm.

26. Michael Shih-ta Chen, William C. Kirby, Tracy Yuen Manty, and Keith Chi-ho Wong, "Xi'an International University: The Growth of Private Universities in China," Case 309-074 (Boston: Harvard Business School, 2009).

Chapter 5

1. Regina Abrami, William C. Kirby, F. Warren McFarlan, Tracy Yuen Manty, and Keith Chi-ho Wong, "Wanxiang Group: A Chinese Company's Global Strategy," Case 308-058 (Boston: Harvard Business School, 2008).

2. "Special Economic Zones and Open Coastal Cities," *China Society for Human Rights Studies*, http://www.humanrights-china.org/meetingchina/Meeti2001112793911.htm.

3. Bin Yang, E. Chen, and F. Warren McFarlan, "UFIDA (A–F)," Cases TU0007, TU0009, TU0011, TU0013, TU0015, TU0037 (Beijing: Tsinghua University School of Economics and Management, 2011–2012).

4. Ziqian Zhao, Jin Zhang, and F. Warren McFarlan, "Kingdee," Case TU0005 (Beijing: Tsinghua University School of Economics and Management, 2011).

5. John A. Quelch and Katherine E. Jocz, "Google in China (A)," Case 510-071 (Boston: Harvard Business School, 2010); also John A. Quelch, "Google in China (B) and (C)," Cases 510-110 and 511-024 (Boston: Harvard Business School, 2011).

6. William C. Kirby, F. Warren McFarlan, and Tracy Yuen Manty, "The Challenges of Launching a Start-up in China: Dorm99.com," Case 307-075

(Boston: Harvard Business School, 2008); also William C. Kirby, F. Warren McFarlan, and Tracy Yuen Manty, "A Chinese Start-up's Midlife Crisis: 99Sushe.com," Case 309-060 (Boston: Harvard Business School, 2009).

7. Donghong Li, Hong Zhang, Lei Li, and F. Warren McFarlan, "Chem-China," Case TU0028 (Beijing: Tsinghua University School of Economics and Management, 2012).

8. William C. Kirby, F. Warren McFarlan, and Tracy Yuen Manty, "Esquel Group: Integrating Business Strategy and Corporate Social Responsibility," Case 307-076 (Boston: Harvard Business School, 2011).

9. Michael E. Porter, "The Five Forces That Shape Strategy," *Harvard Business Review*, January 2008, http://hbr.org/2008/01/the-five-competitive-forces-that-shape-strategy/.

10. William C. Kirby, Michael Shih-ta Chen, Tracy Yuen Manty, and Yi Kwan Chu, "International Agribusiness in China: Charoen Pokphand Group," Case 910-418 (Boston: Harvard Business School, 2011).

11. William C. Kirby, Nora Bynum, Tracy Yuen Manty, and Erica M. Zendell, "Kunshan, Incorporated: The Making of China's Richest Town," Case 313-103 (Boston: Harvard Business School, 2013).

12. Einar Tangen, *The Kunshan Way* (Beijing: Foreign Languages Press, 2010), 130.

13. Ibid., 77.

14. Elisabeth Köll, Lynda M. Applegate, William R. Kerr, and David Lane, "ReSource Pro," Case 812-031 (Boston: Harvard Business School, 2011).

15. Regina Abrami, William C. Kirby, F. Warren McFarlan, and Tracy Yuen Manty, "Sealed Air China," Case 308-051 (Boston: Harvard Business School, 2011).

16. Regina Abrami, William C. Kirby, F. Warren McFarlan, and Tracy Yuen Manty, "Inner Mongolia Yili Group: China's Pioneering Dairy Brand," Case 308-052 (Boston: Harvard Business School, 2011).

17. "China Now World's Largest Luxury Market: Bain Report," *Jing Daily*, December 17, 2012, http://www.jingdaily.com/china-now-worlds-largest-luxury-market-bain-report/22695/.

18. Guoqing Chen, Ziqian Zhao, and F. Warren McFarlan, "China Merchants Bank in Transition," Case TU0017 (Beijing: Tsinghua University School of Economics and Management, 2011).

19. Michael Shih-ta Chen, Keith Chi-ho Wong, and William C. Kirby, "Appellation Shanxi: Grace Vineyard," Case 309-075 (Boston: Harvard Business School, 2011).

20. Amy Cortese, "Wine from China," *New York Times Magazine*, December 12, 2008, http://www.nytimes.com/2008/12/14/magazine/14Ideas-section4B-t-005.html.

21. Ziqian Zhao, Zheng Xiaoming, and F. Warren McFarlan, "The Haidilao Company," Case TU0021 (Beijing: Tsinghua University School of Economics and Management, 2011).

22. David E. Bell and Aldo Sesia, "COFCO Xinjiang Tunhe Co., Ltd.," Case 508-079 (Boston: Harvard Business School, 2009).

23. "The Perils of Private Enterprise: There Was Blood," *The Economist*, August 4, 2012, http://www.economist.com/node/21559950.

24. Ricky Lai and Ali Farhoomand, "Alibaba's Jack Ma: Rise of the New Chinese Entrepreneur," Case HKU-913 (Hong Kong: University of Hong Kong, 2010).

Chapter 6

1. "Issue in Focus: China's 'Going Out' Investment Policy," Freeman Briefing, Center for Strategic and International Studies, May 27, 2008, http://csis.org/files/publication/080527_freeman_briefing.pdf.

2. Eric Martin and Bennett Roth, "Boeing Taps D.C. Lobbyist in Export-Import Bank Renewal Push," *Bloomberg*, 20 March 2012, http://www.bloomberg.com/news/2012-03-20/boeing-taps-top-d-c-lobbyist-in-export-import-bank-renewal-push.html.

3. "2010 Annual Report: China EXIM Bank Operational Highlights," China EXIM Bank website, 2010, http://english.eximbank.gov.cn/annual/2010/2010nb23.shtml.

4. Michael Forsythe and Henry Sanderson, "Financing China Costs Poised to Rise with CDB Losing Sovereign-Debt Status," *Bloomberg*, May 2, 2011, http://www.bloomberg.com/news/2011-05-02/financing-china-costs-poised-to-rise-with-decision-on-cdb-debt.html.

5. F. Warren McFarlan, Guoqing Chen, and David Lane, "COSCO," Case 302-051 (Boston: Harvard Business School, 2002).

6. Dai Yan, "COSCO Interested to Buy Stake in Greek Port," *China Daily*, February 9, 2009, http://www.chinadaily.com.cn/english/doc/2006-02/09/content_518508.htm.

7. Ralph William Huenemann, *The Dragon and the Iron Horse: The Economics of Railroads in China, 1876–1937* (Cambridge, MA: Council on East Asian Studies, Harvard University, 1984); Bodo Wiethoff, *Luftverkehr in China* (Wiesbaden: O. Harrassowitz, 1975).

8. Dan Xizhuan and Wang Baorun, *Dayu xian (Jiangxi) xu zhi* [Dayu County (Jiangxi) Continued Ambitions], vol. 2 (China: Xianfeng yuan nian, 1851); Jean-Baptiste du Halde, *The General History of China*, trans. Richard Brookes (London: J. Watts, 1736), 1, 161; Stanley Fowler Wright, *Kiangsi Native Trade and Its Taxation* (New York: Garland Publishing, 1980), 12, 16.

9. John K. Fairbank, "The Creation of the Treaty System," in *The Cambridge History of China*, vol. 11, part 1, ed. John K. Fairbank (Cambridge, UK: Cambridge University Press, 1978), 245; Jian Youwen, *The Taiping Revolutionary Movement* (New Haven, CT: Yale University Press, 1973), 307; Wright, *Kiangsi Native Trade and Its Taxation,* 12, Appendix A; Liu Daqian, "Dayu shehui jingji zhi xiankuang tan" [On the current situation of Dayu's society and economy] in Jiangxi sheng zhengfu, ed., *Jingji xunkan* [Economic Periodical] 2, no. 14 (May 11, 1934), 15–17; *Jiangxi zhi techan* [Local products of Jiangxi] (Nanchang, 1935), 106.

10. Zhou Daolong, ed., *Gannan wukuang zhi* [Tungsten mines of Southern Jiangxi] (Nanchang, 1936), 121–122; *Jiangxi jingji wenti* [Jiangxi economic issues] (Nanchang: Jiangxi sheng zhengfu, 1934), 255ff; L. Fabel, "Le Tungstène: Minerai le plus important de la Chine" [Tungsten: China's Most Important Mineral Ore], *Bulletin de l'Université l'Aurore* 3, no. 4 (1943), 128.

11. "Shishi wusha tongzhi zhi buzhu" [Steps toward the control of tungsten ore], *Jingji xunkan* [Economic Periodical] 4, no. 5 (February 15, 1935), 5; Liu Daqian, "Dayu," 16–17.

12. Lillian M. Li, *China's Silk Trade: Traditional Industry in the Modern World, 1842–1937* (Cambridge, MA: Council on East Asian Studies, Harvard University, 1981), 200; Terry M. Weidner, "Local Political Work under the Nationalists: The 1930's Silk Reform Campaign," *Illinois Papers in Asian Studies*, no. 2 (1983), 67.

13. Lau-King Quan, *China's Relations with the League of Nations, 1919–1936* (Hong Kong: Asiatic Litho Printing Press, 1939), 219–226; "Quanguo jingji weiyuanhui gongzuo baogao" [Report of the work of the National Economic Council], Second Historical Archives, Nanjing 44, no. 1719 (1937): 33–40; Chin Fen, "The National Economic Council," *Second Historical Archives* 44, no. 2, 78 (March 1935), 67–70; Lau-King Quan, *China's Relations with the League of Nations*; Tao Siu, "L'Oeuvre du Conseil National Economique Chinois" [Work of the Chinese National Economic Council], (PhD diss., L'Université de Nancy, 1936), 73–77.

14. Christian Henriot, *Shanghai, 1927–1937* (Berkeley: University of California Press, 1993); Marie-Claire Bergère, *The Golden Age of the Chinese Bourgeoisie: 1911–1937 (Studies in Modern Capitalism)*, trans. Janet Lloyd (Cambridge, UK: Cambridge University Press, 1989); David Strand, *Rickshaw Beijing: City People and Politics in the 1920s* (Berkeley: University of California Press, 1989).

15. Bergère, *The Golden Age of the Chinese Bourgeoisie*.

16. Elisabeth Köll, "The Rong Family: A Chinese Business History," Case 308-066 (Boston: Harvard Business School, 2010).

17. William C. Kirby, F. Warren McFarlan, and Tracy Yuen Manty, "Esquel Group: Integrating Business Strategy and Corporate Social Responsibility," Case 307-076 (Boston: Harvard Business School, 2008).

18. To be sure, this was not an overnight process, as Hans J. van de Ven has shown in his *From Friend to Comrade: The Founding of the Chinese Communist Party, 1920–1927* (Berkeley: University of California Press, 1991). On the international if not particularly cosmopolitan experiences of Chinese communists in Europe, see Marilyn A. Levine, *The Found Generation: Chinese Communists in Europe During the Twenties* (Seattle: University of Washington Press, 1993).

19. Mah Feng-Hwa, *The Foreign Trade of Mainland China* (Chicago: Aldine-Atherton, 1971), 724.

20. William C. Kirby, "Sino-American Relations in Comparative Perspective," in *Pacific Passage: The Study of American-East Asian Relations on the Eve of the Twenty-First Century*, ed. W. I. Cohen (New York: Columbia University Press, 1996), 163–190.

21. Wayne Morrison, "The Growth of the Private Sector in China and Implications for China's Accession to the World Trade Organization," *Congressional Research Services*, March 28, 2001.

22. James Mann, *Beijing Jeep: A Case Study of Western Business in China* (New York: Simon & Schuster, 1989).

23. "Company News; China Agrees to Buy Vehicles from the Big Three," *New York Times*, July 29, 1992, http://www.nytimes.com/1992/07/29/business/company-news-china-agrees-to-buy-vehicles-from-the-big-three.html.

24. Regina Abrami and Iacob Koch-Weser, "Heavy Metal (A): Baosteel Enters Brazil," Case 912-411 (Boston: Harvard Business School, 2011); Regina Abrami and Iacob Koch-Weser, "Heavy Metal (B): Baosteel Struggles in Brazil," Case 912-412 (Boston: Harvard Business School, 2011); Regina Abrami and Iacob Koch-Weser, "The Comeback (C): Baosteel Stays in Brazil," Case 912-413 (Boston: Harvard Business School, 2011).

25. Robb M. Stewart, "Rio Tinto Accepts Chinese Bid for Kalahari Shares," *Wall Street Journal*, February 1, 2012, http://online.wsj.com/article/SB100014240 52970204740904577195961601888798.html.

26. Emma Rowley, "Uranium Miner Kalahari Agrees Takeover by Chinese," *The Telegraph*, December 8, 2011, http://www.telegraph.co.uk/finance/newsbysector/industry/mining/8944951/Uranium-miner-Kalahari-agrees-take-over-by-Chinese.html.

27. "China Minmetals, Chile's Codelco Set Up 2 bln usd JV," *Metals Place*, February 23, 2006, http://metalsplace.com/news/articles/4030/china-minmetals-chiles-codelco-set-up-2-bln-usd-jv/; "Case Studies: Structured Financing for Codelco with Minmetals," *Asset*, 2013, http://www.assetchile.com/descripcion-de-transacciones/structured-financing-for-codelco-with-minmetals/.

28. Paul Ausick, "Petrobras Seems the Winner in China's $10 Billion Loan (PBR, SNP, XOM, CVX)," *24/7 WallSt.com*, May 20, 2009, http://247wallst.com/2009/05/20/petrobras-seems-the-winner-in-chinas-10-billion-loan-pbr-snp-xom-cvx/.

29. Donghong Li, Hong Zhang, Lei Li, and F. Warren McFarlan, "Chem-China," Case TU0028 (Beijing: Tsinghua School of Economics and Management, 2012).

30. Yan Bian, "Legion of Honor for ChemChina President Ren," *China Daily*, December 20, 2011, http://www.chinadaily.com.cn/cndy/2011-12/20/content_14290290.htm; "Overseas Development," *ChemChina*, 2013, http://www.chemchina.com.cn/en/gjyw/whfz/A601701web 1.htm; Françoise Nicolas, "Chinese Direct Investments in France: No French Exception, No Chinese Challenge," IE Programme Paper IE PP 2010/02 (London: Chatham House, January 2010), http://www.chathamhouse.org/sites/default/files/public/Research/International%20Economics/0110pp_nicolas.pdf.

31. Alexei Barrionuevo, "China's Interest in Farmland Makes Brazil Uneasy," *New York Times*, May 26, 2011, http://www.nytimes.com/2011/05/27/world/americas/27brazil.html; "China Wants to Buy Directly from Brazilian Farmers, Avoid Intermediation," *MercoPress*, August 16, 2011, http://en.mercopress.com/2011/08/16/china-wants-to-buy-directly-from-brazilian-farmers-avoid-intermediation.

32. Kelly Hearn, "China Plants Bitter Seeds in South American Farmland," *Washington Times*, February 1, 2012, http://www.washingtontimes.com/news/2012/feb/1/china-plants-bitter-seeds-in-south-american-farmla/?page=all.

33. "Outsourcing's Third Wave," *The Economist*, May 21, 2009, http://www.economist.com/node/13692889.

34. Sudha Ramachandran, "China's Pearl in Pakistan's Waters," *Asia Times*, March 4, 2005, http://www.atimes.com/atimes/South_Asia/GC04Df06.html.

35. Ziad Haider, "Baluchis, Beijing, and Pakistan's Gwadar Port," *Georgetown Journal of International Affairs* 6, no.1 (2005): 6, 95–103.

36. Farhan Bokhari and Kathrin Hille, "Pakistan in Talks to Hand Port to China," *Financial Times*, August 30, 2012, http://www.ft.com/intl/cms/s/0/5c58608c-f2a6-11e1-ac41-00144feabdc0.html#axzz2ChAaJ3HY.

37. Regina Abrami, "China and the WTO: Doing the Right Thing?" Case 704-041 (Boston: Harvard Business School, 2004).

38. Fang Yang, ed., "Full Text: China-Africa Economic and Trade Cooperation," *Xinhua*, December 23, 2010, http://news.xinhuanet.com/english2010/china/2010-12/23/c_13661632.htm.

39. Geoff Dyer, Jamil Anderlini, and Henny Sender, "China's Lending Hits New Heights," *Financial Times*, January 17, 2011, http://www.ft.com/intl/cms/s/0/488c60f4-2281-11e0-b6a2-00144feab49a.html.

40. "China: The New Colonialists," *The Economist*, March 13, 2008, http://www.economist.com/node/10853534.

41. Nicholas D. Kristof, "China and Sudan, Blood and Oil," *New York Times*, April 23, 2006, http://query.nytimes.com/gst/fullpage.html?res=990CE3D9153FF930A15757C0A9609C8B63.

42. Adriane Tillman, "UC Regents Agree to Divest from Sudan," *SDnews.com*, 2006, http://www.sdnews.com/view/full_story/298651/article-UC-Regents-agree-to-divest-from-Sudan.

43. Jonathan Stempel, "Fidelity, Berkshire Targeted over PetroChina," Reuters, May 1, 2007, http://www.reuters.com/article/2007/05/01/idUSN01231202.

44. "South Sudan 'Agrees $8bn Deal with China,'" *BBC*, April 28, 2012, http://www.bbc.co.uk/news/world-africa-17883321; Jane Perlez, "South Sudan to Get Aid from China; No Oil Deal," *New York Times*, April 26, 2012, http://www.nytimes.com/2012/04/26/world/asia/china-to-aid-south-sudan-but-pipeline-efforts-stall.html.

45. Regina Abrami and Iacob Koch-Weser, "Goldwind USA: Chinese Wind in the Americas," Case 912-416 (Boston: Harvard Business School, 2012).

46. Edward Welsch, Dinny McMahon, and Phred Dvorak, "China Eyes Potash Corp," *Wall Street Journal*, September 2, 2010, http://online.wsj.com/article/SB10001424052748704791004575465440115184752.html.

47. "Nexen Shareholders Approve Cnooc Deal," *Wall Street Journal*, September 20, 2012, http://online.wsj.com/article/SB10000872396390444032404578008162542570432.html; "China Oil Giant Buys into North America," *CNN Money*, July 23, 2012, http://money.cnn.com/2012/07/23/news/companies/cnooc-nexen/index.htm.

48. Regina Abrami and Weiqi Zhang, "China Construction America (A): The Road Ahead," Case 911-408 (Boston: Harvard Business School, 2011).

49. Joseph S. Nye Jr., *Soft Power: The Means to Success in World Politics* (New York: Public Affairs, 2004).

50. Wang Lili, "Strengthen China's Public Diplomacy," *China Daily*, June 2, 2012, http://english.peopledaily.com.cn/90883/7834319.html.

Chapter 7

1. For a stimulating set of papers, see Cheng Li, ed., *China's Emerging Middle Class: Beyond Economic Transformation* (Washington, DC: Brookings Institution Press, 2010).

2. "28,000 Chinese Waterways Dry Up amid Pollution Tidal Wave," *Russia Today*, March 31, 2013, http://rt.com/news/china-pollution-rivers-devlopment-101/.

3. See the superb study by Dai Qing, "The Heritage of Beijing Water," *China Heritage Quarterly*, no. 16 (December 2008), http://www.chinaheritagequarterly.org/editorial.php?issue=016.

4. Edward Wong, "On a Scale of 0 to 500, Beijing's Air Quality Tops 'Crazy Bad' at 755," *New York Times*, January 12, 2013, http://www.nytimes.com/2013/01/13/science/earth/beijing-air-pollution-off-the-charts.html?_r=0; Chi-Chi Zhang, "U.S. Embassy: Beijing Air Quality Is 'Crazy Bad,'" *Huffington Post*, November 19, 2010, http://www.huffingtonpost.com/2010/11/19/us-embassy-beijing-air-qu_n_785870.html.

5. Clifford Coonan, "Beijing Is Left Fighting for Breath as Pollution Goes off the Scale," *The Independent*, January 29, 2013, http://www.independent.co.uk/environment/green-living/beijing-is-left-fighting-for-breath-as-pollution-goes-off-the-scale-8471743.html.

6. William C. Kirby, Nancy Hua Dai, and Erica M. Zendell, "Wanxiang Group: A Chinese Company's Global Strategy (B)," Case 313-096 (Boston: Harvard Business School, 2013).

7. Regina Abrami and Iacob Koch-Weser, "Goldwind USA: Chinese Wind in the Americas," Case 912-416 (Boston: Harvard Business School, 2012).

8. "World's Biggest Airport Planned," *CNN Travel*, September 13, 2011, http://travel.cnn.com/shanghai/life/world's-biggest-airport-planned-328259.

9. "Urban and Rural Areas 2011," United Nations Department of Economic and Social Affairs Population Division, 2011, http://esa.un.org/unup/Wallcharts/urban-rural-areas.pdf.

10. "China to Expand Insurance So Sick Don't 'Lose Everything,'" *Bloomberg News*, September 17, 2012, http://www.bloomberg.com/news/2012-09-17/china-to-expand-insurance-so-sick-don-t-lose-everything-.html.

11. Bryant Ott and Rajesh Srinivasan, "Three in 10 Chinese Adults Smoke," *Gallup World*, February 9, 2012, http://www.gallup.com/poll/152546/three-chinese-adults-smoke.aspx.

12. Wei Tian, "Credit Card Use Up, So Are Risks," *China Daily*, May 9, 2012, *English China News Service*, http://europe.chinadaily.com.cn/business/2012-05/09/content_15244850.htm; and Wang Yuxia,"Young People China's Main Credit Card Users," April 8, 2013, http://europe.chinadaily.com.cn/business/2012-05/09/content_15244850.htm.

13. F. Warren McFarlan, Michael Shih-ta Chen, and Keith Chi-ho Wong, "Li & Fung 2012," Case 312-102 (Boston: Harvard Business School, 2012).

14. John E. Wills Jr., "Chinese and Maritime Europeans," unpublished paper cited in William C. Kirby, "Traditions of Centrality, Authority, and Management in Modern China's Foreign Relations," in *Chinese Foreign Policy: Theory and Practice*, eds. T. W. Robinson and David Shambaugh (Oxford: Clarendon Press, 1994), 21.

15. Gary King, Jennifer Pan, and Margaret E. Roberts, "How Censorship in China Allows Government Criticism but Silences Collective Expression," *American Political Science Review*, May 2013, http://gking.harvard.edu/files/censored.pdf.

16. Andrew Jacobs, "Chinese Officials Find Misbehavior Now Carries Cost," *New York Times*, December 25, 2012, http://www.nytimes.com/2012/12/26/world/asia/corrupt-chinese-officials-draw-unusual-publicity.html.

17. Institute of International Education. "Open Doors Data: International Students: Leading Places of Origin," 2013, http://www.iie.org/Research-and-Publications/Open-Doors/Data/International-Students/Leading-Places-of-Origin/2010-12.

18. Minxin Pei, "China's Troubled Bourbons," *Project Syndicate*, October 31, 2012, http://www.project-syndicate.org/commentary/rising-political-uncertainty-in-china-by-minxin-pei.

19. Jacobs, "Chinese Officials Find Misbehavior Now Carries Cost."

BIBLIOGRAPHY

Abrami, Regina. "Naming Progress, Finding Vice: Class Labeling, Credible Commitment, and the Making of Private Entrepreneurship in Vietnam and China." Unpublished manuscript. 2013.

Academica Historia, Taiwan, 2–12.02.I, file. "Zhongguo hangkong qicai zhizao gongsi" [China Air Materials Construction Company], (1934–1937).

Archibold, Randal C. "China Buys Inroads in the Caribbean, Catching U.S. Notice." *New York Times*, April 7, 2012. http://www.nytimes.com/2012/04/08/world/americas/us alert-as-chinas-cash-buys-inroads-in-caribbean.html.

Ausick, Paul. "Petrobras Seems the Winner in China's $10 Billion Loan (PBR, SNP, XOM, CVX)." *24/7 WallSt.com*, May 20, 2009. http://247wallst.com/2009/05/20/petrobras-seems-the-winner-in-chinas-10-billion-loan-pbr-snp-xom-cvx/.

Barrionuevo, Alexei. "China's Interest in Farmland Makes Brazil Uneasy." *New York Times*, May 26, 2011. http://www.nytimes.com/2011/05/27/world/americas/27brazil.html.

Bedeski, Robert E. *State-Building in Modern China: The Kuomintang in the Prewar Period*. Berkeley: Center for Chinese Studies, University of California, Berkeley, 1981.

Benjamin, Dwayne, et al. "Income Inequality during China's Economic Transition," in *China's Great Economic Transformation*, edited by Loren Brandt and Thomas G. Rawski. New York: Cambridge University Press, 2008.

Bergère, Marie-Claire. *The Golden Age of the Chinese Bourgeoisie: 1911–1937 (Studies in Modern Capitalism)*. Translated by Janet Lloyd. Cambridge, UK: Cambridge University Press, 1989.

Bergsten, C. Fred, et al. *China's Rise: Challenges and Opportunities*. Washington, DC: Peterson Institute, 2008.

Bokhari, Farhan, and Kathrin Hille. "Pakistan in Talks to Hand Port to China." *Financial Times*, August 30, 2012. http://www.ft.com/intl/cms/s/0/5c58608c-f2a6-11e1-ac41-00144feabdc0.html#axzz2ChAaJ3HY.

Bracey, Gerald W. "Heard the One About the 600,000 Chinese Engineers?" *Washington Post*, May 21, 2006. http://www.washingtonpost.com/wp-dyn/content/article/2006/05/19/AR2006051901760.html.

Brown, Arthur Judson. *New Forces in Old China: An Unwelcome but Inevitable Awakening*. New York: F.H. Revell, 1904.

Brown, Rajeswary Ampalavanar, ed. *Chinese Business Enterprise in Asia*.
London: Routledge, 1995.

Burbidge, William F. *Rising China: A Brief History of China and a Biographical
Sketch of Generalissimo and Madame Chiang Kai-shek*. London: J. Crowther,
1943.

Cantlie, James. *Sun Yat Sen and the Awakening of China*. New York:
F.H. Revell, 1912.

"Car Sales Set to Double in China by 2020." *Powder Metallurgy Review*, March
21, 2012. http://www.ipmd.net/news/001631.html.

"Case Studies: Structured Financing for Codelco with Minmetals." *Asset*, 2013.
http://www.assetchile.com/descripcion-de-transacciones/structured-financing-
for-codelco-with-minmetals/.

Chen Guofu. "Gaige jiaoyu chubu fangan" [Draft plan for the reform of educa-
tion], in *Chen Guofu xiansheng quanji*. Taipei: Zheng Zhong shuju, 1952.

Chen Jimin, ed. *Minguo guanfu* [Republican government offices]. Hong Kong:
Jinling shu chubanshe, 1992.

Chen Zhu. "Empowerment, Sinosteel Style." *Caixin Online*, December 17, 2010.
http://english.caixin.com/2010-12-17/100208301.html.

Cheng Chu-yuan. *China's Economic Development: Growth and Structural
Change*. Boulder, CO: Westview Press, 1982.

———. *Communist China's Economy, 1949–1962*. South Orange, NJ: Seton Hall
University, 1963.

Cheng Li, ed. *China's Emerging Middle Class: Beyond Economic Transformation*. Washington, DC: Brookings Institution Press, 2010.

Chin Fen. "The National Economic Council: History, Organization, and Activities." Second Historical Archives of China, Nanjing 44, no. 2 (March 1935), 78.

"China Communist Party Members Exceed 82 Million." *Xinhua*, June 30, 2012.
http://news.xinhuanet.com/english/china/2012-06/30/c_131686357.htm.

"China Confirms Weapons Firms Met Gaddafi Envoys in July." *BBC*, September
5, 2011. http://www.bbc.co.uk/news/world-asia-pacific-14785688.

"China Demands Compensation for Lost Libyan Business." *Libya Herald*,
March 7, 2012. http://www.libyaherald.com/2012/03/07/china-demands-
compensation-for-lost-libyan-business/.

"China to Expand Insurance So Sick Don't 'Lose Everything.'" *Bloomberg*,
September 17, 2012. http://www.bloomberg.com/news/2012-09-17/china-to-
expand-insurance-so-sick-don-t-lose-everything-.html.

"China Has More Than 4,000 Micro-finance Companies." *Xinhua*, January 9,
2012. http://news.xinhuanet.com/english/china/2012-01/10/c_131350905.htm.

"China Minmetals, Chile's Codelco Set Up 2 bln usd JV." *Metals Place*, Febru-
rary 23, 2006. http://metalsplace.com/news/articles/4030/china-minmetals-
chiles-codelco-set-up-2-bln-usd-jv/.

"China Now World's Largest Luxury Market: Bain Report." *Jing Daily*,
December 17, 2012. http://www.jingdaily.com/china-now-worlds-largest-
luxury-market-bain-report/22695/.

"China Oil Giant Buys into North America." *CNN Money*, July 23, 2012. http://
money.cnn.com/2012/07/23/news/companies/cnooc-nexen/index.htm.

"China Rich List." *Forbes*, October 11, 2012. http://www.forbes.com/china-billionaires/list/.

"China Suspends Death Sentence for Wu." *Bloomberg*, April 21, 2012. http://www.businessweek.com/news/2012-04-20/china-s-top-court-orders-new-trial-for-rich-sister-wu-ying.

"China: The New Colonialists." *The Economist*, March 13, 2008. http://www.economist.com/node/10853534.

"China Wants to Buy Directly from Brazilian Farmers, Avoid Intermediation." *MercoPress*, August 16, 2011. http://en.mercopress.com/2011/08/16/china-wants-to-buy-directly-from-brazilian-farmers-avoid-intermediation.

"China's Billionaire People's Congress Makes Capitol Hill Look Like Paupers." *Bloomberg*, February 26, 2012. http://www.bloomberg.com/news/2012-02-26/china-s-billionaire-lawmakers-make-u-s-peers-look-like-paupers.html.

"China's Cash-Strapped Small Firms Ring Alarm Bells." *Xinhua*, October 10, 2011. http://news.xinhuanet.com/english2010/china/2011-10/10/c_131181749_2.htm.

"China's Entrepreneurs Gain More Clout," research paper, *Xinhua*, January 9, 2007, http://news.xinhuanet.com/english/2007-01/09/content_5585156.htm.

Chun Liao. *The Governance Structure of Chinese Firms: Innovation, Competitiveness, and Growth in a Dual Economy*. New York: Springer, 2009.

Cochran, Sherman. "Capitalists Choosing Communist China: The Liu Family of Shanghai, 1948–1956." In *Dilemmas of Victory: The Early Years of the People's Republic of China*, edited by Jeremy Brown and Paul J. Pickowicz. Cambridge, MA: Harvard University Press, 2010.

Cohen, Mike. "China's EXIM Lend More to Sub-Sahara Africa Than World Bank, Fitch Says." *Bloomberg*, December 28, 2011. http://www.bloomberg.com/news/2011-12-28/china-exim-loans-to-sub-sahara-africa-exceed-world-bank-funds-fitch-says.html.

Coleman, Maryruth. "Municipal Politics in Nationalist China: Nanjing, 1927–1937." PhD dissertation. Harvard University, 1984.

"Company News; China Agrees to Buy Vehicles from the Big Three." *New York Times*, July 29, 1992. http://www.nytimes.com/1992/07/29/business/company-news-china-agrees-to-buy-vehicles-from-the-big-three.html.

Coonan, Clifford. "Beijing Is Left Fighting for Breath as Pollution Goes off the Scale." *The Independent*, January 29, 2013. http://www.independent.co.uk/environment/green-living/beijing-is-left-fighting-for-breath-as-pollution-goes-off-the-scale-8471743.html.

Cortese, Amy. "Wine from China." *New York Times Magazine*, December 12, 2008. http://www.nytimes.com/2008/12/14/magazine/14Ideas-section4B-t-005.html.

"Country Comparison: Distribution of Family Income—Gini Index." *CIA World Factbook*. 2013. https://www.cia.gov/library/publications/the-world-factbook/index.html.

Crow, Carl. *400 Million Customers: The Experiences—Some Happy, Some Sad, of an American in China, and What They Taught Him*. New York: Halcyon, 1937.

Dai Qing. "The Heritage of Beijing Water." *China Heritage Quarterly*, no. 16 (December 2008). http://www.chinaheritagequarterly.org/editorial.php?issue=016.

Dai Yan. "COSCO Interested to Buy Stake in Greek Port." *China Daily*, February 9, 2009. http://www.chinadaily.com.cn/english/doc/2006-02/09/content_518508.htm.

Dan Xizhuan and Wang Baorun. *Dayu xian (Jiangxi) xu zhi* [Dayu County (Jiangxi) Continued Ambitions], vol. 2. China: Xianfeng yuan nian, 1851.

DePillis, Lydia. "A Lot of CEOs Get Taken Hostage in China." *Washington Post*, June 25, 2013. http://www.washingtonpost.com/blogs/wonkblog/wp/2013/06/25/a-lot-of-ceos-get-taken-hostage-in-china/.

Dikötteer, Frank. *Mao's Great Famine: The History of China's Most Devastating Catastrophe, 1958–1962*. New York: Walker & Co., 2010.

Downs, Erica S., and Michael Meidan. *Business and Politics in China: The Oil Executive Reshuffle of 2011*. Washington, DC: The Brookings Institution, February 8, 2012. http://www.brookings.edu/research/articles/2012/02/08-oil-politics-downs.

du Halde, Jean-Baptiste. *The General History of China*. Translated by Richard Brookes. London: J. Watts, 1736.

Dyer, Geoff, Jamil Anderlini, and Henny Sender. "China's Lending Hits New Heights." *Financial Times*, January 17, 2011. http://www.ft.com/intl/cms/s/0/488c60f4-2281-11e0-b6a2-00144feab49a.html.

Edmonds, Richard Louis. "The Legacy of Sun Yat-sen's Railway Plans." *China Quarterly*, no. 111 (September 1987).

Erian, Stephanie. "China at the Libyan Endgame." *POLICY* 28, no.1 (Autumn 2012). http://103.14.52.105/images/stories/policy-magazine/2012-autumn/28-1-12-stephanie-erian.pdf.

Fabel, L. "Le Tungstène: Minerai le Plus Important de la Chine" [Tungsten: China's Most Important Mineral Ore]. *Bulletin de l'Université l'Aurore* 3, no. 4 (1943).

Fairbank, John K. "The Creation of the Treaty System." In *The Cambridge History of China*, vol. 11, part 1, edited by John K. Fairbank. Cambridge, UK: Cambridge University Press, 1978.

Fang Xuyan and Lea Yu. "Government Refuses to Release Gini Coefficient." *Caixin*, January 18, 2012. http://english.caixin.com/2012-01-18/100349814.html.

Fang Yang, ed. "Full Text: China-Africa Economic and Trade Cooperation." *Xinhua*, December 23, 2010. http://news.xinhuanet.com/english2010/china/2010-12/23/c_13661632.htm.

Fischer, Elisabeth. "China's High-Speed Rail Revolution." *railway-technology.com*, November 21, 2012. http://www.railway-technology.com/features/feature124824/.

"Ford Exports Increase 33 Percent." *PR Newswire*, August 26, 1992. http://www.thefreelibrary.com/FORD+EXPORTS+INCREASE+33+PERCENT-a012562611.

Forestier, Katherine. "Chinese Troops Turn on Computer Pioneers." *New Scientist*, no. 1671 (July 1, 1989).

Forsythe, Michael, and Henry Sanderson. "Financing China Costs Poised to Rise with CDB Losing Sovereign-Debt Status." *Bloomberg*, May 2, 2011. http://www.bloomberg.com/news/2011-05-02/financing-china-costs-poised-to-rise-with-decision-on-cdb-debt.html.

Freeman, Charles, and Xiaoqing Lu Boynton. "China's Emerging Global Health and Foreign Aid Engagement in Africa." Washington, DC: Center for Strategic and International Studies, November 2011. http://csis.org/files/publication/111122_Freeman_ChinaEmergingGlobalHealth_Web.pdf.

Garnaut, John. "Gaddafi's Overthrow Gives China's Leaders More to Feel Insecure About." *Sydney Morning Herald*, September 16, 2011. http://www.smh.com.au/opinion/politics/gaddafis-overthrow-gives-chinas-leaders-more-to-feel-insecure-about-20110915-1kbrd.html.

Garnaut, Ross, and Ligang Song, eds. *China's Third Economic Transformation: The Rise of the Private Economy*. London: Routledge, 2004.

Garnaut, Ross, et al. *China's Ownership Transformation*. Washington, DC: International Finance Corporation, 2005.

Gerth, Karl. *As China Goes, So Goes the World: How Chinese Consumers Are Transforming Everything*. New York: Hill & Wang, 2010.

"Global 500." *CNN Money*, July 23, 2012. http://money.cnn.com/magazines/fortune/global500/2012/full_list/index.html.

"Global R&D Network." Haier website, 2013. http://www.haier.net/en/research_development/rd_System/global/.

Godley, Michael R. "Socialism with Chinese Characteristics: Sun Yat-sen and the International Development of China." *Australian Journal of Chinese Affairs*, no. 18 (July 1987): 109–125.

Gold, Thomas B. "Urban Private Business and Social Change." In *Chinese Society on the Eve of Tiananmen: The Impact of Reform*, edited by Deborah Davis and Ezra Feivel Vogel. Cambridge, MA: Council on East Asian Studies, Harvard University, 1990.

Graham, Loren R. *The Ghost of the Executed Engineer: Technology and the Fall of the Soviet Union*. Cambridge, MA: Harvard University Press, 1993.

Grinter, Lawrence E., ed. *The Dragon Awakes: China's Military Modernization Trends and Implications*. Montgomery, AL: United States Air Force University, 1999.

Haider, Ziad. "Baluchis, Beijing, and Pakistan's Gwadar Port." *Georgetown Journal of International Affairs* 6, no.1 (Winter 2005).

He, Henry Yuhuai. *Dictionary of the Political Thought of the People's Republic of China*. Armonk, NY: M.E. Sharpe, 2001.

Hearn, Kelly. "China Plants Bitter Seeds in South American Farmland." *Washington Times*, February 1, 2012. http://www.washingtontimes.com/news/2012/feb/1/china-plants-bitter-seeds-in-south-american-farmla/?page=all.

Henriot, Christian. *Shanghai, 1927–1937*. Berkeley: University of California Press, 1993.

Heunemann, Ralph William. *The Dragon and the Iron Horse: The Economics of Railroads in China, 1876–1937*. Cambridge, MA: Council on East Asian Studies, Harvard University, 1984.

Hogg, Chris. "China's Reluctant First Entrepreneur." *BBC*, April 5, 2010. http://news.bbc.co.uk/2/hi/asia-pacific/8487888.stm.

Hong Qingyu. "A Review of the Work during the Early Stages of the Three Gorges Project." In *Megaproject: A Case Study of China's Three Gorges Project*, edited by Shiu-hung Luk and Joseph Whitney. New York: M.E. Sharpe, 1993.

"Innovation: China's Next Advantage?: 2012 China Innovation Survey."
    The China Europe International Business School, the Wenzhou Chamber
    of Commerce, the Benelux Chamber of Commerce, and Booz & Company,
    July 2012. http://www.booz.com/media/uploads/BoozCo_2012-China-Innova-
    tion-Survey.pdf.
Institute of International Education. "Fields of Study of Students from Selected
    Places of Origin, 2011/12." *Open Doors Report on International Educational
    Exchange.* http://www.iie.org/opendoors.
———. "Open Doors Data: International Students: Leading Places of Origin."
    2013. http://www.iie.org/Research-and-Publications/Open-Doors/Data/
    International-Students/Leading-Places-of-Origin/2010-12.
"Issue in Focus: China's 'Going Out' Investment Policy." *Freeman Briefing.*
    Washington, DC: Center for Strategic and International Studies, May 27,
    2008. http://csis.org/files/publication/080527_freeman_briefing.pdf.
Jacobs, Andrew. "Chinese Officials Find Misbehavior Now Carries Cost." *New
    York Times,* December 25, 2012. http://www.nytimes.com/2012/12/26/world/
    asia/corrupt-chinese-officials-draw-unusual-publicity.html.
Jackson, Kevin T. "The China Aviation Oil Scandal." In *Handbook of Frauds,
    Scams, and Swindles: Failures of Ethics in Leadership,* edited by Serge
    Matulich and David M. Currie. Boca Raton, FL: CRC Press, 2009.
Jacques, Martin. *When China Rules the World: The End of the Western World
    and the Birth of a New Global Order.* New York: Penguin, 2009.
Jian Youwen. *The Taiping Revolutionary Movement.* New Haven, CT: Yale
    University Press, 1973.
Jiangxi jingji wenti [Jiangxi economic issues]. Nanchang: Jiangxi sheng
    zhengfu, 1934.
Jiangxi zhi techan [Local products of Jiangxi]. China: Nanchang, 1935.
Johnson, Chalmers. *MITI and the Japanese Miracle: The Growth of Industrial
    Policy, 1925–1975.* Stanford, CA: Stanford University Press, 1982.
Johnson, Eliana. "NSA Chief: Chinese Cyber-Theft 'Most Significant Transfer
    of Wealth in History.'" *National Review Online,* June 23, 2013. http://www
    .nationalreview.com/corner/351786/nsa-chief-chinese-cyber-theft-most-
    significant-transfer-wealth-history-eliana-johnson.
King, Gary, Jennifer Pan, and Margaret E. Roberts. "How Censorship in China
    Allows Government Criticism but Silences Collective Expression." *American
    Political Science Review,* May 2013. http://gking.harvard.edu/files/
    censored.pdf.
Kirby, William C. "China's Internationalization in the Early People's Republic:
    Dreams of a Socialist World Economy." *China Quarterly* (December 2006):
    870–890.
———. "The Chinese War Economy: Mobilization, Control, and Planning
    in Nationalist China." In *China's Bitter Victory: The War with Japan,
    1937–1945,* edited by Steven I. Levine and James C. Hsiung. New York:
    M.E. Sharpe, 1992.
———. "Continuity and Change in Modern China: Chinese Economic Planning
    on the Mainland and on Taiwan, 1943–1958." *Australian Journal of Chinese
    Affairs,* no. 24 (July 1990): 121–141.

————. *Germany and Republican China.* Stanford, CA: Stanford University Press, 1984.

————. "Sino-American Relations in Comparative Perspective." In *Pacific Passage: The Study of American-East Asian Relations on the Eve of the Twenty-first Century,* edited by W. I. Cohen. New York: Columbia University Press, 1996.

Kirchfield, Aaron. "Sany Will Buy Biggest Cement-Pump Maker Putzmeister in Biggest China-German Deal." *Bloomberg,* January 27, 2012. http://www.bloomberg.com/news/2012-01-27/sany-will-buy-cement-pump-maker-putzmeister-in-biggest-china-german-deal.html.

Krarup-Nielsen, Aage. *The Dragon Awakes.* London: J. Lane, 1928.

Kraus, Willy. *Private Business in China: Revival between Ideology and Pragmatism.* London: Hurst, 1991.

Kristof, Nicholas D. "China and Sudan, Blood and Oil." *New York Times,* April 23, 2006. http://query.nytimes.com/gst/fullpage.html?res=990CE3D9153FF930A15757C0A9609C8B63.

Kwoh, Leslie. "Huawei, a Rising Chinese Tech Firm, Aims to Penetrate the U.S. Market." *Star Ledger* (Newark, NJ), July 31, 2011. http://www.nj.com/business/index.ssf/2011/07/chinas_huawei_the_ biggest_comp.html.

"Laid-Off Workers Protest en Masse." Associated Press, March 18, 2002. http://www.weijingsheng.org/doc/labor/Laid%20-%20Off%20Chinese%20Protest%20en%20Masse.htm.

Lake, Eli. "Beijing Spying Feared in Telecom Proposal: Chinese Firm Would Make Parts." *Washington Times,* October 20, 2010. http://www.washingtontimes.com/news/2010/oct/20/beijing-spying-feared-in-telecom-proposal/?page=all.

Lam, Willy. "The 'Latin-Americanization' of China's Domestic Politics." *China Brief* 6, no. 21 (May 9, 2007). http://www.jamestown.org/single/?no_cache=1&tx_ttnews%5Btt_news%5D=3991.

Leafy, William M., Jr. *The Dragon's Wings: The China National Aviation Corporation and the Development of Commercial Aviation in China.* Athens: University of Georgia Press, 1976.

Lee, John. "China's Rich Lists Riddled with Communist Party Members." *Forbes,* September 14, 2011. http://www.forbes.com/2011/09/14/china-rich-lists-opinions-contributors-john-lee.html.

Lenin, V. I. "Report of the All-Russia Central Executive Committee and the Council of People's Commissars on the Home and Foreign Policy to the Eighth All-Russia Congress of Soviets." December 22, 1920. Reprinted in *V. I. Lenin: Selected Works in Three Volumes,* vol. 3. Moscow: Progress Publishers, 1977.

Levine, Marilyn A. *The Found Generation: Chinese Communists in Europe during the Twenties.* Seattle: University of Washington Press, 1993.

Li Jiabao. "Firms Awaiting Libya Loss Compensation." *China Daily,* April 5, 2012. http://www.chinadaily.com.cn/bizchina/2012-04/05/content_14979267.htm.

Li, Lillian M. *China's Silk Trade: Traditional Industry in the Modern World, 1842–1937.* Cambridge, MA: Council on East Asian Studies, Harvard University, 1981.

Li Minqi. *The Rise of China and the Demise of the Capitalist World Economy.* London: Pluton Press, 2008.

Lim, Jason. "Why China Won't Be Innovative for at Least 20 More Years." *Venture Beat*, March 26, 2012. http://venturebeat.com/2012/03/26/why-china-doesnt-innovate/.

Lim, Louisa. "China's Capital of Capitalism Weathers Recession." NPR, March 17, 2010. http://www.npr.org/templates/story/story.php?storyId=124740579.

Liu Daqian. "Dayu shehui jingji zhi xiankuang tan" [On the current situation of Dayu's society and economy]. In Jiangxi sheng zhengfu, ed., *Jingji xunkan* [Economic Periodical] 2, no. 14 (May 11, 1934).

Liu Hua. "Zong qing hou fan jong daneng lujing diaocha" [After Zong's rebuttal, Danone only deepens its investigation] *Sina*, April 12, 2007. http://finance.sina.com.cn/chanjing/b/20070412/09073494827.shtml.

Mah Feng-Hwa. *The Foreign Trade of Mainland China.* Chicago: Aldine-Atherton, 1971.

Mann, James. *Beijing Jeep: A Case Study of Western Business in China.* New York: Simon & Schuster, 1989.

Mao Zedong. "Don't Attack on All Fronts" (Mao Zedong's Speech at the Third Plenum of the Seventh Central Committee, June 6, 1950). In *The Writings of Mao Zedong: 1949–1976, Volume 1, September 1949–December 1955.* Armonk, NY: M.E. Sharpe, 1986.

Martin, Eric, and Bennett Roth. "Boeing Taps D.C. Lobbyist in Export-Import Bank Renewal Push." *Bloomberg*, March 20, 2012. http://www.bloomberg.com/news/2012-03-20/boeing-taps-top-d-c-l obbyist-in-export-import-bank-renewal-push.html.

Ministry of Railways. "National Railway Operating Mileage of 98,000 Kilometers Ranks Second in the World." *chinanews.com*, January 17, 2013. http://finance.chinanews.com/cj/2013/01-17/4496731.shtml.

Miyazaki, Ichisada. *China's Examination Hell: The Civil Service Examinations of Imperial China.* Translated by Conrad Schirokauer. New York: Weatherhill, 1976.

Morrison, Wayne. "The Growth of the Private Sector in China and Implications for China's Accession to the World Trade Organization." *Congressional Research Services*, March 28, 2001.

"Nanjing shi zhi jingji jianshe" [Economic development of Nanjing]. In *Shinianlai zhi Zhongguo jingji jianshe* [China's economic development in the past ten years]. Nanjing: Zhongyang dangbu guomin jingji jihua weiyuanhui [Commission on National Economic Planning of the Central Committee], 1937.

National Academy of Sciences. *Rising Above a Gathering Storm: Energizing and Employing America for a Brighter Future.* Washington, DC: National Academy of Sciences, 2007.

"Nexen Shareholders Approve CNOOC Deal." *Wall Street Journal*, September 20, 2012. http://online.wsj.com/article/SB10000872396390444032404578008162542570432.html.

Nicolas, Françoise. "Chinese Direct Investments in France: No French Exception, No Chinese Challenge." IE Programme Paper IE PP 2010/02.

London: Chatham House, 2010. http://www.chathamhouse.org/sites/
default/files/public/Research/International%20Economics/0110pp_
nicolas.pdf.

Nye, Joseph S., Jr. *Soft Power: The Means to Success in World Politics.*
New York: Public Affairs, 2004.

Orleans, Leo A. *Professional Manpower and Education in Communist China.*
Washington, DC: US Government Printing Office, 1961.

Ott, Bryant, and Rajesh Srinivasan. "Three in 10 Chinese Adults Smoke."
Gallup World, February 9, 2012. http://www.gallup.com/poll/152546/three-
chinese-adults-smoke.aspx.

"Outsourcing's Third Wave." *The Economist*, May 21, 2009. http://www
.economist.com/node/13692889.

"Overseas Chinese Population Count." Overseas Chinese Affairs Council. 2012.
http://www.ocac.gov.tw/english/public/public.asp?selno=8889&no=8889&
level=B.

"Overseas Development." ChemChina website, 2013. http://www.chemchina
.com.cn/en/gjyw/whfz/A601701web_1.htm.

Pei Minxin. "China's Troubled Bourbons." *Project Syndicate*, October 31, 2012.
http://www.project-syndicate.org/commentary/rising-political-uncertainty-
in-china-by-minxin-pei.

"The Perils of Private Enterprise: There Was Blood." *The Economist*, August 4,
2012. http://www.economist.com/node/21559950.

Perlez, Jane. "South Sudan to Get Aid from China; No Oil Deal." *New York
Times*, April 26, 2012. http://www.nytimes.com/2012/04/26/world/asia/china-
to-aid-south-sudan-but-pipeline-efforts-stall.html.

Porter, Michael E. "The Five Forces That Shape Strategy." *Harvard Business
Review*, January 2008. http://hbr.org/2008/01/the-five-competitive-forces-that-
shape-strategy/.

"Premier Wen Says to Handle Ex-Tycoon Death Sentence Based on Facts."
Xinhua, March 13, 2012. http://news.xinhuanet.com/english/china/2012-
03/14/c_131466718.htm.

Quan Lau-King. *China's Relations with the League of Nations, 1919–1936.*
Hong Kong: Asiatic Litho Printing Press, 1939.

Ramachandran, Sudha. "China's Pearl in Pakistan's Waters." *Asia Times*,
March 4, 2005. http://www.atimes.com/atimes/South_Asia/GC04Df06.html.

Rawski, Thomas G. *China's Transition to Industrialism.* Ann Arbor: University
of Michigan Press, 1980.

"Research and Development." Huawei website, 2013. http://www.huawei.com/
en/about-huawei/corporate-info/research-development/index.htm.

Reynolds, Douglas. *China, 1898–1912: The Xinzheng Revolution and Japan.*
Cambridge, MA: Council on East Asian Studies, Harvard University, 1993.

Ross, Robert S., and Zhu Feng, eds. *China's Ascent: Power, Security, and the
Future of International Politics.* Ithaca, NY: Cornell University Press, 2008.

Rowley, Emma. "Uranium Miner Kalahari Agrees Takeover by Chinese." *The
Telegraph* (London), December 8, 2011. http://www.telegraph.co.uk/finance/
newsbysector/industry /mining/8944951/Uranium-miner-Kalahari-agrees-
takeover-by-Chinese.html.

"SANY America." SANY Group website, 2013. http://www.sanygroup.com/
abroad/america/en-us/about/america.htm.

"SANY's New R&D Center to Generate 300 Jobs in Peachtree City, GA." *Area
Development Online*, October 21, 2011. http://www.areadevelopment.com/
newsitems/10-21-2011/sany-peachtreecity-georgia-rd-center-7772523.shtml.

Second Historical Archives of China, Nanjing 44 (1719). "Quanguo jingji
weiyuanhui gongzuo baogao" [Report of the work of the National Economic
Council], 1937.

Sender, Henny. "China's Capital Flight Looks Ready for Take-Off." *Financial
Times*, February 2, 2012. http://www.ft.com/cms/s/0/7f9d917a-4d92-11e1-bb6c-
00144feabdc0.html.

"Shadow Banking in China: The Wenzhou Experiment." *The Economist*, April 7,
2012. http://www.economist.com/node/21552228.

"Shadow Banks on Trial as China's Rich Sister Faces Death." *Bloomberg*,
April 11, 2012. http://www.bloomberg.com/news/2012-04-10/shadow-banks-on-
trial-as-china-s-rich-sister-faces-death.html.

Shanghai Academy of Social Sciences Documentary Collection. Ministry
of Industry file: "Gongye zhongxin" (Industrial center): "Guoying gangtiechang" [State-run iron and steelworks]. Ministry of Industry report,
August 1932.

———. Ministry of Industry file: "Shiyebu chouban guoying gongye" [Minis-
try of Industry preparations for state-run industries]. Ministry of Industry
report, 1936.

———. Ministry of Industry file. "Benbu yinianlai choushe guoying gongye
gaikuang" [Overview of this ministry's preparations for state-run industry in
the past year]. Ministry of Industry report, March 1933.

———. Ministry of Industry file: "Ziyuan weiyuanhui gongba." *Resources Committee Bulletin* 13, no. 4 (October 1947).

Shen Hu. "China's Gini Index at 0.61, University Report Says." *Caixin*,
December 10, 2012. http://english.caixin.com/2012-12-10/100470648.html.

"Shishi wusha tongzhi zhi buzhu" [Steps toward the control of tungsten ore].
Jingji xunkan [Economic Periodical] 4, no. 5 (February 15, 1935).

Shoudu jihua [Plan for the capital]. Nanjing: Guodu sheji jishu zhuanyuan banshichu [Office of Technical Experts for Planning the National Capital], 1929.

Smith, A. Viola, and Anselm Chuh. *Motor Roads in China*. US Department of
Commerce Trade Promotion Series, no. 120. Washington, DC: US Government Printing Office, 1931.

Société des Nations General 50/R5669-71. "Engineering Mission of the League of
Nations in China." Report no. 7. September 7, 1932.

———. "Engineering Mission of the League of Nations in China." Report no. 8.
October 19, 1932.

———. "Highway Inspection Trip to Hunan Province." Report. December 10,
1932.

"South Sudan 'Agrees $8bn Deal with China.'" *BBC*, April 28, 2012. http://
www.bbc.co.uk/news/world-africa-17883321.

"Special Economic Zones and Open Coastal Cities." *China Society for Human Rights Studies*. http://www.humanrights-china.org/meetingchina/Meeti2001112793911.htm.

Springut, Micah, Steven Schlaikjer, and David Chen. "China's Program for Science and Technology Modernization: Implications for American Competitiveness." Prepared for the U.S.-China Economic and Security Review Commission. CENTRA Technology Inc., January 2011. http://china-us.uoregon.edu/pdf/uscc_report.pdf.

Stempel, Jonathan. "Fidelity, Berkshire Targeted over PetroChina." *Reuters*, May 1, 2007. http://www.reuters.com/article/2007/05/01/idUSN01231202.

Stewart, Robb M. "Rio Tinto Accepts Chinese Bid for Kalahari Shares." *Wall Street Journal*, February 1, 2012. http://online.wsj.com/article/SB10001424052970204740904577195961601888798.html.

Strand, David. *Rickshaw Beijing: City People and Politics in the 1920s*. Berkeley: University of California Press, 1989.

Su Hsing Hsueh and Lin Tse-lin Mu-ch'iao. *The Socialist Transformation of the National Economy in China*. Beijing: Beijing Foreign Language Press, 1960.

Sun Yat-sen. *The International Development of China*. London: G.P. Putnam's Sons, 1922.

Suttmeier, Richard P., Cong Cao, and Denis Fred Simon. "China's Innovation Challenge and the Remaking of the Chinese Academy of Sciences." *Innovations* (Summer 2006.

T'ang Leang-li. *Reconstruction in China*. Shanghai: China United Press, 1935.

Tangen, Einar. *The Kunshan Way*. Beijing: Foreign Languages Press, 2010.

Tao Siu. "L'Oeuvre du Conseil National Economique Chinois" [Work of the Chinese National Economic Council]. PhD dissertation. L'Université de Nancy, 1936.

"Three Gorges Dam Has Caused Urgent Problems, Says China." *The Guardian*, May 19, 2011. http://www.guardian.co.uk/environment/2011/may/19/china-three-gorges-dam.

"339,700 Chinese Choose to Study Abroad in 2011." *Xinhua*, February 11, 2012. http://news.xinhuanet.com/english/china/2012-02/11/c_131403850.htm.

Till, Barry. *In Search of Old Nanjing*. Hong Kong: Joint Publishing Company, 1982.

Tillman, Adriane. "UC Regents Agree to Divest from Sudan." *SDnews.com*, 2006. http://www.sdnews.com/view/full_story/298651/article-UC-Regents-agree-to-divest-from-Sudan.

Tsai, Kellee S. *Back Alley Banking: Private Entrepreneurs in China*. Ithaca, NY: Cornell University Press, 2002.

"28,000 Chinese Waterways Dry Up amid Pollution Tidal Wave." *Russia Today*, March 31, 2013. http://rt.com/news/china-pollution-rivers-devlopment-101/.

2010 Annual Report: China EXIM Bank Operational Highlights. China EXIM Bank, 2010. http://english.eximbank.gov.cn/annual/2010/2010nb23.shtml.

"2013 Shanghai Municipal Bureau of Statistics, National Bureau of Statistics Survey Organization Shanghai Information Dissemination Plan." Shanghai Municipal Bureau of Statistics. http://www.stats-sh.gov.cn/data/release.xhtml.

Tyau Min-Ch'ien T. Z. *China Awakened*. New York: Macmillan, 1922.

————, ed. *Two Years of Nationalist China*. Shanghai: Kelly and Walsh, 1930.

"Urban and Rural Areas 2011." United Nations Department of Economic and Social Affairs Population Division, 2011. http://esa.un.org/unup/Wallcharts/urban-rural-areas.pdf.

van de Ven, Hans J. *From Friend to Comrade: The Founding of the Chinese Communist Party, 1920–1927*. Berkeley: University of California Press, 1991.

Vance, Ashlee, and Bruce Einhorn. "At Huawei, Matt Bross Tries to Ease U.S. Security Fears." *Bloomberg*, September 15, 2011. http://www.businessweek .com/magazine/at-huawei-matt-bross-tries-to-ease-us-security-fears-09152011 .html.

Wan Runnan. "My College Upper Classman, Hu Jintao." *China Times*, August 2012. http://www.thechinatimes.com/online/2012/08/4701.html.

Wang Lili. "Strengthen China's Public Diplomacy." *China Daily*, June 2, 2012. http://english.peopledaily.com.cn/90883/7834319.html.

Wang Shuhuai. "Jianshe weiyuanhui dui Zhongguo dianqi shiye de guihua" [The National Reconstruction Commission's planning for China's electric power industry]. Paper presented to the Conference on the Centennial of Sun Yatsen's Founding of the Kuomintang for Revolution, Taipei, 1994.

Wang Yuxia. "Young People China's Main Credit Card Users." *China Daily*, April 8, 2013. http://europe.chinadaily.com.cn/business/2012-05/09/content_15244850.htm.

Wei Tian. "Credit Card Use Up, So Are Risks." *China Daily*, May 9, 2012. http://europe.chinadaily.com.cn/business/2012-05/09/content_15244850.htm.

Weidner, Terry M. "Local Political Work under the Nationalists: The 1930's Silk Reform Campaign." *Illinois Papers in Asian Studies*, no. 2 (1983).

Welsch, Edward, Dinny McMahon, and Phred Dvorak. "China Eyes Potash Corp." *Wall Street Journal*, September 2, 2010. http://online.wsj.com/article/SB10001424052748704791004575465440115184752.html.

Wiethoff, Bodo. *Luftverkehr in China*. Wiesbaden: O. Harrassowitz, 1975.

Wills, John E., Jr. "Chinese and Maritime Europeans." Unpublished paper cited in William C. Kirby, "Traditions of Centrality, Authority, and Management in Modern China's Foreign Relations," in *Chinese Foreign Policy: Theory and Practice*, edited by T. W. Robinson and David Shambaugh. Oxford: Clarendon Press, 1994.

Wong, Edward. "China's Court Overturns a Young Tycoon's Death Sentence." *New York Times*, April 20, 2012. http://www.nytimes.com/2012/04/21/world/asia/china-court-overturns-death-penalty-for-tycoon-in-fraud-case.html.

————. "On a Scale of 0 to 500, Beijing's Air Quality Tops 'Crazy Bad' at 755." *New York Times*, January 12, 2013. http://www.nytimes.com/2013/01/13/science/earth/beijing-air-pollution-off-the-charts.html?_r=0.

"World's Biggest Airport Planned." *CNN Travel*, September 13, 2011. http://travel.cnn.com/shanghai/life/world's-biggest-airport-planned-328259.

Wright, Stanley Fowler. *Kiangsi Native Trade and Its Taxation*. New York: Garland Publishing, 1980.

Xiao Wan. "ChemChina Develops through Acquisitions." *China Daily*, October 24, 2008. http://www.chinadaily.com.cn/cndy/2008-10/24/content_7136469.htm.

Xin Nanjing [New Nanjing]. Nanjing: Nanjing shi zhengfu, 1933.

Yan Bian. "Legion of Honor for ChemChina President Ren." *China Daily*, December 20, 2011. http://www.chinadaily.com.cn/cndy/2011-12/20/content_14290290.htm.

Young, Jack C. "Joint Venture and Licensing in Civil Aviation: A Sino-American Perspective." *Stanford Journal of International Studies* 15 (1979).

Yuk Pan Kwan. "SEC Targets Chinese Pork Processor." *Financial Times*, April 6, 2012. http://blogs.ft.com/beyond-brics/2012/04/06/sec-targets-chinese-pork-processor/#axzz2DYNSoHFw.

Yun Chen. "Dianqi wang" [Electrical power network]. *Jianshe yuekan,* no. 9 (October 1930).

Zhang Chi-Chi. "U.S. Embassy: Beijing Air Quality Is 'Crazy Bad.'" *Huffington Post*, November 19, 2010. http://www.huffingtonpost.com/2010/11/19/us-embassy-beijing-air-qu_n_785870.html.

Zhao Ziyang. "Advance Along the Road of Socialism with Chinese Characteristics" (report delivered at the Thirteenth National Congress of the Chinese Communist Party, October 25, 1987). *Beijing Review*, no. 45 (November 9–15, 1987).

Zhong Shaohua. "Zhongguo gongchengshi xuehui jieshi" [Brief history of the Chinese Society of Engineers]. Manuscript.

———. "Zhongshan shiye jihua yu Zhongguo xiandaihua" [Sun Yatsen's *Industrial Plan* and China's modernization]. *Zhongshan shehui kexue jikan* (Sun Yatsen Social Science Quarterly) 5, no. 4 (December 1990).

Zhongguo jindai gongyeshi ziliao [Materials on the modern history of Chinese industry], vol. 3, edited by Chen Zhen. Beijing: Sanlien shudian, 1961.

Zhou Daolong, ed. *Gannan wukuang zhi* [Tungsten mines of Southern Jiangxi]. China: Nanchang, 1936.

INDEX

ABOUT THE AUTHORS

Regina M. Abrami is a Senior Fellow at the Wharton School, Director of the Global Program at the Lauder Institute of Management and International Studies, and Senior Lecturer in Political Science at the University of Pennsylvania. Prior to this, she was a member of the Harvard Business School faculty for eleven years, where she taught courses focused on government and international political economy, Chinese political economy, and stakeholder management in its MBA and executive education programs. In addition, Abrami served from 2008 to 2011 as the faculty chair of the school's inaugural international immersion program. At HBS, she was twice named a Hellman Fellow and also received the Robert F. Greenhill Award in recognition of distinguished service. Abrami is a frequent commentator on the globalization of Chinese companies, Chinese industrial policy, and the relation between non-market factors and business strategy. In addition to dozens of HBS cases, her work has appeared in such academic publications as *Comparative Politics* and the *Journal of East Asian Studies* and has been published by Cambridge University Press and Oxford University Press. Abrami is a member of the National Committee on United States-China Relations, a faculty affiliate of the Center for the Study of Contemporary China at the University of Pennsylvania, and formerly an Executive Committee member of Harvard University's Fairbank Center for Chinese Studies.

William C. Kirby is the Spangler Family Professor of Business Administration at Harvard Business School and the T. M. Chang

Professor of China Studies at Harvard University, where he has
been named a Distinguished Service Professor. He serves as
Chairman of the Harvard China Fund and Faculty Chair of the
Harvard Center Shanghai.

Kirby's work examines China's business, economic, and political development in an international context. He has taught Executive Education programs on business environments in China and
has written or coauthored more than thirty HBS cases on China.

Before coming to Harvard in 1992, he was Professor of History, Director of Asian Studies, and Dean of University College at
Washington University in St. Louis. At Harvard, he has served as
Chair of the History Department, Director of the Harvard University Asia Center, and Dean of the Faculty of Arts and Sciences.

Kirby holds degrees from Dartmouth College, Harvard Uni-
versity, and (Dr. phil. h. c.) the Free University of Berlin and the
Hong Kong Polytechnic University. He has held appointments as
Visiting Professor at the University of Heidelberg and the Free
University of Berlin. He is a Fellow of the American Academy of
Arts and Sciences.

F. Warren McFarlan, a Harvard Business School faculty member since
1964, is a Baker Foundation Professor of Business Administration and the Albert H. Gordon Professor of Business Administration, Emeritus. He was Senior Associate Dean from 1990 to 2004,
successively responsible for research, external relations, and
China. Since 2009 he has been a guest professor and codirector of
the China Business Case Center at Tsinghua University's School
of Economics and Management. He holds a BA from Harvard
University and an MBA and DBA from Harvard Business School.
A prolific case writer, McFarlan has written over two hundred
cases during his career and authored or coauthored fourteen
books, the most recent of which are *Chinese General Management:
Tsinghua–Harvard Text and Cases* (2009) and *Joining a Nonprofit
Board: What You Need to Know* (2011). His most recent article is
"China's Growing IT Services and Software Industry: Challenges

and Implications," which appeared in *MIS Quarterly Executive*. For the past fifteen years, McFarlan's primary role has been developing HBS's presence in China and preparing cases and technical notes toward that end. He serves on the board of Li & Fung and several other firms and is a trustee of several nonprofit organizations.